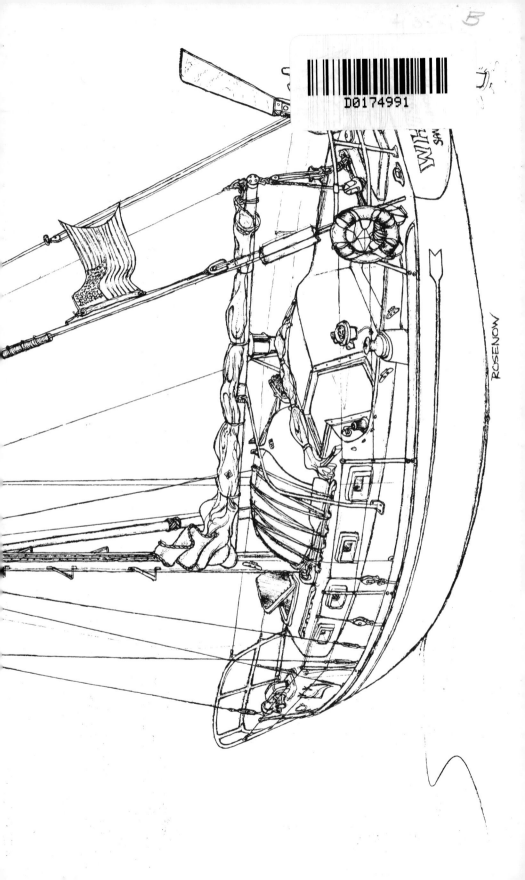

AFTER 50,000 MILES

AFTER 50,000 MILES

by Hal Roth

Photographs by the author and drawings by Frank Rosenow

W W Norton & Company Inc.
New York London

Published simultaneously in Canada by George J. McLeod Limited, Toronto. Printed in the United States of America.

Library of Congress Cataloging in Publication Data

Roth, Hal.
    After 50,000 miles.
    Bibliography: p.
    Includes index.
    1. Yachts and yachting. 2. Sailing. I. Title.
GV813.R63   1977   797.1   77–1920
ISBN 0–393–03202–7

        7 8 9 0

This book was designed by Patricia Dunbar
Typefaces used are Electra and Bernhard Modern Bold
Manufacturing was done by Haddon Craftsmen

This book is dedicated to John and Barbara Haddaway, who have encouraged my writing and photographic efforts for more than twenty years. In scores of letters and dozens of visits and trips together I have always profited from their wisdom, their freely given advice, and their cheery sense of hopeful optimism.

Contents

〜〜〜〜〜〜〜〜〜〜〜〜〜〜〜〜〜〜〜〜〜〜〜〜〜〜〜〜

1. The Pleasure and the Freedom   1
2. The Corpus Itself   21
3. A New Yacht   37
4. The Rig   51
5. Self-Steering   71
6. The Anchor Game   85
7. The Practice of Anchoring   107
8. Heat and Cooking   127
9. Planning the Trip   141
10. Can You Be Seen at Night?   151
11. Managing without Refrigeration   161
12. Wrinkles   171
13. What Does World Cruising Cost?   189
14. The Cruising Engine: Necessity or Monster?   199
15. The Dinghy Problem   213
16. Questions and Answers   223
17. Storm Management   239
18. Storm Tactics   247
19. Schooling at Sea   263
20. Foreign Paperwork   271
21. Which Yacht for Me?   279
22. The Accommodation Puzzle   289
23. The Dream and the Reality   299

Notes   307
Appendices
   1. Addresses   309
   2. Conversion Table for Meters, Feet, and Fathoms   312
   3. Conversion Tables for Metric System   315
Index   319

Illustrations

~~~~~~

Whisper approaches Isla Pinta in the Galápagos   xvi
Ed Boden and his Vertue, *Kittiwake*   8, 9
Amateur-constructed yachts at Pete's Harbor, Redwood City,
    California   15
Sauvage, a French-made aluminum vessel   20
Cliff Niederer, Inverness, California, at work on a wooden hull   23
Steel and aluminum hulls under construction   26, 28
Chilean barkentine *Esmeralda*   36
Viking 34 racer-cruiser   41
Hull-deck renovation aboard *Whisper*   43
Cockpit renovation aboard *Whisper*   45
Gypsy Moth V   50
Myth of Malham   52
Lever and sheave for running backstays   54
Inner forestay   57
Turk's head   57
Storm trysail storage bag   59
Gazelle   60
Tom Colvin   61
Roller reefing   64
Mainsail reefing on *Whisper*   67
Self-steering devices   70, 75
Fisherman anchor   84
CQR anchor   87
Anchor recovery with windlass   89
Disconnecting the anchor chain   91

Drum storage of anchor warp   93
Spare anchor stowage   95
Wishbone anchor   100
Anchor gear connections   106
Golden Feather aground   110
Grapnel with adjustable flukes   113
Fisherman anchor   116
Connecting an anchor spring   119
Al Petersen hanks on a jib aboard *Stornoway*   122
Coffee making in a thermos   126
Taylors kerosene heating stove   129
Stove flue shield   130
Single-burner Tilley stove   131
Aftermath of a gas explosion   134
Dickinson cookstove   136
Touching up with a Tilley kerosene iron   137
Cataloguing the charts   140
More planning   145
Whisper and *Gaucho* meet in Buenos Aires   148
Masthead light on *Whisper*   150
Other navigation lights, good and bad   153, 155, 157
Fresh baked bread   160
Greasing eggs   163
Saro Jane   168
Collecting rainwater   170, 173
Mast steps   175
Burgee mounting   177
Aldis signaling lamp   179
Spinnaker pole mounting, raising, and lowering   180
Tilley wick for Primus stove   182
Topping lift   183
Safety harnesses   184, 185
Stornoway   191
Blue Water Medal of the Cruising Club of America   195
Engine overhaul aboard *Whisper*   198
Whisper under way   202
Engine cooling and exhaust system of *Cimarron*   206, 208
Rowlock socket   216
Brigantine *Anna Maria*   222
Lisa Pittoors at her Read's sewing machine   226

Sail decoration   231
Whisper running north from Bermuda under full sail   238
Portlight closure   242
High seas in the South Atlantic   246
Boom gallows   249
Mary Adams studies aboard *Eileen*   262
Unseaworthy construction   278, 284, 285
Interior of *Whisper*   288
Jester   298
Ornamental taffrail woodcarving   301
Schooner, cutter, and ketch in Lesser Antilles   305

Drawings

IOR Measurements   6
Vertue profile   10
Vertue interior   11
Pidgeon's *Islander* in profile   16
Yacht hull with parts shown   22
DeRidder self-steering vane   76
Miranda-type self-steering vane   77
Anchor and flukes   98
Whisper's topping lift   183
Whisper interiors   293

Acknowledgments

I would like to thank Bill Robinson of *Yachting* (U.S.), *Cruising World* (U.S.), Hans Strepp of *Die Yacht* (West Germany), Gerry Kidd of *Pacific Yachting* (Canada), Peter Campbell of *Modern Boating* (Australia), and David Pardon of *Sea Spray* (New Zealand) for their kind permission to use some of the material which appeared originally in their magazines.

AFTER 50,000 MILES

A landfall on a new island after a long sea passage is a magical moment. The discovery of the island on the horizon, the gradual unfolding of the contours and hills, the strengthening of the colors, and the first fragrance of the vegetation all combine to make a pleasure unique to small ship sailing. Here Whisper approaches Isla Pinta in the Galápagos after a 29-day passage from California.

1

~~~~~~

The Pleasure and the Freedom

For a good many people the game is simply one of taking a yacht from a marina for a pleasant afternoon sail. For others the fun is the chase and overtaking of similar sailboats. A third category of people lives for the two-week vacation cruise in a nearby bay or delta or string of islands. I belong to a fourth group—a dedicated and zany collection of distant horizon seekers who eschew the old and safe for the distant and beyond.

I have written this book for people who want to cross oceans, who hope to make extended blue-water passages, and who plan to live aboard small sailing vessels for long periods. The chapters that follow describe in detail some of the experiences of two people who elected to sail extensively and to earn their way while living aboard a thirty-five-foot yacht.

During the past eleven years my wife and I have sailed our little sloop *Whisper* from Canada to California, through the South and western Pacific to Japan, east across the North Pacific to the Aleutian Islands and to the Bering Sea, to Alaska, Canada's Queen Charlotte Islands, and back to our home port of San Francisco. On another trip we sailed to British Columbia and circled Vancouver Island.

More recently Margaret and I voyaged south to Ecuador and the Galápagos Islands, sailed along the extensive coasts of Peru and Chile, had a look at the Southern Ocean, the Strait of Magellan and Cape Horn, and visited Argentina, Uruguay, and Brazil. Just now we are in Bermuda. Altogether we have logged some 50,000 miles in *Whisper*.

1

Margaret and I have pottered about in rivers, explored groups of islands, and sailed on the oceans of the world for a very long time. We have had moments of sublime joy and of nerve-jarring agony. We have been on the yacht continuously, in all seasons, in all kinds of weather, and in all sorts of countries. We have run with the trade winds behind us for weeks and have also bashed into the trade winds for weeks to get to difficult windward destinations. In our travels we have been robbed, rammed, had holes shot through the yacht, and skirted the edges of political revolutions. We have been welcomed and assisted by port officials (usually) and at other times have been grossly insulted and humilated by them (rarely). We have made hundreds of wonderful friends and have been treated to marvelous hospitality. We have visited many parts of the earth that a tourist never sees, and we have enjoyed a whole world of sailing.

I think back to some of our delightful anchorages: the ethereal turquoise of the lagoons in the Tuamotus; the charming, butterfly-like villages of the fishermen along the southeast coast of Japan; the nose-tingling fragrance from the tall cedars and spruces around the bays of southeast Alaska; the rose-colored flamingos flying overhead in the Galápagos; the chilling immensity of the frosty, ice-blue glaciers that loomed above *Whisper* in Beagle Channel in southern Chile; the calm quietness of the tropical jungles of Brazil. . . . Then my mind becomes a kaleidoscope of twisting colors, out-of-focus landscapes, of storms and calms, of sail changes and anchoring. My ears ring with the babble of strange languages, sea sounds in the night, and the hooting of big ships in distant harbors. I smell the cloying sweetness of drying copra in the tropics. I turn my head to sniff the iodine seashore at low water in the far north. I think of dolphins breathing alongside the yacht; of boobies plummeting into the ocean after food; of frigate birds circling ever higher, at the far edge of my eyesight. I think of pleasant, lingering meals with new friends, and the fun of shopping in strange markets with curious money. All these thoughts make up the essential stuff of happy memories, of a short lifetime at sea.

This is supposed to be a technical book, however, and already I am wandering from the mark. You see, I am an incorrigible romantic; otherwise who would travel at a snail's pace in an era of speedy air transport?

The birch-bark canoe of the American Indian and the creaking, six-horse stagecoach of 150 years ago belong to another age. The small sailing yacht is hopelessly antiquated, too. It is slow, often intolerably uncomfortable, difficult to build, and expensive to maintain. Yet the popularity of sail for long-distance traveling is increasing at a surprising rate. How can we explain this? By any rational analysis a sailing vessel should be tucked away like a museum replica of an extinct bird. Can you imagine taking three or four weeks to sail from San Francisco to Tahiti when a jet aircraft can do the trip in a few hours and at less cost?

The answer is that life under sail—especially in your own vessel—is highly appealing because it is simple and basic and infinitely challenging. Your existence gets back to first principles. At a stroke you erase 90 percent of the trivia of modern life. You travel to new places at your own pace, and can linger as much or as little as you wish. In no other activity except perhaps mountaineering are you so independent and so accountable for your own actions.

You alone put food on board. You alone bend on the sails and adjust them. You alone choose your sailing waters. You alone are responsible for finding your way on the sea. You alone select the anchorages. You alone are in charge of the upkeep of the yacht. If you get into trouble, it's generally you alone who must bail yourself out. The business of solving your own problems, making your own repairs, and looking after yourself is satisfying, and grows into nice feelings of independence, confidence, and self-respect. In no other activity can I think of such a propitious combination of attractions. In no other endeavor can I think of so many satisfied people replete with enjoyment and self-determination.

I believe it was the famous Hawaii-based sailor, Bob Griffith, who spoke of "the pleasure and the freedom" inherent in world cruising. What a lovely phrase: "the pleasure and the freedom . . ."

Yet before we hypnotize ourselves with words, we must be realistic. Listen to this wise counsel from Guy Cole:

. . . for every one engaged in long-distance cruising there are probably a thousand others who dream about it. The trouble with many of these dreamers is that they seek to project themselves from an environment which they find completely unsatisfactory, into one which they regard as wholly desirable, without considering the steps which come between. Therein lies many a personal tragedy. Much of this can be laid directly as a charge against the people who write books about long-distance cruises. They make it all sound fatally easy. "The wind had now worked up to Force Eight and we pulled down a couple of reefs in the main. . . ." Impatiently, the reader flips over the page to see what happened next. Yet, concealed within that careless sentence, is half an hour of bitter struggle, wrestling with refractory canvas, in the blackness of a rain-squall, while being thrown around the decks of a small boat pitching and tumbling in an ocean swell.

Worse still are those who write books describing how they simply bought a boat, and sailed away—just like that—without any knowledge of seamanship, or navigation, or anything else. It has been done. There is no denying it. But in order to survive for long enough to enable them to acquire the necessary knowledge to carry on with their cruising these people must have been extraordinarily lucky. And we hear nothing of those who failed miserably, or never got started, through inexperience.[1]

Cruising under sail is a thousandfold more complex than merely buying a suitable yacht. The marinas and harbors of the world are dotted with private pleasure craft of many kinds. There are tens of thousands of boat-owners but very few sailors. *Lots of boatowners but few sailors.* And a sailor you must be if you're going to try ocean voyaging. You need a modicum of sailing aptitude, some grasp of mechanical concepts, and a willingness to pitch in and work. Most veteran world sailors fall into the classification of restless adventurers who are always looking at distant horizons. Generally speaking these people are remarkably competent. They have all served fairly intensive apprenticeships to learn about the sea, the management of themselves, and the care of their vessels.

To learn the fundamentals of sailing you must go to a special school for a week or two. You will be taken out in a dinghy to learn something about sail handling, knots, tacking, jibing, docking, and maneuvering in restricted waters. Then you must practice as often as possible and serve as crew for friends on their yachts. Every time you sail on a new vessel you learn something, for every captain has different ways of doing his job. You need to practice stitching sails, to learn about anchors and rigging, and to get some notion of marine painting and general upkeep, for life under sail is a never-ending round of maintenance and small repairs. To learn celestial navigation requires specialized study and practice, although the mysteries of the sextant and related calculations are a good deal exaggerated.

You must have patience to learn the craft of sailing, which has set and orderly ways of doing each operation, schemes of success that have been polished for generations. Even the nautical vocabulary is specialized, for it is necessary to be able to describe every part of a vessel and to talk about each maneuver and action with unmistakable precision.

You can learn the fundamentals quickly, but half a lifetime seems scarcely enough to perfect your techniques. A good sailor is always studying and learning and asking questions. People who travel and work on the sea tend to be literate souls who often write books. There is an astonishing library of nautical volumes that you can digest bit by bit to hurry your learning process. But in spite of the help to be got from books, you must learn about sailing at first hand. You do not become a seaman by reading. You need practice. You need to get your hands dirty.

Age is no barrier. My good friend, the late Colin Darroch, fulfilled a lifetime ambition by singlehanding a small vessel from San Francisco to Hawaii and back when he was sixty-eight. Jean Devogué circumnavigated when he was sixty-nine. I have read account after account of members of Great Britain's Royal Cruising Club who have paused in the midst of great sailing adventures "to celebrate my seventy-fifth birthday," or "to take note that I was seventy-nine today." Conversely, Robin Lee Graham began his circumnavigation when he was sixteen.

A main problem for people who want to buy a yacht for cruising is that most yachts are designed for racing. Though these vessels are often called racer-cruisers (or cruiser-racers), their designs are based on faddish racing rules which have produced groups of similar yachts designed to compete with one another like horses or racing greyhounds. Within the narrow limits of some rule or other, the magic word has always been *performance,* which sometimes has taken precedence over safety and which quite often has eclipsed comfort. Damn the well-being of the crew. Damn the expense of custom gear. Damn the height of the mast. Damn any difficulties at all. The main thing is performance and the rating. The builders and naval architects want to sell yachts to make money. A winner sells best.

What have been the guidelines of racing rules for the past century?

When the racing criterion was *over-all length,* the designs reflected maximum waterline length with plumb bows and sterns—ugly-looking and very wet vessels. When the racing criterion was *waterline length,* the bow and stern overhangs became excessively long (and unseaworthy), because the unmeasured length of the hull meant that when the yacht was heeled, its immersed waterline was greater and the yacht went faster. When the racing criterion was *a fixed sail* area, the naval architects drew plans for high and efficient sailing rigs on light hulls with heavy keels (to give stability to the tall rigs). Otherwise the nautical lawyers sought to use unmeasured sail area in various ways. When the racing criterion was *displacement,* the builders produced long and fragile yachts built to go fast in light and medium airs (the yachts stayed home in heavy weather).

More recently the vessels constructed for racing under the formulas of the Cruising Club of America, the Royal Ocean Racing Club, and the International Offshore Rule have used combinations of earlier rules plus a large number of additional measurements to encourage seaworthiness and to attempt to perfect handicaps. CCA yachts like *Finisterre* (Sparkman & Stephens, 1954) and RORC designs such as *Outlaw* (Illingworth & Primrose, 1963) would make excellent cruising yachts today. Both were constructed of wood and drawn in an era when the racing efforts were

International Offshore Rule Measurements

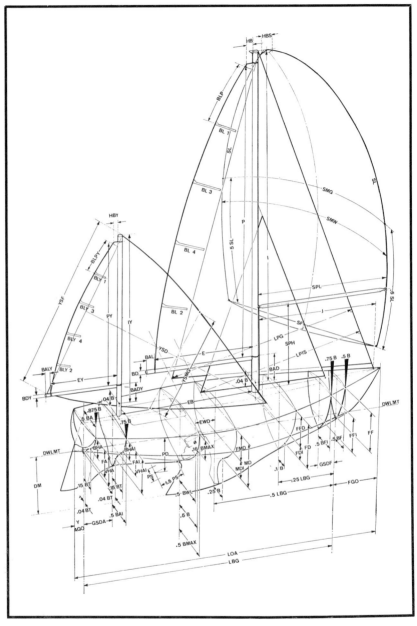

This drawing of the required measurements to obtain an IOR racing certificate shows the idiocy of using a racing yacht for cruising purposes. Few of these measurements have anything to do with sailing qualities. (Drawing courtesy of Yachting World magazine)

keen but not ruthless. I feel that the naval architects of a generation ago were more gentleman designers than the cold-blooded engineers of today, although the firm of Sparkman & Stephens has worked in both eras.

The newer IOR rule has been successful at handicapping yachts for even racing, although the designs have become drably uniform. The trouble is that the yachts started out well under the rule, but the regulations have gradually been exploited to produce extreme types. The rule itself is so complex that it defies understanding except by specialists who use computers. (There has even been an appeal for money to help finance a Massachusetts Institute of Technology computer study to determine the course and direction of racing rules and handicaps.) To be competitive today you need a very expensive, all-out racing machine that is useless for anything else. For a fractional improvement in speed or a microscopically lower rating, no sacrifice or expense is too much. Like racing sails, a racing yacht that is two years old is considered old and outmoded. Perhaps to the ultimate disadvantage of the sport, innovators are quickly cut down by the establishment. We have seen the cat ketch and retracting bilge boards penalized when both, if modestly encouraged, might have brought a few fresh breezes into the stultified calms of IOR design.[2]

The trends for supposed oceangoing yachts are frightening. I do not like the acutely pinched IOR bows, which may lack sufficient buoyancy in big seas if the yacht is overloaded; the incredibly tall, weakly supported masts with masthead shroud angles as low as 8 degrees instead of the 12 degrees to 15 degrees usually found on offshore yachts ("We love the repeat business," a spar builder told me); and the shoebox accommodations designed to keep the crew's weight in the middle of the yacht.

Edward Brewer commented wryly about a typical IOR racing design in the November 1975 issue of *Sail* when he wrote: "She sleeps six in comfort that would do credit to any county jail cell and has sufficient facilities to keep the crew alive for a few days."

I am a bit aghast at hull plating of ⅛ inch aluminum for a thirty-eight-foot yacht (*America Jane III*, a 1975 Scott Kaufman design). Several light-air designs from California (the Erickson 46, for example) have not only done poorly in heavy-weather Bermuda races, but the bulkheads have come loose and the hulls have been severely strained because of flimsy construction.

"An arc of a circle gives the smallest amount of wetted surface for a given displacement which is why the sections of many modern racing boats look as if they have been drawn with a pair of compasses," writes naval architect John Teale. "Such a shape achieves its various objectives

These three photographs show Ed Boden's Kittiwake, a Vertue designed by Laurent Giles and built of wood by E. F. Elkins and Son of Christchurch, England. A real pocket cruiser only 25 feet 6 inches over all, this heavy displacement sloop (9,447 pounds) is probably the minimum size for ocean sailing. The speedy and close-winded Vertue handles particularly well under sail with enough weight and draft to help her shoulder her way through seas that stop most other designs of similar dimensions. Her narrow beam of only 7 feet 2 inches, however, and generally small size restrict her to two people for any extended adventures. Many Vertues are sailed without

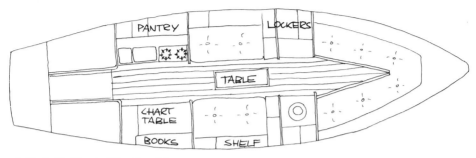

VERTUE INTERIOR

engines—as is Kittiwake—and get along quite well. The captains—from
necessity—become excellent seamen and seem to develop a fine spirit of
adventure. Whether the owners have this before they acquire their Vertues is
something I'm unable to say, but as a group the Vertue people are an
adventurous lot. Bill Nance and John Struchinsky have each completed
singlehanded circumnavigations in Vertues, while Ed Boden, the man in these
photographs, continues slowly westward on his great sailing voyage. Vertues
have made dozens of ocean crossings and hundreds of notable shorter cruises.
At least three owners have reported 24-hour runs of over 150 miles, which
is astonishing for a yacht only 21 feet 6 inches on the waterline. These
long-keeled yachts generally change hands like antique Mercedes-Benz cars,
and the sellers are usually more concerned with the new owner's sailing plans
than with the selling price. The Vertue was designed in 1936 along the
lines of a pilot-fishing boat and was originally gaff-rigged with a topsail and a
long bowsprit. The yacht carries 4,438 pounds of lead ballast. A near sister
to the first Vertue was built in 1936 and christened Wanderer II by a
young sailor named Eric Hiscock. Some 175 have been built so far, with at
least half a dozen under construction in 1977. With the exception of two
steel hulls made in Holland, the 175 have been built of wood, practically all
carvel planked. The architects have recently completed a set of drawings
for fiberglass construction using the C—flex method, which should result
in a lighter, roomier, and more economically viable Vertue. Everyone is
agreed, however, that the remarkable hull lines should never be changed.

but . . . it restricts space inside and does nothing to dampen rolling. As you can imagine, a barrel would be the ideal roller and a modern yacht designed with the IOR rules in mind is often little more than a sophisticated barrel with a fin keel attached."[3]

What has all this to do with ocean cruising, living aboard, and sailing for pleasure? Quite a bit, because racing rules have so dominated yacht design, publicity, and advertising that few vessels other than racing oriented vessels have been available. Racing has been the *ne plus ultra*, the end goal, the great attraction for the competition-minded owners who after all have financed the game. Racing has been the economic mainstay just as cargo carrying was the reason for commercial sail a century ago.

But wait a minute! Many builders have discovered that their customers don't care a whit about racing. The interests of these buyers lie elsewhere—in sailing to places, in living aboard, and in enjoying a beautiful yacht for itself. A large recreational boating market based on the ocean cruising yacht has appeared so quietly (and fully developed) that many people are not aware of its breadth and significance. Today men and women are living longer, are better educated, have more money and leisure time, and often retire at an early age. There are more customers for an attractive idea.

I don't want to seem to be endlessly picking and grumbling about racing yachts and their designs, which are perhaps excellent for a specialized purpose. The situation with cruising yachts, however, is that they are derived mostly from racing craft. But along with the derivation have come a lot of unnecessary and undesirable racing ideas and hardware, concepts and fittings that are of little use to ocean cruising sailors. Racing designs and cruising designs are acquaintances and half brothers, not lovers and intimates.

The notion of a small, well-equipped ocean cruising yacht is fairly recent. Her design demands are at least as much and as specialized as any racing yacht—perhaps more. Like larger cargo and passenger-carrying ships, the ocean cruising yacht is a tiny self-contained entity capable of an independent existence for a long time, not merely the duration of a race. Seakeeping ability, considerable space for stores, and some thought to comfort of the crew are paramount.

The ocean cruising yachts I speak of are between twenty-five and fifty-five feet on deck. Most are thirty to forty feet or so. I believe that twenty-five feet is the minimum size for ocean cruising, and is best typified by a Folkboat, a Vertue, or some of the more modern lightweight fiberglass designs. The Vertue was designed by Laurent Giles of Lymington, England. This pocket cruiser sails very well but is handicapped by the weight of gear she must carry. All these yachts—big or small—require a clutch of anchors, a dinghy, lots of food and water, extra sails, and a thousand things more. The twenty-five-footer, which may displace as much as four and a half tons, must carry all these items (albeit smaller) just like a forty-footer, which may displace twelve tons. The cruising equipment (say one ton) for a long voyage amounts to 22 percent of the smaller yacht's weight and takes up a great deal of her room, while the figure for a larger yacht is only 8 percent (or maybe 10 percent because of heavier gear). Also, a ton of stuff—not so much, really—easily disappears into the roomier shelves and lockers and bilges of the larger vessel. Considerations such as these are completely alien to the racing yacht.

I hope you will understand that I have nothing against racing, which is a good way to learn the fine points of sail adjustment, how to sail in light winds, helmsmanship, the importance of a clean hull, and so forth. We owe much of the development of yachting to racing, particularly sails, winches, flush through-hull fittings, and a hundred things more. Nevertheless, I do not think that racing design slanted to artificial standards is a logical way of getting the best vessels for the sea.

In Howard Chapelle's book *The Search for Speed Under Sail* the author speaks of racing enthusiasts who seek speed under sail in craft whose qualities are determined by "whim, fashion, and arbitrary rating rules." This prominent naval architect's analyses show that racing craft are seldom better and are usually poorer in performance than many commercial vessels of the past two hundred years. Modern racing yachts— with their improved rigs and sails—are superior only to windward. Most commercial sailing of a century ago was across or with the wind (as is most yacht cruising), so designers were not especially concerned with windward work. Windward performance remains important but is not fundamental; the need is for good all-around sailing qualities.

As recently as 1965 the remarkable record of 2,200 miles in ten days was established during the downwind Los Angeles–Honolulu race by a seventy-three-foot ketch-rigged yacht named *Ticonderoga*, designed by Francis Herreshoff. A mathematical comparison (speed-length ratio) with large commercial sailing vessels shows that *Ticonderga's* record was the fastest sustained run of all time.* The hull of this handsome yacht shows the form of the best small commercial ships of the 1850 era. Yet the yacht rates poorly under any modern rating rule.

---

* This record has been slightly bettered by *Windward Passage*, an outstanding design by Alan Gurney, but I believe my point remains valid.

Fortunately for cruising enthusiasts, several dozen conscientious naval architects who are not bound by racing rules are busy designing yachts solely for sailing on the sea. These men are concerned with hull forms and ballast arrangements that will give easy motion and good steering; with plenty of sail area to drive the vessels in light airs but capable of being shortened easily; with pleasant and commodious accommodations that have ample accessible stowage; with sizable safety margins for the mast, rigging, and ground tackle; with heat for cold weather, bookshelves, boom gallows, rubbing strakes, steering vanes . . . The job of the architects is big and difficult, but their products are steadily getting better because the designers have the incentive of sales in a market that is getting firmer and bigger every year. A recent boat show annual of cruising yachts listed ninety-five designs that actually were being built. Two-thirds of these were large enough for two people to take on long trips. With all this effort, the competition for sales, and customer feedback, the average vessel will certainly improve.

At this moment lots of ocean cruising yachts already exist. Colossal numbers of new ones are being built. "How many?" you ask. On a world basis no one can ever know, but a sampling of indicators is astonishing even if we use very conservative figures. Naval architect Bruce Roberts-Goodson, who specializes in plans for amateur builders, reported in November 1975 that he had sold six hundred sets of drawings for just five of his recent ocean cruising designs. In the July 1975 *Bulletin* of the Seven Seas Cruising Association a letter noted that eighty yachts were in New Zealand to wait for the passing of the hurricane season (ten years ago the figure was eight). At least seventy-five yachts made the east to west Atlantic crossing from the Azores to the West Indies in 1975. In the 1976 Capetown to Rio de Janeiro race South Africa entered ninety-three yachts, half of which were cruising vessels. A dozen builders of wind-vane steering devices (average cost $600) sold fifty or more units. Eight years ago there were four nationally distributed yachting magazines. Today there are six, plus a dozen or so regional magazines and tabloid newspapers. Major equipment suppliers such as North Sails and Barient now direct sizable advertising and production effort toward the cruising market. There have been incredible lines of people waiting to inspect cruising yachts displayed at boat shows (in New York and London, for example). The New York–based Dolphin Book Club, which specializes in the sale of nonfiction sailing books and which hardly existed a dozen years ago, now has 50,000 members and is a multi-million-dollar business. The photograph (taken in September 1973) on page 15 is not of a wartime

What is yacht cruising coming to? Where will all the vessels go? Are the oceans large enough? How much pressure can Tahiti stand? Here in a corner of Pete's Harbor in Redwood City, California, is a fleet of ten nicely built, amateur-constructed ferro-cement yachts. These ten yachts will represent an investment of between a quarter and half a million dollars when ready for sea. But more than mere monuments to money, each yacht is owned by a man with his own hopes and dreams and aspirations.

shipyard but of yachts belonging to ten amateur builders at Pete's Harbor in Redwood City, California, a scene that has been duplicated in dozens of places all over the world. A few days ago I visited an English yacht named *Paille-en-Queue* that had just come from Europe. The captain told me that France claims to have 6,000 cruising yachts. This figure presumably includes many small coastal cruisers, but even if we take only 10 percent of the number, it is impressive.

Many of these bits of evidence are circumstantial. Nevertheless, the list can be extended until even a disbeliever realizes that ocean cruising has become big time. Much of the interest might be thought to be only hopes and dreams, but the substantial sums of money changing hands in bro-

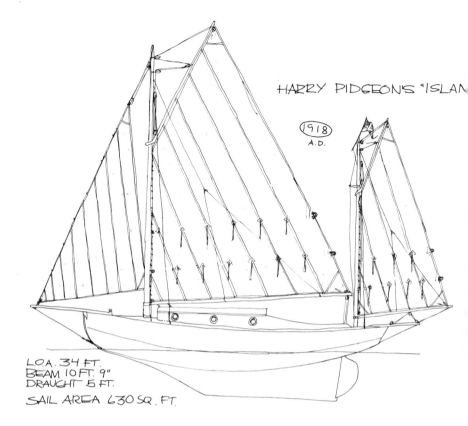

HARRY PIDGEON'S "ISLAN

1918 A.D.

LOA. 34 FT.
BEAM 10 FT. 9"
DRAUGHT 5 FT.
SAIL AREA 630 SQ. FT.

kerages and the arrivals of large numbers of yachts in foreign ports are not fantasies.

In 1895–98, Joshua Slocum sailed around the world in his famous *Spray*. Harry Pidgeon, who was fifty-one when he began, circumnavigated in *Islander* in 1921–26. Both yachts were home-built and both men were simple, salt-of-the-earth sailors whose direct and pithy accounts of their trips seem eternally fresh. Think, for a moment, of the astonishment that Slocum and Pidgeon might exhibit if they were alive to view some of today's cruising vessels. Both *Spray* and *Islander* were rigged as gaff yawls, both had plenty of sail area for their size, and both could be made to steer themselves by adjusting their sails (with the help of the small mizzen). Both yachts were engineless, both were easy to beach for bottom cleaning, both were built for very little money, and both made ocean passages that would be considered excellent today.

Can it be that we have lost something by trying to turn expensive racing yachts into vessels for ocean cruising? Must we have a 50 percent ballast ratio, twenty bags of Hood sails, half a dozen electronic instruments, a single side-band radio, a hydraulic backstay adjuster, and rod rigging to go to sea? Deck-sweeping genoas that pick up water and ruin visibility to leeward are not seaworthy. A low, droopy main boom that cracks people on the head is not humane. Why have cockpit coamings (to keep the helmsman dry) and toe rails (to brace your feet against and perhaps keep you from falling over the side) been eliminated in the quest to save a few pounds of weight?

Observers of the competition scene know that the slender, bendy masts of ocean racers break far more often than the owners care to admit. Instead of safety equipment lists that have become silly in their complexity and cost, the rules should ensure hulls and riggs that *will not fail*. Let's get our priorities in order. Spend the money on the yacht to make her supremely seaworthy in the first instance, not on rescue attempts after a Mickey Mouse hull and rig have failed. There is not a reason in the world why all ballasted monohulls cannot be made unsinkable by installing flotation between an inner and outer skin.

And while we are criticizing racing trends, what about cruising trends? Can it be that we have fallen into the trap of trying to make some of our beamy, shoal draft cruising vessels into shoreside apartments (with king-size beds, electric cooking, shag rugs, and deep-freeze units)? Some of the engine rooms of fifty-foot cruising yachts look more like the main propulsion rooms of World War II German submarines. Air conditioning may be nice at times, but why pay the price of machinery and engine time? Why not go where there is some wind and open a hatch?

It is obvious from their products that many builders who make cruising yachts do or have done very little sailing themselves. They are not interested in cruising but in selling so many units per month. In addition, many racing companies are hurrying to get into the cruising act, and as we have seen, the requirements are quite different. Marketing experts know that a woman's vote is important, so the builders have become more concerned with headroom for apartment styling than with draft for windward ability; more worried about refrigeration than about adequate anchors; more likely to install a pressure hot- and cold-water system than to provide a proper dinghy. Yet these people mumble about world cruising capability in the same breath that they discuss bank financing. Perhaps the truth is that most yachts will never unplug their yellow electrical umbilical cords and go anywhere anyway, so the dockside apartment marine living *is* more important.

I hope not.

The uneasiness and antagonism between many of the owners of mono-hulls and multihulls are discouraging. We should remember that we're all sailors and can learn much from each other. Even the most mossback monohuller is generally delightfully astonished at the acceleration and speed of a trimaran on his first ride. The recent multihull capsizes have been horrifying, but instead of endless criticizing and holier-than-thou pontificating by monohull owners, all of us should encourage naval architects to come up with a positive system of self-righting for oceangoing catamarans and trimarans. This is a problem of first priority. Certainly if naval architects like Dick Newick can design such brilliant, eye-catching, and high-performance trimarans as *Three Cheers, Gulfstreamer,* and *Val,* they can invent a system of righting an upside-down craft. *They must.*

Finally, must yachts look so alike. A splendid variety of rigs and hulls is available. There are five hundred years of traditional designs from which to choose. We have the gaff ketch, the staysail schooner, the Chinese lugsail rig, the cat ketch, the lateen—the list goes on and on. We have bluff-bowed hulls, long slender hulls, double-enders, hulls with reverse sheer, those lovely hulls with the gorgeous sheer that John Alden used to draw for his *Malabar* schooners.

What I am saying is that a cruising yacht can be distinctive, pretty, sail reasonably well, and still be simple and moderately priced. The more complex a vessel is and the more maintenance and money she requires, the less an owner will enjoy his voyages because too much of his time will be spent on upkeep and repairs.

Remember when we started out to see the world and to meet people in different lands we spoke of the delight and independence that an ocean cruising yacht can give? Let's not forget that magical phrase: "the pleasure and the freedom."

This book is full of nuts-and-bolts information. I express opinions frequently. I name people and products. My standards are demanding because I use marine gear for years and years, not for one quick trip. Often I must make repairs in difficult, out-of-the-way places. If I seem exasperated at times, it's because I consider that some trends on ocean cruising yachts are disastrous. We can begin the list with cockpits that are much too large for safety, paltry anchors, too many gadgets, and hopeless navigation lights. I have no admiration at all for the over-dependence on large, complicated, and inaccessible engines, useless refrigeration systems, the lack of suitable dinghies, and keel designs that make yachts difficult or impossible to haul out of the water in remote places.

At the end of this book is an Appendix with the names and addresses of many nautical firms and various sailing specialists. If you want more information, please write directly to the manufacturers, suppliers, and designers (not to me or the publisher).

2

~~~~~~

The Corpus Itself

The hulls of sailing yachts are made of wood, steel, aluminum, ferro-cement, and fiberglass. Each material has advantages and disadvantages. None is perfect and none is simple or cheap. The cost of the hull of a yacht is roughly 20 percent of her total no matter what the material, so a saving of 10 or 20 percent (so widely advertised) is really only an economy of 2 to 4 percent, not a large consideration because the hull, after all, is the heart of a vessel. The costs for the ballast, mast, spars, rigging, interior woodwork, tanks, and machinery do not vary no matter what hull material is used.

The main structural members of a hull are the *stem, keel,* and *stern-post.* Curved athwartship *frames* are erected above and on each side of this central backbone. The frames are let in or welded to the keel and

The staysail schooner Sauvage *was built in France to designs of Dominique Presles. Her aluminum hull is quite fair and no filling of any kind was used. The owner wanted a low maintenance yacht, so—like many French aluminum vessels—the topsides are unpainted. The bottom is coated with an arsenic base paint. With the exception of the stainless steel propeller shaft, all underwater parts—including the propeller—are made of the same aluminum alloy to reduce possible galvanic action. Her electrical system uses a two-wire ungrounded wiring scheme. Sauvage's measurements: 47′11″ x 40′4″ x 13′1″ x 6′5″. Displacement 13 tons (14 tons loaded).*

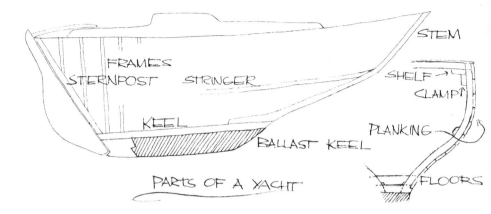

stem; to add to the strength of the frames and to tie opposite frames to each other and to the keel, transverse *floors* are laid across the frames just above the keel. The athwartship floors bind the frames and keel into a single unit of great strength. (The floors are structural members and have nothing to do with the cabin sole.)

The *ballast keel* is usually a massive lead molding that is bolted to the wooden (or metal) keel. With steel and aluminum the lead ballast is sometimes melted into place inside the hull; with fiberglass the ballast is often put inside in small blocks. The hull is *planked* or *plated* with longitudinal planks or plates of metal. *Stringers* are fore-and-aft wooden or metal strengthening pieces that run inside the frames from the stem to the stern. The *clamp* (or sheer clamp) is a structural member that runs fore and aft on the inside and just below the tops of the frames. A second structural member called the *shelf* is bolted to the clamp (sometimes one piece of wood or metal is used for both), and the shelf takes the athwartship deck beams which support the deck. All through the construction each piece is screwed or bolted or welded to its neighbor to make a rigid and unyielding structure of great strength.

There are five ways to build with wood: carvel planking, clinker planking, strip planking, plywood, and cold-molded.

Here boatbuilder Cliff Niederer of Inverness, California, works on the wooden hull of a 42-foot Howard Chapelle traditional American design. About 30 percent of the fir planking is in place and the hull is beginning to fill out with a smooth and graceful shape.

The traditional wood construction (still widely used in many countries for work and fishing craft) is *carvel planking*, in which longitudinal planks, say 1¼ x 5 inches (for a thirty-eight-foot vessel), are nailed or screwed to transverse frames erected on heavy fore-and-aft timbers that make up the stem, keel, and sternpost. The seams between the planks are caulked to make the hull watertight. Such a hull relies on strong fastenings to hold its hundreds of separate pieces together, each of which has been named and its function carefully worked out during centuries of trial and error. Because of the many skilled hand operations and the difficulty of buying suitable wood, few carvel-planked yachts are built today.

Clinker planking, sometimes called clench or lapstrake, is similar to carvel except that the planks are overlapped slightly and through-fastened. This makes an extremely strong hull which requires no caulking and is quite watertight. Unfortunately, the hull is not smooth because of the projecting plank edges. Varnished clinker planking is common in Scandinavia.

Strip planking is a scheme of wooden hull construction in which the planks are generally square (perhaps 1 or 1½ inches). The top of each strip is cut slightly concave and the bottom shaped a little convex so that each plank will fit nicely into the next when working up or down the curves of the hull. Every plank is glued and edge-nailed to its neighbor, which results in a rigid, watertight, and very strong monocoque hull that is well suited to amateur construction. Since small sizes of wood air-dry more rapidly, the problem of getting suitable wood is easier than with carvel planking.

Plywood can be bent only one way, so its use is limited to a hard chine hull with parallel topsides and a V bottom. The sides of the V are sometimes split and angled outward a second time, which results in a double chine or a more rounded hull section. This type of building is good for amateurs except that the rabbets in the chine logs (the longitudinal pieces that take the edges of the pieces of plywood) are difficult to cut. Many yachts with hard chine hulls are superb sailing vessels, especially the famous Grumete and Cadete designs of Germán Frers Sr. of Argentina. Eric Taberly's *Pen Duick VI,* the winner of many races, has a hard chine hull form although built of aluminum.

The fifth type of wooden boatbuilding is *cold-molded,* in which thin layers of hardwood (say ⅛ or 3/16 x 5 inches) are formed over a male mold. The hull is built upside down, and initially a single laminated piece that forms the stem, keel, and sternpost is put into place along the top of the mold. The first layer of planking over the male mold is followed by the second, resorcinol-glued and stapled, with the grain of the wood aligned in a different direction. The grain of each succeeding lamination crosses at a different angle, resulting in a plywood-like, one-piece hull of great strength and lightness. From three to nine laminations are built over the form before the hull is removed from the mold and the internal framing installed. The famous yachts *Stormvogel, Windward Passage, Gypsy Moth IV,* and *Gypsy Moth V* all have cold-molded hulls. An advantage of cold-molded is that wafer-thin planks are used and the wood can be seasoned quickly. The hulls are costly, however, because craftsmen of great skill and integrity are needed.

The strength of wood is reduced significantly when wet. The American Plywood Association notes that stiffness, for example, is lessened about 11 percent with a moisture content of 16 percent or more. Allowable stress in bending is reduced 25 percent and compression as much as 39 percent. The WEST system of the Gougeon Brothers—in which cold-molded wood is saturated with thin epoxy to make an almost new material—has much to recommend it.

All five types of wooden construction require frames (steam-bent, sawn, grown, laminated, or made of metal), floors of wood or metal, a clamp and shelf, and stringers.

Decks are often made of several layers of plywood with their joints carefully scarfed and staggered. The plywood is screwed or nailed to the deck beams, which are bolted to the shelf, which in turn was bolted to the clamp, as we have seen. The decks are sometimes covered with teak planking for appearance and non-skid, or more often fiberglassed with paint and sand for non-skid or a covering such as Treadmaster.

Wood is subject to rot, especially wood of poor quality that is improperly seasoned. Careful design, however, together with adequate ventilation and chemical treatment, can minimize such deterioration. Wood immersed in the sea is attacked by marine borers which can destroy unprotected timbers in less than a year. Shipworms (teredo and bankia) and gribble (limnoria) can be kept away either by putting sheets of thin copper over the wood or by covering it with heavy toxic paint. With strip-planked, plywood, and cold-molded hulls you can get perfect protection from marine borers by putting a single layer of fiberglass cloth and polyester or epoxy resin on the hull. This is not possible with carvel construction because of the expansion and contraction of the planks.

Steel is excellent for larger yacht hulls. The metal is by far the strongest of all hull materials and can be easily and positively fastened by welding. Steel is quite cheap, and it is simple to have it shot-blasted and painted before use. A surprising amount of the paint stays on during the cutting and handling. Either hard chine or conventionally curved hulls can be built. The procedure starts with steel frames being erected on the stem, keel, and sternpost pieces, which are also cut from steel. Longitudinal stringers fair out the hull and form the substructure. The plating ($\frac{3}{16}$ inch for a 42-footer) goes on in large rectangular pieces that can be rolled, pounded, or forced into the necessary curves.

It is impressive to watch a metalworker plate a new vessel. After raising a plate (say 3 x 6 feet) into position over the framework, the builder

Construction of a 46-foot Buchanan steel cutter in California using ³/₁₆-inch plating. (Photo by Tee Jennings)

clamps one or two edges and fastens them down with tack welds. Then with powerful clamps, purchases, bars, and much ingenuity the metal-worker begins to bend the plate little by little until after several hours or a day's work the plate is pulled and pushed into its final curve.

I remember watching Alex Jacubenko—an extremely skilled craftsman —at work in Sausalito. "A steel plate is like a woman," he said. "It will yield only to a stronger mind and a superior force." Then Alex would grunt a little and lever a big hydraulic jack into position.

After the plates are all tacked into place, they are welded together into a structure of tremendous strength, the only sort of hull that has a chance on a coral reef. The decks can be made of steel (heavy) or plywood (lighter).

Unprotected steel rusts quickly and must be zinc-sprayed and painted, or painted after sandblasting to protect the metal from salt water. In addition, it is generally necessary to sandblast the hull down to bare metal every four or five years. A builder must be careful not to use bronze through-hull fittings, for example, because galvanic action (two nearby dissimilar metals electrically connected and immersed in an elec-trolyte) begins at once in salt water. The steel hull, the less noble metal, begins to decay, and in time holes will be eaten in the plating next to the bronze fittings. (Steel hulls made today generally have iron or plastic valves.) It is customary to attach small sacrificial plates of zinc to the propeller shaft and any underwater fittings made of metal different from the hull. The zincs, being anodic, or least noble, are eaten away before the underwater fittings, and it is simple to replace the zinc plates during a haulout. Most steel commercial vessels use zincs.

These points suggest that a steel hull requires a lot of maintenance. It is, however, extremely strong. The bottom of the keel can be made of 1-inch steel plate if you wish; the heavy plate acts as both ballast and an indestructible bumper. A steel hull is easy and fast to repair because you can find competent welders all over the world. The metallic shell has watertight integrity, and has no problems at all with shipworm. With careful design and the use of stainless steel in a few places (in the chain plates and for the bulwarks, for instance), the maintenance can be reduced.

Aluminum is much lighter than steel and in the alloy used for boatbuilding (4 percent magnesium) is quite free from corrosion. Aluminum can be welded with special equipment and is ideal for yacht hulls (a 45-foot vessel uses $\frac{5}{16}$-inch plate). The main problems are the high cost of the material and the greater expense of welding. The metal is excellent for decks.

In good hands an aluminum hull can be a thing of great beauty, besides being lightweight and leakproof. It is possible to skip deck and topside painting altogether, though these areas are normally painted for aesthetic reasons (the paint adhesion problems have not been entirely solved). In the early 1950's, Tom and Ann Worth circumnavigated in *Beyond*, a Laurent Giles forty-three-foot cutter that was constructed of riveted Birmabright, an aluminum alloy. At the moment aluminum is used mostly for large custom racing vessels, although naval architect Tom Colvin elected to use this metal for the hull of his new cruising yacht *K'ung Fu-ste*. The slowly increasing use of aluminum for custom building is evolving a technology that should eventually trickle down to the ordinary cruising market.

Electrolysis, the corrosion caused by stray electrical currents seeking a ground, can be serious in a steel yacht and catastrophic in an aluminum hull. The electrical wiring must be faultless. A two-wire, non-grounded system is favored by most engineers. Taking aboard electric power from the shore is risky. Harbors full of powerboats and commercial vessels often have stray currents in the water and are a poor environment for metal-hulled vessels.

Aluminum alloy may well be the hull material of the future because it is lightweight, strong, and can be positively fastened by welding. Each year brings improvements in handling, and with the continuing price rises of fiberglass materials and resin, aluminum becomes more attractive. The topsides of aluminum yachts can be left completely unpainted if desired. Bottom paints with copper are not normally used, but there are excellent paints that employ tin or arsenic compounds. The aluminum hull in the photograph has long bars of T-shaped stock tacked in place on the outside of the plating to keep it smooth during construction.

In addition, galvanic action—quite distinct from electrolysis—is not to be ignored. The problem is not new. A century ago when a giant New York racing yacht with an all-bronze hull (!) was moored with a group of its rivals (perhaps with iron cables to a common iron buoy?), the other yacht captains began to complain that their underwater iron was disappearing.

During the past ten years there has been much talk about *ferro-cement* hulls. In one system, frames of iron pipe are erected on a metal backbone. Longitudinals of 1/4-inch iron rods (or high-tensile steel) are tacked in place, spaced about every four inches from the keel to the bulwarks. Then layers of square welded mesh (or chicken wire) are laid over the hull on both the inside and outside and tied to one another and to the longitudinal metal rods with small wires. The entire hull is then plastered with a dense, cement-rich concrete mix.

This all sounds fast and cheap, but the amount of handwork is considerable. Care is necessary with the lofting, the setting up of the frames, and at every step. The plastering is critical and expensive, and unless a first-class hull results, the amateur builder will be quite disappointed and own a product that is completely unsalable.

Ferro-cement yachts tend to be heavy, often a good deal more so than their designers admit, and the sailing performance suffers because the vessel is under-rigged for its weight. Because of its inherent weight, ferro-cement construction is best for large yachts, say forty-five to fifty-five feet. In particular, ferro-cement decks and bulkheads are disastrous because of their great weight, which robs the usual iron ballast (lead is so much better) of much of its effect. The desperate novice owner then installs a big engine and large fuel tanks, whose weight handicaps the sailing even more. A ferro-cement hull must be insulated for cold-weather sailing; painting is not easy, and sometimes the wavy lines in a hull are enough to make even the strong weep. It is important to get complete penetration of the metal armature when the vessel is plastered; otherwise the hull will be in trouble from the beginning. To guard against voids, uneasy builders often drill hundreds of holes and pump in epoxy or grout under pressure.

In spite of these problems, a ferro-cement hull designed by an expert can take an owner a very long way. The voyages of Bob and Nancy Griffith in their fifty-three-foot *Awahnee* have been exemplary, although the hull was fiberglassed a few years ago to reduce rust bleeding, cracking, and peeling. I have seen beautiful ferro-cement yachts from New Zealand, from Vancouver, and from England. All, however, were constructed by experts who would have done a good job in any medium.

Naval architect Bruce Bingham, who has made an intensive study of ferro-cement (and has even done a book), wrote in *Sail* magazine in August 1973:

When it gets down to laying mesh, applying rods, twisting wires and fairing out the ferro-cement armature, the inexperienced amateur may be in for a further shock. The process takes untold patience, much more than the proponents dare to admit. A comparable strip-planked hull, for instance, may be constructed and faired in about one fourth the time required for ferro-cement, and a one-off fiberglass hull can usually be completed in slightly more than half the time of ferro-cement, using a male mold process. Aluminum construction is well beyond the amateur capability, but construction of a hard-chine plywood or steel hull can still beat ferro-cement on the time scale.

Regrettably, ferro-cement building—which actually may have a good future—has suffered enormously from the misleading publicity of a few unscrupulous promoters who have implied to unwary plan buyers (by way of magazine advertisements that should never have been printed) that they could easily build a yacht that could sail around the world. All they needed was a few bits of iron pipe, some iron rods, a little chicken wire, and a few bags of cement. I am writing this in 1977, and I defy anyone to build a first-class forty-foot ferro-cement yacht ready for the sea with ballast, deck, interior, engine, spars, sails, and ground tackle for less than $25,000. It can't be done.

A dozen years ago another promoter, who was pushing trimarans, promised the same sort of pie-in-the-sky. A born salesman who could have sold ice to Eskimos, this man claimed that for a few sheets of plywood, a little glue, and a few odds and ends that you probably have in your garage, you could put together a multihull in which you could sail off into the blue and retire from the world. This was manifestly untrue, misleading, and quite dishonest, as many gullible people discovered after wasting a lot of time and money. Aside from the question of multihull seaworthiness, which I will mention in a later chapter, it is not possible to build any sort of reasonable yacht with bits and scraps unless you are resourceful and ingenious to an extraordinary degree and are willing to put up with considerable discomfort and some hardship. It is notable that this man didn't go around the world in one of his vessels, nor have the ferro-cement promoters.

An encyclopedia salesman gives away a lot of free words, but he never gives away free books.

It is too bad that these people exist, for they cause harm to everyone and give the sport of sailing a bad name. All, however, is not lost, because most builders and designers are scrupulously honest. I am impressed with the efforts of the commercial English and New Zealand ferro-cement builders and the *Journal of Ferro-Cement* under the editorship of Ian Baugh.

We have talked briefly about wood, steel, aluminum, and ferro-cement. Now let's discuss *fiberglass* yacht construction, a scheme that started commercially in the United States in 1958, when William Coleman began to build the forty-foot Bounty design of Phillip Rhodes at Aeromarine Plastics in Sausalito, California. From time to time I still see Bounties sailing. They may need painting, and some of the fittings may be a little worn, but the vessels are still afloat and presumably seaworthy.

Fiberglass vessels are constructed of thin glass filaments that have been made into various kinds of fabrics. When a hull is laid up, these fabrics, a layer at a time, are saturated with liquid polyester resin. When the resin becomes hard, a new substance is formed that has strength properties superior to either the glass fabric or the resin. A comparison can be made with the steel and cement of reinforced concrete. In a fiberglass laminate the amount of strengthening glass filament runs about 30 percent, a great deal more than the percentage of steel in reinforced concrete.

Fiberglass (often called GRP or FRP for "glass-reinforced plastic" or "fiberglass-reinforced plastic") is a remarkable material. It is strong, free from rot, unaffected by marine borers, has a useful life of twenty years or more, and is ideal for molding complex shapes that are hard to construct in wood. GRP is lightweight (in suitable design and execution), and repairs are easy as long as you have a dry environment, heat, and a powerful disk sander. Some 90 percent of all U.S. yachts use fiberglass for their hulls. Worldwide for cruising yachts the figure is considerably less—my guess is 40 or 50 percent—though the figure is increasing. There is much talk of fiberglass, but away from the United States and Europe you see many wooden and steel yachts.

Fiberglass also has drawbacks. The materials are expensive. The usual polyester resin is not fireproof. Abrasion resistance is low. The work is a messy, smelly business. When you use a disk sander on fiberglass, the resulting dust is extremely irritating, and the hell of fiberglass itch is well known. Generally a costly female mold is needed for a hull, although progress is being made with one-off male molds. A GRP hull and deck need to be carefully insulated if the vessel is to be used in cold weather (see Chapter 8).

It is necessary to protect a fiberglass layup from the effects of water seepage and ultraviolet rays. This is done with gel coat, whose colors are so shiny and gorgeous when new. Gel coat, however, is a soft, difficult, and unstable material that gives much trouble to builders and shipyards. Severe underwater blistering is common and is such a problem that some builders now paint the below-water parts of hulls with special epoxy or polyurethane paints from the beginning. The offending agent in the gel coat may be the colored pigment, and several prominent builders, among them Nautor of Finland and Tyler of England, paint the bottoms of their yachts with unpigmented gel coat. Besides the bottom problems, which are considerable, gel-coated topsides become faded, dull, and scratched after four or five years and are usually painted with epoxy products. I look for gel coat to be phased out as paints are improved.

A fiberglass hull is usually constructed in a wax-coated female mold which has been made from a strip-planked plug. The first step is to spray a layer of gel coat resin inside the mold. Then the laminators climb inside the mold and, working from a scaffolding, carefully press a layer of fiberglass cloth against the gel coat. The cloth is saturated with polyester resin, and any air bubbles are rolled out. Then the main building commences. This is a layer of heavy mat—a material with short fibers in random directions—followed by a layer of roving—bundles of continuous fibers woven into a sort of coarse, thick cloth. To simplify somewhat, mat has superior bonding properties but only moderate strength. Roving is a very strong material but its bonding qualities are poorer. So alternate layers of mat and roving are used—each saturated with resin and any air bubbles removed—until a suitable hull thickness is built up, say from $\frac{5}{16}$ to 1 inch depending on the location. Next go in longitudinal stiffeners, perhaps floors and a sheer clamp, and finally the bulkheads. It is a good idea to keep the hull in the mold until the stiffeners and bulkheads are glassed into place so the hull will maintain the exact form of the mold. Chainplates are often added at this point so that the hull can be lifted conveniently.

It is unpleasant to work with strong chemicals and irritating glass materials deep inside a hull. For this reason and because it is difficult to supervise semiskilled labor, some companies build fiberglass hulls in two halves, which are joined with many layers of mat and roving. In England two-piece hulls are usually strengthened with substantial floors, which are a good idea for one-piece hulls also. A few custom builders, Frers & Cibels, for instance, construct a longitudinal I-beam inside the hull along the entire length of the stem, keel, and sternpost to reinforce the hull for high rigging tensions. If the design uses a fin keel, floors are necessary to take the keel bolts. In any case, some sort of interior structure is necessary for a foundation for the interior joinery. Such structures might as well serve as useful strengthening members. This may sound obvious, but many builders construct the hulls and interiors separately and merely tack the furniture in place instead of strongly glassing in settee fronts, shelves, partial bulkheads, and so on.

Another common GRP hull building scheme is to use $\frac{1}{2}$ or $\frac{3}{4}$-inch end grain balsa or Airex (a special closed-cell polyvinyl chloride foam that comes in 3 x 6-foot sheets) between two layers of fiberglass layup. This foam core, or sandwich construction, is more trouble to make but gives considerable strength, excellent insulation, and is lightweight. Through-hull fastening areas require a solid layup or special spacers to keep bolts, for example, from crushing the foam. The keel area is commonly strengthened by solid GRP. The decks of yachts are often built with a balsa core to give a more solid feel and to stop condensation by adding a layer of insulation.

Fiberglass hulls can also be built of a single layup or sandwich construction over a male mold. Naval architect Jerry Cartwright has designed several stout cruising yachts built over male molds using C-flex, a material that incorporates long, thin glass rods within a fiberglass fabric. The C-flex "planks" come in long rolls and can be bent in two directions to follow compound curves. I think this technique has a good future, especially for one-off hulls.

Fiberglass yachts built in the United States generally have thick skins, bulkheads, and minimum internal framing, while vessels built in England have thinner skins with more internal longitudinal and transverse stiffeners. Large unsupported flat areas of a hull are vulnerable to oil-canning; also, if an American-style hull is fractured, the damage can extend as far as a bulkhead. Adequate longitudinal and transverse framing tends to localize damage and to maintain hull form. I favor such internal framing, which is simple to install when the hull is molded. If 1½-inch softwood dowels are sliced lengthwise, tacked in place to make a latticework of 12-inch or 15-inch squares, and covered with three or four layers of mat, the gain in hull rigidity is amazing. The bottom area should have adequate floors. Lloyd's scantling rules specify a 9-inch-deep floor spaced every 16 inches for a thirty-five-foot hull. Each floor should have two limber or drainage holes.

Unfortunately, in the United States there is a phobia about hull thickness ("How thick is she?"), which, though important, is not the complete answer. Fiberglass becomes a costly and heavy material when laid up in 1-inch thickness. The hull, of course, varies from the deck to the keel, but in general I believe that an average thickness of ½ or ⅝ inch plus floors, internal stiffening, and a stout hull-deck joint is optimum for a forty-foot hull.

In my judgment the best ballast arrangement is to use an external one-piece lead molding that is substantially bolted to heavy floors that are well glassed into the hull. If you go aground with such an exterior keel, the mass of lead takes the punishment. Putting lead inside the hull is simple, cheap, and quick but much less satisfactory to the man who sails the yacht. The resistance of GRP to abrasion is poor, particularly if you put the full weight of the yacht on a small area of fiberglass. If you go aground with a fiberglass keel and are unfortunate enough to pound for a few hours, rocks will chew right through the fiberglass and reduce it to a useless hash. Such damage is extremely tedious to repair even when you are hauled out, because you can seldom get the keel area high enough into the air to work on it properly. Lying on wet ground and grinding fiberglass and copper paint above my head with the GRP fibers and paint dust falling into my face is not my idea of fun.

A grounded yacht is always in a chancy position; yet vessels with lead keels have pounded for days with only superficial dents and gouges. The sailor with a fiberglass hull with the ballast inside the keel area is less fortunate. If your builder at least encapsulated the ballast inside the hull and securely blocked its chamber off from the rest of the hull, you are lucky and your yacht will not fill with water. In theory, interior lead is supposed to be massively cemented in place with a mixture of resin and asbestos fibers or resin and sawdust, but all too often the high-school dropout who was doing the job was dreaming of a White Christmas and left large voids. This means that a rupture of the keel area may lead to flooding. If you think that I am a chronic complainer, I can tell you that twice I have knocked small holes in the keel area of my vessel *Whisper*, and twice my wife and I have had to pump non-stop for several days. The only way to fix a fiberglass hull with voids between the shell of the hull and the ballast inside is to tap for voids and then to drill several dozen small holes and to either pump in or suck in epoxy under pressure so the entire keel area becomes a one-piece whole that cannot leak into the interior of the yacht (this begins to sound like ferro-cement).

Occasionally builders use lead shot or small bits of lead for ballast. I have heard of an unfortunate Englishman who punched a hole in the keel area of his vessel and lost his entire ballast, which ran out like watery soup. Builders use encapsulated ballast for only one reason: it is cheaper. There is much talk about keel bolts leaking, but substantial monel bolts (you need fewer than a dozen) and stout floors need not leak a drop if properly caulked at building time.

A second reason for favoring an external bolted-on keel is that the lead will take the shocks and strains of haulouts. In both remote and near places, haulout cradles are sometimes misaligned, ill-fitting, and tottery. A block of lead three or four feet long gives a good margin for error if the yacht comes out of the water with the cradle in the wrong place. We hauled *Whisper* out in Pichidangui, Chile, at a small yacht club whose members swore by their marine railway. They even sent down a diver to be certain that the car on the marine ways was set correctly. Unfortunately, it was not, and when the yacht emerged from the water, the entire weight of the vessel rested on the edge of a thin steel brace that ran athwartships across the end of the marine car. Part of the fiberglass keel area was crushed and cracked. I spent three weeks repairing the damage— mostly waiting for the area to dry out and trying to get sanding disks and heat lamps from Santiago by an occasional bus.

A third reason for using an exterior keel and keel bolts is that it is simple to fit one or two lifting eyes to the tops of several keel bolts. A stout cable can be led from the eyebolts vertically through a skylight or overhead ventilator to the lifting hook of a crane. In many places a 25-ton (or more) crane is available which can easily lift a yacht for bottom painting. If copper paint is sprayed over a smooth, well-sanded bottom, complete coverage is ensured and a perfect job is possible.

Such a lifting arrangement is ideal because no paint-gouging straps or cables need be used around the hull. You dispense entirely with cumbersome marine railways. In Callao, Peru, for example, there are several 50-ton cranes at the naval shipyard; no other haulout arrangement is available for a yacht. In Buenos Aires the Argentine yachtsmen use this system to perfection and routinely haul their vessels for a two-hour scrub. I have seen yachts lifted similarly in Japan. Sometimes it is possible to get a friendly cargo ship captain to lift you on board in a perfectly calm harbor if the ship has no pressing business. The advantages for shipping a yacht are obvious.

3

~~~~~~

A New Yacht

I have nothing but admiration for naval architects, for their job is hardest of all. Not only must they juggle several dozen complex design variables and think about safety (make it heavy), but they must concern themselves with performance and good sailing (make it light). Naval architects answer many inquiries and deal with clients whose sailing experience, whose desires and hopes, and whose finances range from 0 to 100. A naval architect often turns into a sort of family adviser, referee, and juggler of dreams. He is, of course, a mathematical expert who works with such things as wetted area, prismatic coefficients, centers of effort, righting moments, and wringing stresses. He thinks about water flow, buoyancy, quarter waves, and deadrise. He must know about rigging strains, plating thicknesses, propeller cavitation, mast tangs, sail battens, and Herreshoff's scantling rules.

One of the excitements of traveling on the oceans of the world is that every day is different. While north of Bermuda we sailed in company with this great Chilean barkentine Esmeralda. *Aboard the 100-meter four-master were 167 officers and 170 midshipmen. When I took this photograph, the winds were light—12 to 14 knots—which drove* Whisper *along at five knots. In the same wind the* Esmeralda *could do not better. We sailed together for some hours until with a freshening wind our tall sister left us far behind. In the photograph all sorts of regular and unusual sails are set on the four-master. I count 26. What do you get?*

In addition to all this, the successful naval architect must be a bit of an artist. Who but a man with an inspired hand could draw the eye-pleasing lines of a John Alden, Bill Garden, Germán Frers Sr., Laurent Giles, and Robert Clark? Indeed, some of these men are excellent painters and musicians. We know that the best naval architect is both a traditionalist and an experimenter who cheerfully blends new ideas and bold approaches with a heady admixture of time-honored common sense. Above all he must keep a measure of respect for the sea, which is strong, unyielding, and quite nasty at times. No matter what else happens, the structure and the rig of the vessel *must not fail.*

Think, for example, of the design problems of a hard chine cruising yacht thirty-five feet long built of plywood. If the hull sections are too flat, she will pound. If the sections are too soft, she will be impossibly tender. How much ballast will she need? How heavy should the plywood be? What sort of fastenings, frames, and floors will she need? What about the details of the rudder? The engine? The mast? The keel? The cockpit? (The poor architect can do a perfect job on the entire yacht, but if the slope of the cockpit coaming doesn't fit the owner's back, the architect's payment will be a hailstorm of curses.)

Take just one detail, the main boom. How long should it be? What is the best shape? Size? What material? Is the boom to bend in strong winds to flatten the mainsail? What about the gooseneck arrangements at the forward end and the outhaul hardware at the after end? How is the mainsheet to be attached? If the boom is to be aluminum, what is the best extrusion size? Availability? What about corrosion protection? Cost? Weight? Reefing arrangements?

Each of these design points—I can list fifty categories more—may necessitate a separate session of thinking and drawing, for a builder can only follow the actual plans and drawings and specification sheets of a naval architect. Unless an amateur builder is talented to an extraordinary degree, he should work from the plans of a professional architect. The product will be a hundredfold better, particularly in pleasing and effective hull lines and clever design details that are mastered only with long practice.

But we all know this and try to buy from established people who construct first-class vessels based on the best designs. We compare specifications of different yachts, go for trial sails, talk to owners, and think hard about the costs.

Yet in spite of the flint-hard figures of finance and the uncompromising lines on drawings, you buy a yacht because she is pretty. In your mind you have certain size and performance limits, of course, but beyond that the vessel must appeal to you. Something about her must catch your eye. Some combination of color, the sheer of her hull, the rake of her masts, the jaunty tilt of her bowsprit, or the appeal of her tall white sails. Maybe it is not folly that a ship is always called by the feminine pronoun, for she is very much like a woman. Full of curves, contradictions, pleasure, trouble, expense, and delight.

As is true of most sailors, the shape and appearance of a vessel mean a lot to me. A little more than twelve years ago, when Margaret and I were hunting for a new yacht, we traveled to Seattle, Washington, to look at yachts at Shilshole Bay Marina. We saw a sleek black sloop glide silently into her berth pulled along by a half-lowered jib. The yacht was the size we wanted. She charmed us at once.

"Is she for sale?" we asked the owner. "What is her design?"

"Not at all," he replied, answering our questions in turn. "She is a Spencer 35 built across the border in Canada. The designer is John Brandlmayr and the builder is Phil Hantke. Go see them. A small yard. Nice people."

We did as the man suggested. We became friends with the designer and builder, both competent professionals, and eventually bought hull No. 29 of a series production. With the approval of the architect we made a few minor changes and additions. Our new child was launched in February 1966, a date that seems ages ago. I marvel at what Margaret and I have been through with our little vessel since the first day she floated in salt water.

"What have been your experiences with your yacht as a cruising vessel?" and "What would you change?" are questions that we have heard again and again during our travels.

Whisper was constructed by Spencer Boats, Ltd., of Richmond, British Columbia, and with 25-foot waterline and a 9-foot 6-inch beam she was representative of design of that period. She has a masthead sloop rig and, as built, had a six-ton displacement, a cockpit 8 feet 6 inches long, and four large portlights set in a small doghouse raised above a low coach roof that extended from the cockpit to five feet forward of the mast. Our new yacht also had a wooden mast. But more about that later.

Her bow has a moderate overhang with rounded V-shaped sections, and the hull ends in a graceful counter of medium length. Her stern and midship sections are quite hard, and she carries 4,200 pounds of lead ballast near the bottom of her hull, which had a designed draft of 5 feet 3 inches when built. Both a 35-gallon diesel tank and a 39-gallon water tank are in the bilge. The rudder is attached to what corresponds to the sternpost in the traditional manner. John Brandlmayr gave *Whisper* an eight-foot flat-bottomed keel that was horizontal in profile and continued forward into a gently rounded forefoot. Although various details differed, our little vessel resembled an Alberg 35, a Pearson Vanguard, a Nicholson 32, and various of the Allied, Cal, and Columbia yachts before general adoption of spade or skeg-hung rudders and separate keels in pursuit of less wetted area, the current Holy Grail.

The keel shapes of cruising vessels is a subject on which people have strong opinions. A long-keel design (even with a cutaway forefoot) has more wetted area than a hull with a fin keel and spade or skeg-hung rudder. More wetted area means more drag, so if everything else is equal, the fin-keel design will outperform the long-keeled vessel by a small margin.

The problems of keel design are not black and white, however. The rudder of a long-keel design is generally stronger because the stock is fastened along its length, and protected against flotsam or the strain of grounding. You seldom hear about the loss of such rudders. Damage to or the loss of a separate spade or skeg-hung rudder is more common. As a practical matter for sailing performance the small increase in wetted area of a long-keel design is not as important as a clean bottom.

To me the only significant aspects of the question are (1) the integrity of the rudder and (2) the ease of hauling, which is so important for a world cruising yacht. The slight hydrodynamic advantages of fin keels and spade or skeg-hung rudders are of no practical significance to a cruising yacht.

In a fin-keel design the propeller is usualy located in the open area between the keel and rudder with the propeller shaft held by a bronze, stainless, or monel strut. Under power the propeller is more efficient because it works in clear water away from the hull. But when sailing, the propeller is still out in the open and gives substantial drag. To solve this problem designers have gone to folding propellers, an absolute curse for cruising vessels. If the folding propeller fails for any reason and an unbalanced propeller starts to rotate, the vibration may well fracture and break the propeller shaft strut. A feathering propeller, it seems to me, is eminently more suitable. Either that, or you must carry a spare strut.*

---

* I don't wish to burden this chapter with horror stories, but I have firsthand knowledge of a Columbia 45 named *Sea Song III* that got a sheet wrapped around her propeller, not an uncommon occurrence. Usually the engine stalls. Not so in the case of *Sea Song III*. The propeller strut—with no backing plate—pulled out and took a piece of the flimsy hull with it. The yacht sank in five minutes (on February 2, 1972), fortunately in a shallow part of San Diego Bay. A second occurrence was in

*People in the business of selling yachts often call a vessel such as this
Viking 34 a racer-cruiser, but where in the world can you haul out such
a yacht except where there is a crane and slings or a Travelift?*

The propeller of a long-keel design generally revolves in an aperture; during sailing, the propeller can be aligned vertically inside the hull aperture to reduce the drag of the blades.

With her long keel *Whisper* sails spendidly, although she is at her best in medium airs, say 12 to 20 knots. She is easy to steer and is steady on the helm. Her deep wineglass sections allow a spacious and pleasant accommodation. The vessel is simple to haul on a marine railway, and an accidental grounding is not the disaster that it might be for some configurations of spade rudders and fin keels that seem to me more suited to the design of dainty ballet slippers than ocean cruising yachts. I have looked at recent designs billed as racer-cruisers that can only be hauled by specialists using a Travelift or a crane and slings, an absurdity for a cruising vessel because these facilities don't exist except in relatively few isolated places in the world and only in some yacht yards.

Our fiberglass hull has been magnificent. Except for three mishaps which were no fault of the hull, it has never leaked a drop or given us a moment of doubt. Likewise the molded deck, coach-roof, and cockpit

---

Salvador, Brazil, in March 1976, when the crew of a South African yacht named *Port Rex*, which was next to us, suddenly felt a horrible thumping when the engine was put into gear. Drying out against a seawall revealed a broken strut because a pin that kept one blade of the Martec propeller from folding incorrectly had come adrift. As soon as the engine was put into gear, there was a huge imbalance; vibration immediately sheared the strut.

structure have been outstanding—no leaks and reasonably easy to keep clean. The bond between the hull and deck, however, gave us a lot of trouble for four and a half years because it leaked in a manner that was devilishly hard to track down and repair. To have finally condemned the hull-deck joint as the ultimate culprit took ages of agonizing detective work and the following of false leads.

The problem was that the hull and deck moldings were bonded together on the inside with a 6- to 8-inch-wide buildup of glass mat from $\frac{1}{4}$ to $\frac{5}{16}$ inch in thickness, quite a stout bond, really. This joint along the outer edge of the deck—not glassed on the outside—was then pierced 140 times (every 6 inches) for bolts to hold on a teak toe rail. What happened during hard sailing was that the hull worked slightly and allowed water beneath the toe rail, even though it was well bedded and bolted. The water ran along the hull-deck crack and came out inside the hull by way of a bolt hole or at the chainplates, which, though massively strong, were fabricated in such a way that water could trickle inside from the hull-deck outer crack beneath the toe rail.

"What's all this about a few drops of water?" you might ask. The leaks were more than a few drips and, of course, were most severe when the weather was worst. The leaks meant wet bedding, soaked food, mildewed charts, a ruined camera, and a radio receiver flooded out with salt water.

After a good deal of thought I ripped off the entire toe rail and filled in the 140 bolt holes. (Why is it that yachts must have more than 250 holes drilled through the deck? With a little planning half the holes— potential leaks—can be eliminated.) Margaret and I then filled the hull-deck crack (it is impossible to get a perfect match on two moldings) with a mixture of fine sawdust and polyester resin, and with a disk grinder we cut a $\frac{1}{2}$-inch radius along the joint on the outside of the hull. We then put a strip of 10-ounce fiberglass cloth $\frac{1}{2}$ inch wide over the rounded joint. This was followed by a second strip 1 inch wide, then 2 inches, 4 inches, and so on up to 8 inches (we used five gallons of resin). The six to eight strips we put on around the entire hull-deck joint (70 feet plus 5 feet for the transom) added about $\frac{1}{4}$ inch of strong fiberglass material, which sealed and strengthened the hull-deck joint on the outside and gave us a total thickness of $\frac{7}{8}$ to 1 inch with no holes and no cracks. In the chainplate area I added many layers of additional mat on the inside. An expert friend then smoothed off the glasswork with a special high-speed disk grinder, and we filled and painted the area.

Left: When I glassed Whisper's hull and deck joint together on the outside, the first step was to remove this teak toe rail and its 140 hold-down bolts, and to plug the holes.

Right: After the hull-deck joint work was completed, we added a 1 x 4-inch teak bulwark a little over 33 feet long on each side. The bulwarks are bolted to ⁵⁄₃₂ x 3¼ x 3¼-inch Everdur plates raised ¾ inch above the deck. The bulwarks have been a big improvement because (1) all water that lands on deck runs off immediately, and (2) the higher bulwarks are easier to brace your feet against. I thought that boarding waves would soon break these long teak pieces, but evidently the wood flexes a little, and some of the force of the water may (?) be eased by the water space beneath.

The result? The annoying leaks stopped immediately, and we feel the hull and deck mating area is much stronger. You can see no trace of the work except a slight flare at the deck level.

In place of the toe rails we added a 1 x 4-inch teak bulwark 34 feet long set ¾ inch above the deck on each side. The bulwarks are fastened every six feet to vertically placed fore-and-aft Everdur plates (⁵⁄₃₂ x 3¼ x 3¼ inches) that I had welded on the outsides of the bronze stanchion bases. The bulwark has been a complete success because it is higher (for safety) and because the ¾-inch space underneath allows any water that lands on deck to run off at once. Our decks are much drier than previously. Also, the space under the bulwarks reduces some of the force of boarding waves that might otherwise tend to break the bulwarks.

When we visited Tahiti, Edward Alcard, the famous English single-handed sailor, came to dinner one night. "Excuse me for saying this," he said, "but your yacht is first-rate except for two things. The portlights are big and vulnerable and the cockpit is too large."

We were well aware of both problems. During various passages we had filled the giant cockpit perhaps fifteen or twenty times. In conditions when a wave slopped into the cockpit we generally rolled out half of the water on the next swell, but even so it took fifteen minutes for the 1½-inch drains (we started out with 1¼-inch) to empty the 8½-foot cockpit, which held two tons of water if you caculated it up to the tops of the coamings. The big cockpit had to be changed.

The danger is that the weight of the water in a large cockpit might depress the stern and overcome the buoyancy of the after part of the hull. In this case, the yacht could be swept by succeeding waves whose weight and battering force might fracture the bridge deck, the main hatch entryway, vulnerable portlights, and the coach roof itself. Such waves could also sweep crew members into the sea. If the cabin were to be breached and water continued to come aboard, the yacht could fill and sink.

We had always carried storm shutters for the portlights, but I continued to worry about the vulnerable portlights of ¼-inch Plexiglas. During a severe storm off the Oregon coast in December 1970, a fair-sized wave broke on board and we were lucky not to have had the portlights stove in.

In May 1971, I took *Whisper* back to the Spencer yard and tore off the entire raised portion of the coach roof (8½ feet). I extended the coach roof three feet aft, which shortened the cockpit to 5½ feet—still a sizable well. We lowered the house by four inches, which eliminated the doghouse entirely and gave an unbroken line for the full length of the coach roof. We traded the four 39-inch portlights for six that measured 5 x 12 inches. Now we had stowage room for a dinghy up to 9½ feet long if we chose. We could store spinnaker poles and awning battens along the unbroken coach roof.

In our opinion the appearance of the yacht was improved; surely she was stronger and safer. In the process we had lost four inches of headroom—74 to 70 inches—but we considered that trifling.

The actual structure of the new coach roof was formed over a

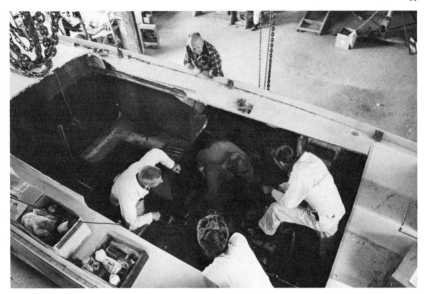

Ah, the joys of major projects in boatyards! Here we have chopped away
Whisper's coach roof from the mast to the cockpit and have cut away
some of the cockpit itself preparatory to building a male mold to lay up a
longer coach roof. The mess is indescribable. The late Phil Hantke, the
ever-cheerful builder of Whisper, *watches amusedly from a ladder at the*
starboard rail.

wooden male mold and built up as a foam sandwich with two layers
each of mat and roving, ½-inch Airex, and four more layers of glass
and resin.

The job was a major alteration and not for the faint of heart. (You
should have seen the mess!) We enlarged the galley, installed an oil
stove and the usual kerosene cooker, and incorporated lots of new
drawers and stowage areas. We built in an athwartship chart table with
a seat, made the quarter berth more usable, and found space for an oilskin locker.

When *Whisper* was first built, she had eight holes through the hull
below the waterline: two for the head, two to drain the cockpit, two for
the galley and head sinks, one for the engine intake, and one for the
salt-water pump in the galley. Since every hole through the hull below
the waterline is not only potential disaster but a high maintenance
item, we eliminated seven of the eight. During earlier modifications I
had cut out the cockpit floor and had reversed its forward tilt so that any

water drained aft. I removed the forward cockpit drains and at the back of the cockpit floor I installed two 1⅞-inch inside diameter pipes that were unobstructed by bends or valves. The lines emptied above the waterline near the transom. I eliminated the head sink (we pour washing water into the head), and we use a small Whale pump to empty the galley sink into a deck-level discharge. The salt water for the galley comes from a T connection to the engine cooling water.

We built a nicely finished wooden box with a deluxe toilet seat to hold a bucket for the head. This eliminated another high maintenance item and got rid of a source of odor, since the rinsing water pumped in to flush a mechanical head is sometimes polluted and terribly smelly. The bucket head is simple, quick, foolproof, noiseless, and cheap. When we are in harbors with shore facilities we use them. In passing, I might add that in eleven years of world cruising I have been in only two harbors with shore facilities (in spite of a lot of talk).

This leaves only one hull opening below the waterline—the engine cooling water intake—whose nylon and stainless steel ball valve we always close when the engine is not running. I have given much thought to an air-cooled engine so that I can eliminate the sole remaining hole in the hull (except for the propeller shaft). Ideally I would have none. Getting rid of seven out of eight, however, is an improvement of 87.5 percent.

In a wooden vessel, bilge drainage and ventilation are taken care of by limber holes cut in the bottoms of the floors, which, as we have seen, are the athwartship strengthening pieces that connect the port and starboard frames to each other and to the keel. Unfortunately, steel, aluminum, and fiberglass vessels share a common fault in that it is easy for a builder to make a tank by simply dropping a top on two bulkheads beneath the cabin sole. Wonderful! You have a simple, cheap, quick-to-make tank. The fact that bilge drainage and ventilation in the way of the tank are stopped is generally dismissed with a grin and a statement such as: "Oh, don't worry. No water is going to come in."

To anyone who has crossed a few oceans, such talk is nonsense. Of course water gets inside a vessel. From a leak, burst plumbing, water through an open portlight, a wave that sneaks on board when the hatch is open—from a dozen causes. Then how do you get rid of the water? With a sponge and bucket? Or if there is enough to rise above the cabin sole, the water will run into the engine bilge, where hopefully you have powerful pumps. But pity the contents of any food, clothing, and tool lockers near the cabin sole in the meantime. Heaven help the engine! Fortunately for them, the producers of vessels without adequate bilge drainage have seldom had to eat the spoiled food, they have seldom had to wear the wet clothing, they have seldom had to clean the rusted tools, and they have seldom been plagued with rebuilding a flooded engine when water has risen above the cabin sole.

Built-in tanks should always have large-volume fore-and-aft bilge drainage pipes constructed at the bottoms when the tanks are made. I feel strongly, however, that built-in tanks are basically poor engineering.

A supposed advantage of built-in tanks is that you get a hull with a double bottom; hull penetration merely punctures a tank, and the hull will not be flooded. This type of safety engineering may be applicable to an oil tanker whose hull is merely a covering for a labyrinth of tanks and plumbing, but not to a yacht with built-in tanks that occupy only a small amount of the space in the hull. In *Whisper's* sailing accidents (severe groundings) the hull was holed in areas where there were no tanks.

Water and fuel tanks should be made separately from the hull so the tanks can be removed for inspection and cleaning. Separate tanks facilitate bilge drainage beneath, and removable tanks mean that the hull can be inspected and repaired without tearing half the yacht apart. Though the tanks may cost more in the first place, in the long run removable tanks are cheaper and more satisfactory. By all means use the best-quality material for the tanks, fittings, and piping, have the tanks pressure-tested when built, and install first-class non-ferrous shut-off valves at the outlets. "Drinking water quality" clear plastic tubing and stainless steel hose clamps (with adjustment screws of stainless steel, not cadmium-plated iron) are ideal for water-tank plumbing. The tubing goes around obstructions with ease, and the tubing can sometimes be arranged to indicate how much liquid is in a tank. The non-conductive tubing also breaks possible galvanic and electrolytic action between different metals. I I have found that GRP is a good material for a diesel tank. Both GRP and stainless steel are suitable for water tanks. Pinhole corrosion is said to be a difficulty with stainless steel, but I have not had this problem. I suggest that you use no iron or plain steel in any tanks or plumbing because the environment of tanks is notoriously damp and the iron never stops rusting. Carry a small magnet in your pocket and be unyielding on this point.

Have adequate cleanout openings installed so that *all* areas of *all* tanks can be reached for cleaning; baffles may necessitate several cleanout openings. With regard to water, it is better to use several 25-gallon tanks than a single 50-gallon tank. For 60 gallons I would use three 20-gallon tanks (which sometimes can be purchased ready-made). If essential fluids are split up, you have some insurance against loss or contamination. In addition, it is easier to keep track of the contents of smaller tanks. They are simpler to locate and to mount, and the weight of a small tank situated some distance from the center of a vessel affects the trim less.

In *Whisper's* case, one problem was to drain the chain locker, which held 35 fathoms of chain that always came in wet. We glassed off the after chain locker bulkhead and ran a 3/4-inch hose by devious routes to the engine bilge in the after part of the hull.

To get rid of a troublesome drainage and damp problem in another area we filled a void beneath the head compartment with foam-in-place plastic. Ideally, however, through-bilge drainage should be built in during early construction before any bilge tankage is completed. There should be adequate drainage beneath all tanks, plus at least 2-inch port and starboard limber holes in the floors or bilge bulkheads so that a glass of water spilled in the chain locker or in the transom locker will run quickly to the bilge pump pickup points located low in the midpart of the yacht. *This should be a primary design and construction point.* The drainage capacity of the limber holes should exceed the combined capacity of all hand, electric, and engine-driven pumps.

The changes in *Whisper* that I have discussed were costly and a lot of trouble. It would be simple for me to say that the builder and designer were at fault. It's easy to criticize, but I don't want to overlook the many good features of *Whisper's* design and construction. The hull is marvelously seaworthy and safe; the interior is well built and a delight. Perhaps it is just that Margaret and I have put our little ship to a lot of hard and specialized usage that has exposed faults which we have tried to correct. All complex machines are compromises. Yachts are no exception.

4

~~~~~~

The Rig

In recent years small ship sailors have circled the globe with every conceivable rig. There are devotees of the sloop, cutter, ketch, yawl, and

The unusual staysail ketch Gypsy Moth V was built for the last solo ventures of the late Sir Francis Chichester. This 57-foot vessel was designed by Robert Clark, who as usual drew lovely lines for Gypsy Moth's sleek hull, which was built of triple diagonal wooden planking by the Crosshaven Boatyard in Cork, Ireland. The five separate sails total 1,372 square feet but the largest—the main topsail—is only 370 square feet. The other four sails run from 252 to 270 square feet, which means that each sail in the rig is manageable by one person (a 510 square foot jib can be set in light weather). The mizzen, the mizzen staysail, and the main staysail are boomed so that when going to weather in strong winds (perhaps with a reefed mizzen for balance) the rig is self-tending. An advantage of the sail plan (and long, slim hull) is that the mizzen boom stops well short of the end of the hull so the transom is unobstructed for the Gunning wind vane steering gear. For running, two 300 square foot sails are held out on 25-foot aluminum poles. Even with her cut-up sail plan, however, this large vessel is a handful for one man. Yet at the age of sixty-nine, Chichester managed a phenomenal 4,000-mile Atlantic-Caribbean crossing in a little less than 23 days, averaging 179 miles per day, a remarkable achievement for a young man or an old man. Gypsy Moth V displaces 17 tons and has 7½ tons of iron on a fin keel. Her measurements: 57′ x 41′8″ x 12′ x 8′4½″. (Photo by Lisa Pittoors)

schooner—each of whom will fill your ears with reasons why his sail plan is superior. Most people prefer a bermudian rig these days, but there is a hard core of gaff advocates who are vocal enthusiasts of short, strongly stayed masts and low profile rigs. The bermudian sail plan with its long luff, however, is clearly superior to windward and is much simpler with no willowy topmasts and fewer strings to pull. The bermudian sail plan is also less subject to chafe and has no troublesome gaff jaws. But in spite of all the talk about modern design, a stumpy, solid gaff mast will stand, be it known, when all bermudian masts have long been leveled. Fancy new yachts come and go, but John Hanna's gaff-rigged Tahiti ketches and Colin Archer's famous gaff cutters continue to do a good job crossing the oceans when that old wind is at the side or behind. Since most cruising is off the wind—and world-wandering sailors go to fantastic lengths to find fair winds—I suppose you can make a good argument for a gaff rig, especially with a short gaff boom, perhaps even made of aluminum, although I think that the idea of a light alloy gaff would cause the traditionalists to gag.

Today most cruising yachts have a single mast and are sloops or cutters for the simple reason that the majority of cruising vessels are derived from racing designs. A bermudian sloop is an efficient, simple rig with only two sails. As long as the sail area suits the wind strength, the sloop rig is ideal. When the wind increases, you must reef the mainsail and change to a smaller headsail. If you use a sloop rig to cross an ocean in the high latitudes, your shoulder development is assured. During a passage that Margarget and I made from Atka in the Aleutian Islands to southeast Alaska, for example, we reefed and unreefed the mainsail and changed headsails sixty-one times during a nineteen-day passage eastward through a series of depressions. It was on that trip that I decided to make *Whisper* into a cutter.

The mast of a cutter is located about halfway along the over-all length

John Illingworth's Myth of Malham *was designed by Laurent Giles and built lightly but strongly of double-skinned mahogany with intricate internal framing of metal and wood. Constructed in 1946, with a 50 percent ballast ratio, and without an engine, she was the terror of ocean racing for fifteen years. Here she slides along in the Solent with her cutter rig pulling her like the ocean greyhound she was. Note the double hatches in the companionway and how the staysail is sheeted inside the topmast shroud. Her measurements are 37.7 feet over all with a waterline length of 33.5 feet, a beam of 9.3 feet, and a draft of 7 feet. (Photo by Beken of Cowes)*

Left: To set up running backstays you can either take the hauling part of a
tackle to a winch or use a lever. I prefer a lever because you always get
the same tension and there is less fumbling. When the after end of this
lever (at the lower left) is raised and taken forward, the slide in the lever
arm runs forward to give additional slack to the backstay. The round,
hemispherical object in the photograph is the top of a mushroom ventilator.
The smaller circular metal piece with the two curved slots screwed to the
bulwark is a mount for a Walker's Knotmaster log.

Right: A sheave for a running backstay needs to be very strong and well
mounted. Surprisingly, a well-made deck-mounted sheave is as expensive as
the lever itself.

of the hull (or, more precisely, 40 percent of the load waterline length
behind the forward end of the LWL). This puts the mainmast in the
heart of the vessel at her widest beam, where good athwartship staying
is possible. With a cutter you generally have a high-clewed jib and a low-
clewed, deck-sweeping staysail. If you include a few reef points on the
staysail, and tack and clew cringles or grommets part way up the luff
and leech, you have a choice of four headsail sizes without physically
manhandling sails. You can set both the jib and staysail, the jib alone,
the staysail alone, or a reefed staysail (which is close to the size of a

storm jib) *all without unhanking, bagging, dragging around, and stowing sails.* If you use a jib or genoa with a deep reef in the foot, you have even more choices. In terms of physical effort, ease, and speed, this scheme offers substantial advantages to sailors.*

During the past few years some sailmakers have begun to speak of a double headsail rig as if they had invented it. Captain John Illingworth was winning ocean races with the *Myth of Malham*, a masthead cutter, thirty years ago. English gaff cutters (with topmasts and bowsprits of incredible length) go back hundreds of years.

A cutter requires either jumpers or running backstays to balance the pull of the inner forestay on which the staysail is flown. Running backstays are superior to jumpers, because if substantial tension is cranked into the masthead backstay, the jumpers will most certainly be overloaded. A second point is that the inner forestay in combination with the running backstays nicely stabilizes the mast when you're banging about in a sizable ocean swell. A third advantage is that if you are unfortunate and lose a forestay, a standing backstay, or a topmast shroud, the running backstay and inner forestay may keep the mast up until you can do something. At worst you will save three-quarters of the mast, not a small consideration when you are quite alone on an unfrequented ocean.

Anyway, for me the choice was quite simple: a cutter rig as I have described. I added substantial mast and deck fittings for an inner forestay, and I had running backstay levers fabricated by the Moonlite Marine Corporation of Costa Mesa, California.† In reply to the argument that runners are too much trouble, I can only say that I am quite unimpressed by sailors who readily crank enormous headsail sheet winches yet who complain about setting running backstays—which take only a moment. In light weather it is not necessary to set up the runners. My one regret with *Whisper's* cutter rig is that the staysail isn't larger. This is not possible because *Whisper's* mast is too far forward and impossible to move. A proper cutter should be designed when the sail plan is first drawn.

There is much talk about the ketch rig among cruising people, but sailors who have used this sail plan report that the mizzen is often useless. If the mizzen is close to the mainsail, the mizzen tends to blanket the main when running; when going to windward the mainsail tends to backwind the mizzen. The mizzen sail, therefore, spends a good deal of

---

* When you do remove and bag headsails, and replace one sail with another, a useful idea is to feed a sail tie through the hanks when the sail is down but before you remove the hanks from the stay. A tie keeps all the hanks together and in order and makes sail changing easier.

† For the address of this company and many others, see Appendix.

its sailing life rotting on its boom. In addition, the mizzen boom interferes with the mounting of a wind-vane steering gear, and downdrafts
from the mizzen sail affect the wind-vane blade itself. The mizzen is
better when reaching, and a mizzen staysail can be set when the wind
is at certain angles. I have seen an expert back a ketch out of a tight berth
using only a mizzen with a wind from ahead.

A ketch has the advantage that she can drop her mainsail and jog along
with a small headsail and the mizzen when the weather is windy or she
wants to maneuver slowly under sail. As Frank MacLear has pointed out,
however, the owners and admirers of ketches often forget the heavy price
they pay for being able to do this.

The mainmast of a ketch is stepped farther forward where the beam
is less, which means the athwartship staying cannot be as efficient. Because three smaller sails occupy the place of two larger sails (of a sloop,
say), the ketch lacks sail area. To get around this problem, the ketch is
given a bowsprit, another structural complication, to enable larger headsails to be set. The combined weight of the bowsprit and the forward
stepped mast places a lot of weight toward the bow—just where it is not
wanted.

All considered—the expanse, weight, clutter, and complexity—work
against the practicality of a ketch. I put the yawl in the same class except
that a yawl's mizzen is even more useless; most yawl owners find that
their vessels sail better with the mizzen entirely removed.

I think a staysail schooner rig is the best two-masted sailing plan.
There is plenty of sail area with a jib, forestaysail, main staysail, and mainsail. In light weather a fisherman staysail can be set between the
masts. This sail is easy to handle if its luff runs up a track set on the
back of the foremast. For running, the eased mainsail is often balanced
with an opposite poled-out headsail, although there are various choices.

In Rio de Janeiro, I spoke with Antoine Muraccioli, a French singlehander who was sailing a green forty-eight-foot steel staysail schooner
named *Om*. The design was a Damien II, with a four-and-a-half-ton retracting keel, by the architect Michel Joubert.

"I find the staysail schooner perfect for me," said the bearded owner
when I talked with him. "When the wind changes, I simply put one or
two sails up or down. Furling or hoisting is easy. Taking off sails is slow
and too much hard work."

When I had *Whisper* built, I fitted twin forestays to facilitate sail
changing. At first the twin stays were separated by two inches; later I

Left: The lower end of Whisper's *inner forestay is connected to a stout U-bolt with a pelican hook so that the inner forestay can be disconnected in case of a lot of tacking with a large sail flown on the (outer) headstay. In strong winds the combination of a running backstay and an inner forestay gives substantial support to a mast and serves to partially back up the main headstay and backstay. Even though a pelican hook has a holding ring, a lashing should always be used in addition.* Whisper's *deck is reinforced under the U-bolt by a stout oak beam that extends the width of the deck and is bolted in place.*

Right: Noise, chafe, and terrible grooves in the spinnaker poles can be easily avoided by tying Turk's heads made of ¼- or ⁵⁄₁₆-inch diameter manila line. Turk's heads are fun to make and should be part of every sailor's knot repertoire.

increased the distance to four inches, but I found that the luff of the headsail still chafed on the unused forestay. In addition the idle forestay was forever catching the jib hanks of the sail flying on the other stay. Dozens of times I found four or five hanks open and the sail madly chafing on the leeward stay. Worse yet, the hanks would get around the wrong stay or both stays, which made lowering the sail difficult. We eventually got to the point of always lowering the sail and hanking it to the leeward stay when on the same tack for an hour or more. I finally junked the twin forestays, their weight, windage, and problems, and went to a single 5/16-inch diameter forestay.

Over the years Margaret and I have found that two of our most useful heavy-weather sails are a storm jib of only 70 square feet and a storm trysail of 85 square feet. The trysail substitutes for the more fragile mainsail and is a most important sail that allows us to work the ship in hard going and to ease the violent motion on a stormy ocean.

For the sheet I run a single part ½-inch nylon line directly to one of the mooring cleats on the transom. If I must get the sheet in, I run it to a winch by way of a snatch block. I have the sheet marked at its correct length, however, and seldom have to change it in trysail weather. You will recall that a trysail has its tack located eight feet or more above the deck. We keep the tack pendant permanently attached to a pad eye at the back of the foot of the mast. The trysail is fixed to the mast with nylon slides (three grouped at the head are sewed on with stainless steel wire), but in addition we have worked eyelets spaced along the length of the luff, so if the mast track is unusable for any reason, we can lace the trysail to the mast and hoist the sail as high as the spreaders.

The trysail is a good sail for *Whisper*, and when it's up I get a wonderful feeling of security. When the wind has begun to moan and the seas have grown big and tall, I like to pull the main boom down into the gallows and to lash the mainsail. The tough, loose-footed, boomless trysail steadies the yacht, pulls hard, and with no boom we have no fear of jibing.

The biggest problem with the trysail is the actual work of setting it in storm conditions. I don't think a newcomer to sailing realizes how much time and energy it takes:

1. Let go the halyard and pull down the mainsail.
2. Get the main boom into the gallows and secure the mainsail with ties.
3. Remove the mainsail slides from the mast track.
4. Find, unbag, and straighten out the trysail.
5. Feed the trysail slides on to the mast track.
6. Change the halyard, secure the tack pendant and sheet, and hoist the sail.

When water is flying around, the yacht is rolling madly, and you spend half of your energy holding on, setting storm sails is hard work. At night (50 percent of all sail changes are at night) the job is more

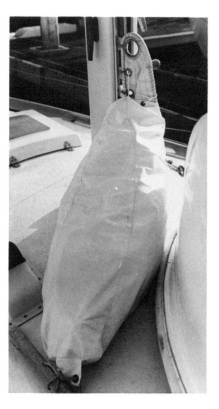

On Whisper *we carry the storm trysail together with its sheet and tack line in this bag, which is stored permanently at the foot of the mast. The trysail slides are kept inserted in a separate mast track. To use the sail it is simply unbagged and hoisted. The bag has large drainage holes at the bottom so water can run out.*

tedious because you can't see as well. My estimate of the time required for one person to set a trysail in whole gale or storm force winds is between one and two hours. In practice this means that you delay putting up the trysail until the wind is quite strong. This makes the job even harder—particularly if you are not feeling too well.

To improve our trysail handling, we installed a separate stainless steel track that runs up the mast alongside the mainsail track. The trysail track extends from the top of the coach roof to above the spreaders and is fastened every three inches. At the top the track is bolted through the mast (the bolthead also serves as a stop so the slides can't escape at the top). We keep the sail permanently bent on and stow it, the sheet, and the tack pendant in a small bag at the foot of the back of the mast. During normal sailing we forget about the bag (which has drainage holes in the bottom). When we want to use the trysail, all we do is pull it from the bag, attach the sheet and halyard, and hoist away. The system is quick, and there is no fumbling with slides or hammering

*Tom Colvin's 42-foot steel-hulled Gazelle with her Chinese lugsail rig.
Colvin, unlike British designers, prefers sails with curved leeches. These
necessitate double sheets, that is, sheets or sheetlets led to each batten on
both the port and starboard sides (otherwise the sheets get fouled by the
roach when the sail swings across). By adjusting the sheetlets going to each
batten, the sail shape can be infinitely varied. In light airs, Gazelle carries
850 square feet of sail area in three lowers. As the wind increases, the jib
is handed first, followed by sail reduction in the easily reefed fully battened
sails. The masts are heavy-walled (5/16 inch) aluminum pipes. The shrouds are
set up loosely—just enough to keep the masts from whipping.*

Tom Colvin adjusting the sheetlets on Gazelle's *reefed mainsail. Colvin, a long-time designer of cruising yachts, runs a small shipyard in Miles, Virginia.*

on corroded trysail transfer tracks. The arrangement also makes it easy to get the trysail down and out of the way when the wind drops and we want to hoist the mainsail again. The trysail stays on deck and is easy to use instead of moldering away at the bottom of a locker.

I have flown a trysail a good deal and have had plenty of time to think about it. Having and using a trysail not only saves the mainsail but gives you a second chance in case of damage to the main. A boomless, loose-footed trysail definitely has utility for ocean cruising, and when I next replace my sails I am going to have a larger, lighter trysail that is cut very flat, has taped edges, and one reef or a bonnet. I plan to use this sail unreefed instead of the triple-reefed mainsail. This will mean only two rows of reefing points on the mainsail, which can be simpler, cheaper, and smoother. The mainsail will not normally be used in gale conditions, so it can be made of less heavy material which should work better and be easier to furl.

My notions about trysails and their handling might be extended to three tracks (one extrusion?) on the mast with a storm trysail, a medium-weather trysail, and a light-weather mainsail that is not reefed at all.

Instead of asking a sailmaker to produce a sail to be used in widely varying wind strengths (an impossibility, really), each of the three sails
could be designed for a specific wind range and might work much better.
I don't think that a mainsail that sets well in 12 knots is helped at all
by being exposed to prolonged blasts of 30- and 40-knot winds.

Dacron sailcloth is remarkable material of incredible strength and
durability. Sailmakers are prone to use quite heavy weights, especially
when you tell them you are going to distant seas of tumultuous reputa-
tion. "That cloth is as strong as sheet steel," they say. Unfortunately, the
heavy cloth furls like sheet steel as well. Sometimes you coin pet names
for every square foot when you have to fist it into a bag or onto a
boom.

I don't want to talk of storm conditions too much, for you can get the
wrong idea. A substantial percentage of the winds in the trade-wind
areas and elsewhere is 15 knots or less, and a sailor spends part of his
life scouting the horizon for a better breeze or whistling for wind when
he is becalmed. Most of the time the wind conditions are light or
moderate, for you try hard to sail with fair winds in summery conditions.
People who talk about reduced rigs for ocean cruising are simply un-
informed. The ideal rig is one that can hold up clouds of sails when the
going is light and be shortened down easily when the wind increases.
This is what makes the Chinese lugsail rigs designed by Blondie Hasler,
Jock McLeod, and Tom Colvin so appealing.

I have sailed on three modern yachts with Chinese lugsail rigs and can
report that the performance was a good deal better than I had anticipated.
You can tack and jibe without touching a sheet, which minimizes the
actual work of sailing. Reefing is incredibly easy. If you get into trouble,
all you have to do is to let sheet and halyard go and the whole rig folds
up effortlessly with the fully battened sail falling neatly between lazy
jacks. There are, of course, no jibs to fool with at all.

Sailing to windward with a Chinese rig requires some new thinking
because the luff of the sail doesn't shake as you head up. You need to
pay attention to your speed through the water, because if you go closer
and closer to the wind you will suddenly find that you have come to a
complete stop.

The other big change from a bermudian rig is the use of an unstayed
mast which is, of course, shorter and a great deal stouter. Such a mast
bends a bit, but freestanding masts have been used in sailing vessels for
centuries. One problem that hasn't been fully solved is the batten
material. Battens of fiberglass, wood, aluminum, PVC pipe, and bamboo
are all under trial.

Our running rig on *Whisper* is an eased mainsail held out with a nylon preventer line led from the end of the boom to the stem to prevent, or at least ease, accidental jibes. We pull the main boom down vertically with a powerful vang tackle or kicking strap that leads from the boom to the genoa track to flatten the sail and to keep it from chafing on the shrouds and the end of a spreader. We balance the drive of the main by poling out a headsail of suitable size on the opposite side. This gives us more area than twin headsails—which are essentially square sails for running—and because we have some fore-and-aft canvas set (the main is never squared right off), the yacht doesn't roll as much. In very light going we sometimes put up a second jib to leeward of the mainsail. The second jib adds to the total headsail area and pulls nicely with a quartering wind. Like most short-handed cruising yachts, we don't carry a spinnaker because of handling problems; nevertheless, we find that even in light airs we move along at 2 or 3 knots. Not as fast as with a big spinnaker, but we generally manage to log 70 or 80 miles a day in light winds.

To jibe the rig, I ease the windward headsail sheet until the spinnaker pole is against the head stay. I then go forward and pull the trip line on the pole to unhook the eased sheet. Then I haul on the mast-end pole lift to slide the pole up the mast until I can dip the outer end of the pole beneath the inner head stay (I stow the pole by running the mast end up a track on the mast; see page 180). I then hook the leeward headsail sheet in the outer end of the pole fitting and lower the mast end of the pole so that it is horizontal again and ready for use.

I then uncleat the preventer for the main boom from a stemhead cleat, and walk with it back to the cockpit, unhooking the vang as I go. I then haul in the leeward headsail sheet (behind the main), jibe the rig with the steering vane, and walk forward to cleat the main boom preventer on the new side. The procedure is easy and simple in either light or heavy going, presuming, of course, that you don't have too much sail up for the wind conditions. If there is a fresh breeze, I haul in the mainsheet to ease the boom across when it jibes; in light airs I simply swing the boom across, taking care to keep a bight of the mainsheet from coiling around my neck!

There is a lot of talk about twin headsails and trade-wind rigs. I have found that a mainsail and a poled-out headsail are superior in all ways. My list of disadvantages of twins includes:

1. Considerable rolling.
2. The necessity for two sets of twins (for winds above and below 12 knots).

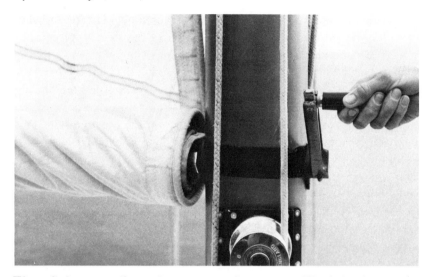

Through-the-mast roller reefing gear on a Contessa 32. The halyard is eased and the boom is cranked round and round, which winds up the sail like a window shade. The boom is then held in a locked position by the handle, which folds down against the mast. The system is ideal for furling the sail. This gear is made by Kemp Masts of England.

3. The requirement that the wind be almost dead astern.
4. The necessity for two poles, two lifts, and a way to secure the sheets to the tiller, a tricky job for one person in a fresh breeze. (Some yachts will steer with twins without leading the sheets to the tiller).
5. The time required to set the twins (more than you think).
6. The time needed to change back to the fore-and-aft rig. This point may seem trivial, but if you want to sail to windward quickly (man overboard or a sudden danger to leeward), it is helpful to have the mainsail up and usable quickly.

If I wanted more area for downwind work, I would consider a square sail patterned after the one used by Tom Steele on *Adios* and described in the December 1964 *Yachting*.

We have a 20-foot yardarm, suspended from a bridle, which is hoisted on the forestay, using the jib halyard. This yardarm can be left aloft or raised and lowered at sea. To the yardarm a square sail is set flying, hauled up to the yard by three halyards, one of them being in the center of the head of the sail. The foot of the sail has three sheets. The center one is belayed tight, as is the center halyard. With the two clew sheets leading aft through blocks to the tiller the square sail, in effect, forms a V-shape and works on the principle of twin staysails. This rig is extremely effective and positive in its steering ability. In addition to being used before the wind, the yard can be braced well around, and with the tack or weather clew led to the end of the bowsprit, the sail flattens beautifully, will claw right up into the wind, and can be used in combination with the fore-and-aft sails.

I recently inspected through-the-mast roller reefing on a British-built Contessa 32. The main boom has no vertical sliding gooseneck at the mast at all, being held in a fixed position by a large horizontal stainless steel pin that goes through the mast. The pin is connected to the boom with a double pivot so that the after end of the boom is free to move up or down or to swing from side to side. The forward end of the pin has a convenient handle (at the front of the mast), which, when turned, rotates the entire boom like an axle. The mainsail requires no setback at the bottom of the luff and rolls up on the boom like a window shade. The entire sail can be rolled up if desired, certainly a marvelous idea for furling. When I tried it, the mainsail rolled up fairly well, with only a few creases.

This scheme is an advance over old types of worm gear roller reefing because you apply the turning motion to the boom from a convenient position forward of the mast. With a long handle you have plenty of power. The reefing handle may be permanently attached, locking the boom so it cannot turn. Designs vary somewhat, and the gear for boats around 40 feet and over may have internal gearing and a standard socket to take a detachable sheet winch handle. The system has been used on 65-foot ocean racers.

However attractive roller reefing is, I prefer slab or tied reefs (now often called jiffy reefing), because the mainsail sets better and there are fewer strains on the sail, which is sometimes reefed for days in strong winds. With tied reefs you get away from dependence on a possibly faulty roller reefing gear, and you can have a lighter boom with improved sheeting arrangements. The costs are about even. You save on the mechanical gear, but each row of reefs on a mainsail is expensive.

When we tie in the first reef on *Whisper's* mainsail, we ease the mainsheet and tighten the topping lift enough to take the weight of the main boom. We then ease the main halyard until the luff reefing grommet reaches a snap shackle kept permanently mounted on the gooseneck. This step takes only a minute.

Next we pull down the leech reefing grommet by taking up on the leech reefing pendant (rove permanently), which is tightened by a small winch mounted on the boom near the mast. The leech pendant runs from a pad eye on the port side of the boom near its after end, up through the leech grommet, and down through a cheek block mounted on the starboard side of the boom near its after end (opposite the pad eye on the other side). The leech pendant then goes forward to a Clamcleat and to the winch. The pad eye and cheek block are positioned a little aft of the clew location of the reefed sail so that when the leech reefing pendant is tightened, there is equal tension on both the foot and leech of the sail. It takes only a minute to winch some tension into this line. Then the main halyard is tightened, the topping lift is eased, and the mainsheet is adjusted. Total time: less than five minutes. Except for putting a lashing in place (see below), all the work of reefing has been done from a safe position just aft of the mast. We gather up the loose foot of the sail by tying six or eight reef points, short lines kept permanently rove in the reefing patches. It is helpful to have different-colored reef points for each reefing row so the points won't get mixed up.

For a second reef I repeat the procedure above. To free the winch, I use a short lashing between the clew reefing grommet and the boom to hold the tension set up by the first reefing pendant.

The only trouble I have had with this scheme is chafe on the reefing pendant at the leech reefing grommet. When the yacht rolls and pitches on ocean swells, the mainsail pulls and jerks on its clew. Even when set up hard with a winch, the reefing pendant (of $3/8$ or $7/16$-inch Dacron braid) stretches a little along its 25-foot length and works back and forth across the grommet. The line chafes and breaks.

To solve this chafe problem (the pendant always broke in the middle of the night or when we were beating up to a harbor in traffic), I pass a separate short tie (an old, hard piece of $1/2$-inch diameter Dacron line about 40 inches long) around the boom, through the cheek block, leech grommet, and pad eye, then tie the ends of the lashing together with a reef knot. Next I ease the reefing pendant from the forward end of the boom so the lashing takes the load. This extra step is inconvenient when running because the boom end is not handy; nonetheless I have found it necessary.

To check whether this chafe problem was unique to Whisper, I looked through a few books on board. Sure enough, Conor O'Brien, writing in The Small Ocean-going Yacht (Oxford, 1931), says on page 64: "The pendant should only be regarded as a means of getting the reef down till the lashing is put on, for it is bound to slack up more or less when it will chafe the sail, and itself."

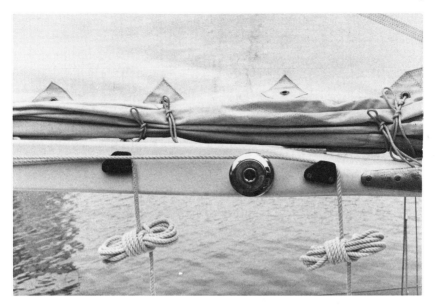

Whisper's *mainsail reefing arrangements with two reefs tied in. The photograph shows the second reef pendant winched tight and its tail held in the Clamcleat at the right. Earlier the first reef pendant was winched tight. Note, however, that you cannot use a Clamcleat (or any type of jamming cleat) where high line tensions are involved because the line jams and you cannot release it. (A sheet stopper would be a possibility if line stretch were not a factor.) I always add a lashing between the clew reefing grommet and the boom after the tension is set up with the pendant on the winch. This lashing holds the pertinent reefing grommet in place, and you then can ease the reefing pendant on the winch, take off the line, and hold it in a handy Clamcleat (or any sort of cleat), as I have done at the left. This frees the winch for other lines. I use a lashing at the boom end because the long reefing pendant stretches a little and after a time will chafe at the nip of the leech grommet.*

I might mention that jiffy reefing, a supposed invention of sailmakers during the past few years, was described by William Cooper in *Yachts and Yachting* in 1873. The technique was also well covered in *A Manual of Yacht and Boat Sailing*, by Dixon Kemp, in 1882.

These days there is much discussion of roller furling headsails. Notice that I said roller furling, not roller reefing, because most sailmakers are agreed that it is impossible to cut a single variable-sized sail that will set well in both light and heavy winds. The draft changes as the sail is rolled upon itself. Also, the sheet leads must be moved forward as sail area is reduced; otherwise the sheet will put too much tension on the foot of the sail and none on the leech.

Although improvements have been made to roller furling mechanisms, I do not think such systems have a place in ocean sailing. The proponents of roller furling headsails do not always admit the considerable cost, complexity, corrosion problems, additional lines, and extra weight and windage aloft. There are difficulties getting adequate luff tension; protecting the furled sail from the sun is troublesome. Most roller furling fans use oversize gear, and practically everyone I have talked to starts off with a list of suggested changes (usually to beef things up).

When a wire luff roller system is used, the wind must be brought abeam or forward of the beam; otherwise the sail may get mixed up with the slack head stay. Grooved aluminum head-stay arrangements require sails with special boltropes instead of hanks. These sails are, of course, useless with ordinary stays. Grooved head-stay arrangements are not easy for a person to use by himself. I would hate to be in a storm at sea with roller furling hardware problems and sails that could not be hanked to a normal headstay.

In my opinion, roller furling headsails are just one more thing to go wrong. We must ty to keep the mechanisms and strings and contraptions to a minimum. There is enough complication already on a cruising vessel. I often look at the unstayed single mast and sail of a Finn or Laser dinghy and marvel at the simplicity and beauty of the rig. O that we could have such a mast and sail for the ocean!

Instead of roller furling sails, a more seamanlike approach—at least for me—is to use headsails with deep reefs in the foot, as I mentioned earlier in this chapter. A second cringle or grommet on the luff and leech plus a few reef patches are all that's necessary. To change the sail's area, you merely ease the halyard and sheet and adjust the clew and tack positions. The foot of the sail is kept tidy with three or four reef points rove through reef patches. An alternate to a headsail that can be reefed is a sail with a removable foot or a bonnet.

When I replaced *Whisper*'s mast several years ago, I chose spruce. It cost more than an aluminum extrusion and is heavier, but I like to put fittings where I want and perhaps to change something around once in a while. Repairs are possible. I once broke a forestay turnbuckle on a former vessel because I failed to have a toggle on the turnbuckle. The wooden mast bent severely, but it didn't break. An aluminum mast would have jackknifed and been ruined.

On *Whisper* we hoist the sails entirely with halyards made of ½-inch Dacron (Terylene). Rope halyards are ideal—easy to use, cheap compared with wire, soft on the hands, simple to coil, and quick to replace (or turn end for end). Either Margaret or I can hoist or hand the sails in a few seconds, sometimes a handy procedure in close maneuvering. At the masthead we have wide-faced, 6-inch diameter sheaves of plastic material that were beautifully made for us by Julio Baquerizas in Buenos Aires.

We fought the battle of wire halyards for years and came to hate the slow hoisting, the horrible broken strands (meathooks), the troublesome wire-to-line splices, wire around the mast steps, grooves worn in the mast, and the dangerous wire winches which are prone to snarls and overrides when you are in a hurry. If you forget to remove the handle of a wire winch and the brake is released accidentally the handle becomes a lethal weapon, perhaps *the single most dangerous item on board*. I have personal knowledge of four serious accidents from wire winch handles. Such mishaps are no rarity in the racing circuits. Experienced foredeck men approach wire winches under high load as if they were filled with dynamite. Why don't the winch companies devise a design with the brake release *underneath* the handle so the handle *must* be removed before the brake can be actuated?

I will never use wire halyards again and advise all sailors to stick to pre-stretched Dacron and open-barrel winches. If you are concerned about halyard tension, you can go to larger barrel winches that can be as powerful as you want. Halyards of line are easy to tie off to prevent the halyards tapping against masts, a thing that drives me wild. I am probably outspoken, but I feel that anyone who allows a halyard to tap against a mast in an anchorage where someone is trying to sleep is simply not housebroken.

Again and again Margaret and I have made small changes to make sail handling safer, quicker, and easier. I hope you don't think that we have a heavy, slow boat that is sailed in ultra-conservative fashion. We like to keep our rig well tuned and to crack on all the canvas we can. Our best run for one week has been 1,003 miles, not world-beating certainly, but quite adequate for us. We like to make smart passages; when the wind changes, however, we want to be able to handle our gear efficiently so that we can continue to press on in a seamanlike manner.

It seems that you are forever pitting one thing against another. Shall I have one mast or two? A new mainsail or bunk cushions this year? Shall we buy a fancy new depth sounder or put the money into the Tahiti fund? Cruising in small ships, like life, is one compromise after another. It's just that we try to make little improvements to make the whole glorious process a little easier.

5

~~~~~~

Self-Steering

Blue-water sailors are more conservative than bankers in taking aboard new gear and ideas, and the wide acceptance of self-steering devices on cruising yachts during the last ten years has been the biggest change since Dacron replaced cotton for sailcloth.

When I mounted a Hasler unit on *Whisper*'s transom in San Francisco in 1966, Margaret and I were generally obliged to spend thirty minutes a day explaining the use and operation of the strange-looking wind-vane gear to curious people on the dock. Today, however, you see complex frames of iron pipe, intricately curved stainless steel rods, and queer-looking aluminum castings hanging over the sterns of dozens of cruising yachts. Above the machinery thin blades of wood, Plexiglas, aluminum, or fabric-covered ovals of tubing swing on delicate bearings and either feather noiselessly into the wind or rock nervously from side to side. The wind blades are of all sizes and shapes and often reflect the personalities of their owners with regard to color and design.

When you walk along the waterfront docks and marinas where the cruising yachts live, the wind blades flap into action with each passing breeze, nodding and spinning like old men whose heads automatically turn when a pretty girl goes by. I sometimes wonder where all the hopeful

Unless self-steering equipment is carefully engineered and built with thought and purpose, the vane will wind up like Fritz.

cruising yachts are headed, and whether the steering vanes were bought to go somewhere or were added for reasons of prestige and acquisitiveness.

We often read articles and promotional material about self-steering devices written by technically oriented people who get involved with force diagrams and boring discussions about articulated hydrofoils and theoretical considerations that are miles from practical seamanship. Shore-based analyses and a trial trip or two with one type of gear hardly justify some of the extravagant descriptions. To learn something about self-steering equipment, you must sail on an ocean with different kinds of vane gears in both light and heavy going on all points of sailing. It's good to talk to sailors who have used self-steering equipment on long passages and to hear about successes and failures.

Self-steering gears must be robust and well able to take bashing about in heavy seas and nasty weather. The equipment must stand up to occasional knocks at rough commercial docks where you sometimes tie up stern to. You should be able to operate the gear from a safe and convenient location, which means some form of remote control. Self-steering gears need power to deal with unbalanced sail settings and weather helm, and the control linkages require feedback arrangements to prevent over-steering. You ought to be able to make reasonable repairs at sea. Enclosed bevel gears, tricky bearing mechanisms, delicate welds, mixtures of alien metals, hidden shafts, vibration in high winds, fouling of underwater parts by kelp, corrosion in bearings—all these things ought to be designed out at the drawing-board stage or eliminated by testing experimental models.

By its very nature a vane gear is a device that responds to a wind change after the yacht has changed course. The vane gear always follows a change in conditions; there is no possibility that a vane gear can ever anticipate a change as can a human helmsman (here comes a puff of wind; here comes a big wave).

Claims that a vane gear will never get off course more than one or two degrees are ridiculous. Out in the ocean with from 0 to 40 knots of wind (or more) and corresponding seas, a small yacht gets shoved first one way and then another. A vane gear may *average* a certain course, but it can never steer more accurately than an alert human hand. (Under hard going at sea a man has to work diligently to keep within a 15-degree range of steering; on large ocean racers the helmsmen are often changed at thirty-minute intervals when the steering is difficult.)

I think that if in average conditions (not a smooth bay) a vane gear can keep the ship within 10 or 12 degrees of the course on either side, then the device is doing a good job. The important thing is the *course made good*, whether steered by a man or a machine. Once these limits are recognized and accepted, the vane gear becomes a useful assistant to small ship sailors. The reason we often hear the phrase "The gear steers a better course than I can" is that many sailors—including me—are rotten helmsmen.

A wind vane can be a wonderful assistant. In 1967 I wrote:

Our vane does not complain, get tired, become bored, or require endless cups of coffee and sandwiches. The magic helmsman needs no oilskins, never flies into a rage or tantrum, and cheerfully steers at 0300 as well as at high noon. As long as the wind works the vane will work too. It will guide you faultlessly from Newfoundland to Scotland as well as to steer you straight into a reef or sandbank two miles away. No matter how good the vane it can never take the place of a man on watch who can think, reason, and respond.

The basic problem of self-steering in yachts is that some scheme of amplifying the power of a wind blade is necessary. In a model yacht that sails on a pond in a park you can couple the wind blade directly to the rudder. But in a thirty- or forty- or fifty-foot sailing vessel you need more muscle. A small vane gear without a power-amplifying scheme may work in strong winds, but it will not function in light breezes unless the wind blade or sail is quite large. At the present time there are three main systems of wind-vane gears. I have put mechanical self-steering systems into a fourth group.

1. The Hasler pendulum servo gear invented by Blondie Hasler uses the action of water on a narrow blade in the water to generate steering power. An airfoil-shaped blade about 6 inches wide and 4 feet long is placed vertically downward in the water with the airfoil section parallel with the fore-and-aft line of the vessel. When the yacht is moving and the blade is parallel to the centerline of the ship, no side force is produced on the blade, but when the blade is rotated slightly about its vertical axis by a linkage from the wind blade above, a powerful side force is generated. The top of the water blade is fastened to a metal framework that pivots from side to side on the longitudinal axis of the yacht. Lines from the metal framework are led to the tiller or wheel, which then steers the yacht through the main rudder.

The narrow blade in the water (sometimes called a paddle or oar) *is not a rudder* and does not control the yacht directly. The blade is a lever, a power-generating device, that amplifies the movements of the wind blade and gives it force.

A pendulum servo self-steering unit is a complicated mechanism that requires a wind blade, a water blade mounted on a double pivot, and various linkages and rods and blocks and lines—depending on the maker. The clever inventors and manufacturers have, however, given their designs a high degree of reliability as proven by the voyages of Chichester and Rose and the many singlehanders in the Atlantic races. The Hasler vane uses the action of a vertically pivoting wind blade, while the Aries, Atoms, and Gunning gears use smaller blades that pivot on a horizontal axis.

I have been shipmates with three commercially-built pendulum servo units, all well made. Two of the three performed splendidly in both strong and light winds from all directions. I am, however, the first to admit that pendulum servo units are complicated devices with lots of parts thrashing around. Chafe is a problem with the steering lines, which are a nuisance in the cockpit. The complexity of the pendulum servo units translates into high prices. The Hasler originally sold for $600 in the United States, but now costs $1,498, which unfortunately has priced this excellent gear out of the market.* The Aries sells for about $583, and the Gunning, the most powerful of all but crudely built compared with the Aries, sells for $435 in the United States. The French Atoms vane costs $600.

The trend of pendulum servo units is to smaller devices and lighter linkages operated by horizontally pivoted wind blades. The French Navik trim tab pendulum servo unit uses a tiny air blade to turn a small tab on the water blade, which in turn forces the larger water blade to one side or the other. The advantage is that a smaller air blade can be used, which is more sensitive to wind shifts. The unit is small and easily mounted. A vane doesn't have to be massive and heavy to be powerful. It's a question of design.

2. The second class of self-steering gears is an auxiliary rudder with a trim tab that is attached either directly to the auxiliary rudder or placed a little distance behind it to increase the effect of the tab. The trim tab is connected to the wind blade by a linkage. Movement of the wind blade turns the trim tab, which forces the auxiliary rudder in the opposite

---

* The Hasler MP gear made by M. S. Gibb of England can be bought in the U.K. for £344, or about $592, say $600. A U.S. agent trying to charge $1500, or a markup of 150 percent, on the U.K. *retail* price shows the idiocy of such pricing. It's a pity, but this type of dealing on imported items is common. The policy seems to be to both overcharge the buyer and to make him furious at the same time. If these agents were satisfied with a 40 percent markup above their cost price, their total sales volume might increase significantly. The companies use the excuse of shipping, insurance, and duty, but in truth these costs are modest. The biggest ripoff of all is on imported electronic items and diesel engine parts. I could easily expand this footnote into a chapter. No magazine will touch this subject because it might lose a few advertisers (but some hard-hitting articles would serve readers, and champion the supposed goals of journalism).

Left: One model of an Aries vane gear made by Nick Franklin on the Isle of Wight in England. This gear uses a horizontally pivoting air blade whose setting can be remotely controlled by a clever adjustment device. The gear is robust, well made, and many long-distance sailors have found the Aries gear to be excellent.

Right: An auxiliary rudder and trim tab can furnish plenty of self-steering power, and in addition can provide an emergency system of hand steering in case of problems with the main rudder. Such units are usually added to a yacht as an afterthought and tend to be bulky and somewhat unsightly. The drag of an auxiliary rudder and its hardware is a factor, and the transom often needs internal reinforcement. This is a Riebandt auxiliary rudder vane gear, which employs a wedge-shaped section in its air blade.

direction with considerable power. With this type of vane gear the main rudder is not used and is generally lashed amidships.

A trim tab device is much simpler than a pendulum servo unit, but the auxiliary rudder scheme has its own set of problems. There is an astonishing amount of pressure on anything placed over the side of a vessel hurrying along at 6 or 7 knots. If the rudder unit strikes a piece of driftwood

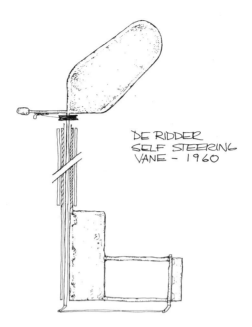

DE RIDDER
SELF STEERING
VANE - 1960

or a collection of floating kelp, the parts in the water can be torn off in an instant if everything has not been built stoutly. The drag of an auxiliary rudder and its associated parts is considerable, and the unit must be kept well painted with anti-fouling.

The main advantage of a trim tab gear is that you steer the yacht with it and gain an extra rudder, a fair exchange for the drag of the unit. This safety feature is dear to the hearts of all cruising sailors, for few people have encountered bad weather without worrying about the rudder. A second advantage is that trim tab units are relatively simple and self-contained and don't clutter up the cockpit with blocks and lines. Third, the trim tab units can be constructed by amateur builders. I have seen excellent vanes made from scraps of material—mostly iron pipe—and a few days of work. The vanes were sometimes heavy and crude, but Al and Beth Liggett, for example, successfully took their yacht *Bacchus* around the world with a DeRidder auxiliary trim tab gear made on the waterfront in Tahiti for less than $50.

Perhaps the most copied trim tab gear is the ingenious design of Michael DeRidder of *Magic Dragon*. The DeRidder rudder—gradually improved since its conception in 1960—is built around a long piece of 2-inch heavy-walled iron or stainless steel pipe placed vertically through the center of the transom or held immediately behind the transom on a strong metal

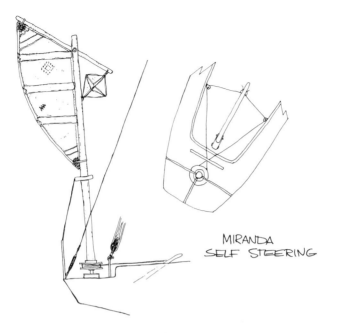

MIRANDA
SELF STEERING

frame. (We will call this pipe No. 1.) An auxiliary rudder is hung from a second, smaller pipe (No. 2) that extends downward through the main vertical pipe (No. 1). To drive the auxiliary rudder, a small trim tab is placed *one foot or more behind* the rudder on supports extending astern from the auxiliary rudder. A wind blade some distance above deck level directs the trim tab by means of a linkage from the bottom of a long vertical shaft that runs inside pipe No. 2.

The separation of the trim tab from the auxiliary rudder gives the system enough power to steer a yacht in almost any circumstances. Unfortunately, there is a good deal of drag from the unit, which is vulnerable to damage if the yacht strikes anything while going astern. To work on the underwater parts generally means hauling the vessel or some long breath-holding.

Self-steering can easily be added to a vessel with a transom-hung rudder or to a double-ender with an outboard rudder. It seems pointless to hang a complex pendulum servo unit immediately behind a stern-mounted rudder whose water flow may upset the working of the servo water blade. It is simple and cheap to mount a trim tab on the main rudder itself or a few inches behind it to gain more force.

3. The third type of wind-vane steering gear is the Miranda configuration worked out by the late Sir Francis Chichester for his singlehanded Atlantic trips in the 1960's. The Miranda gear is actually a tiny mizzen

sail set on a small rotating mast. The bottom of the mast turns a large sheave or crossbar from which a single pair of crossed lines is led directly to the tiller. The advantage of the Miranda gear is that all the parts are on deck and easily serviceable. You get no drag from underwater appurtenances, and the unit is simple and direct. The drawback is that you need a fairly clear counter with an offset backstay, and you may need to reef the vane sail in strong winds.

Several years ago in the South Pacific, Margaret and I sailed in company with Eric Hall, a singlehander who was taking a Nicholson 32 from England to New Zealand. For a steering gear Eric used a 12-foot aluminum mast 3¼ inches in diameter mounted on the transom. The bottom of the mast rested on a small ball bearing thrust bearing; the rotating mast was supported 4½ feet from its base by a tripod of metal supports that angled upward from the stern pulpit. The steering sail (with three light battens) had about 15 square feet of area and turned the mast by means of a short gaff (at the top of the sail), which projected through the mast. The gaff extended through the mast about two feet and was a handy place to hang a radar reflector, which nicely balanced the weight of the sail, battens, and gaff.

I thought this self-steering arrangement was ideal, although Eric's yacht was well balanced and did not require heavy tiller pressure.

4. There are various mechanical schemes for self-steering. Everyone knows about conventional autopilots with their large electric motors and high electrical demands. There are, however, various miniaturized autopilots that control either tillers or wheel steering by means of servo units, and use very little electrical power—on the order of .5 ampere.

It is only a question of time until some enterprising person markets a pendulum servo or auxiliary rudder steering gear controlled by a tiny, sealed, waterproof electric motor guided by either a compass unit or a small air blade (either on command). The compass unit will sense a course change and will send an input to the small electric motor, which will turn a water blade (or the tab on a water blade) on a pendulum servo unit, or the tab on an auxiliary rudder–trim tab device. Oversteering can be controlled by an adjustable feedback device. When the electric half of the unit is switched off (or inoperative), the vane gear will be governed by the wind on the air blade.

An autopilot is of course ideal for motoring in calms. As with all complex gadgetry, however, things can go wrong, and if the ship's power is gone—to list only one possible failing—the autopilot is finished. I believe that an autopilot should be installed below deck, where the parts can be fully protected against salt water. A "water resistant" unit might be satisfactory for use on lakes or bays but is not robust enough for the ocean, where a lot of water is often flying around. Repairmen don't live in Samoa or Madeira or in the Falkland Islands.

I want to mention the problem of getting complicated things repaired when you are thousands of miles away from the place of manufacture. Marine goods are often produced by small shops that have little understanding of the difficulty of overseas repair and the impossible procedures of customs. This problem applies to many things—autopilots, compasses, quartz crystal clocks, radios, refrigeration units, engine parts, cameras, and so forth.

Not only do you have the difficulty of packaging a delicate item, but you often must send it from a doubtful post office (at considerable expense), which may merely forward it to the local customs people, who may or may not send it on. Then, if the item is lucky enough to get to England or France or Germany or the United States, a second customs barrier must be overcome before the item reaches the manufacturer. This whole troublesome process must be reversed in order for you to receive the repaired part. Is it any surprise that four out of five such parts disappear? Foreign post offices, foreign customs, customs and post offices in the country of manufacture, the manufacturer himself, and payment from abroad in different currencies add up to insuperable problems. It's regrettable to write that bribes are common for international shipments. Is it any wonder that the most traveled yachts are the simplest?

Another scheme to power an electric autopilot is to drive an alternator by means of a V-belt from the propeller shaft. To get enough revolutions (say 6 to 1) at low speed, an intermediate layshaft may be required. You also need a sailing clutch and brake. In a large yacht with a big propeller the alternator begins to charge at 3 knots or so and can easily drive an autopilot such as Sharp & Co.'s Mate, a 1/8 horsepower steering unit. The sensing unit can be either a compass or a small wind blade. Such an arrangement was successfully used by Gerard Dijkstra on his seventy-one-foot yacht *Second Life* in the 1972 transatlantic singlehanded race. A variation of this scheme is to use hydraulic power generated by a trailing propeller.

Such devices have the advantage of eliminating an exposed and vulnerable wind blade device at the transom. All these electric and hydraulic schemes are complicated and expensive, however, and are liable to failure unless a clever repairman with plenty of spare parts is on board.

Two recent electric generating developments are small wind-driven generators and solar cells, both of which were used with reasonable success by a number of entrants in the 1976 singlehanded transatlantic competition. The output is very small but continuous as long as the wind and sun last. At the end of the race I was amazed to see a trimaran that had weathered a series of Force 10 storms come gliding into Newport with a mizzen masthead wind-driven generator still churning away (day and night, silently, and at no cost). But the solar cells are even more attractive, being small, silent, with no windage, easy to mount, and not conflicting with other masthead hardware.

My first steering vane was a Hasler pendulum servo gear with a vertically pivoting air blade. The Hasler gear performed admirably in all kinds of weather and on all points of sailing during a 20,000-mile Pacific trip. When I returned to San Francisco, my friend, the late Colin Darroch, was set to go off on a singlehanded venture to Hawaii. Colin needed the gear, so I let him have it.

Always searching for something better, I then bought an English Aries vane gear built on the Isle of Wight by Nick Franklin. This pendulum servo device used a horizontally pivoted wind blade and had a clever system for remote control, so you could adjust the setting from the companionway hatch. The gear was well built and designed around a massive magnesium-aluminum casting with stout bevel gears and heavy shafts that ran on plastic needle bearings. Unfortunately, my Aries vane gear never worked properly. Its action was sluggish, and it seemed to have too much friction in the various linkages and shafts. At one stage we struck some wreckage in the sea, and the breakaway device on the water blade failed to shear. This bent the main shaft. Nick Franklin sent me new parts, but the patient never recovered. I sold it to another sailor, who had no better luck. I am certain the poor operation of my gear was an exception, because many sailors swear by the good performance of the Aries steering device. Nick Franklin now has an improved model.

I needed a vane steering gear for a trip to South America, so I decided to try a Riebandt auxiliary rudder device which steered with a separate small rudder actuated by a trim tab hooked directly to the air blade. Instead of a piece of flat plywood for an air blade like the Hasler and Aries units, the Riebandt gear used a wedge-shaped air blade made of aluminum tubing covered with blue cloth.

The auxiliary rudder unit was powerful and steered *Whisper* with ease. Right from the beginning, however, I complained to the builder about his mixing of bronze and aluminum parts and the crazy requirement that different parts of the gear needed to be coated with different kinds of anti-fouling paint. By the time I had sailed 15,000 miles with the Riebandt gear, small pieces of the auxiliary rudder skeg had been eaten away because of galvanic action between the aluminum and bronze parts. In addition, there was no way of setting the gear from the cockpit. You had to climb on the transom and engage or adjust the steering gear by means of a Morse control lever that was frozen with severe corrosion. The Riebandt gear was good, but it needed further design work. The bulk of the auxiliary rudder and trim tab certainly caused some drag in the water and slowed the yacht perhaps half a knot at high speed; the unit was vulnerable around docks and when tying up stern to. But I liked the idea of an extra rudder. The main failing of my Riebandt unit was **galvanic** action between the principal parts, and the poor engagement device, faults that I believe have now been corrected.

In Buenos Aires I saw a French-built Atoms gear on *Lou*, a Chance 37 that belonged to Louis Brioni, a French singlehander on his way to Cape Horn. Since the Riebandt gear had been sacked, I purchased my fourth (and final?) vane gear, the rather elegant Atoms pendulum servo unit. The Atoms vane gear uses a horizontally pivoting air blade and the usual water blade. The concept for the French gear is a small unit of stainless steel with clever linkage rods and an excellent scheme for remote control. On *Whisper* most of the gear fits inboard of the pulpit and is a neat and practical device that works well. On a passage between Punta del Este, Uruguay, and Ilha de Santa Catarina in Brazil we had several days of following 40-knot winds with large seas during which the Atoms vane gear steered faultlessly.

So for what it's worth you have my experiences with four wind vane gears. Two excellent and two faulty (for minor reasons). I note that in general all the devices steered fairly well. The failings were in mechanical details, areas that can be dealt with by small design improvements.

We must not forget that another system of self-steering exists—the use of power derived from the force of the wind on the sails. For example, if the weather sheet from a backed staysail is led to the weather side of the tiller (balanced on the other side with shock cord or thin rubber hose), you have a form of self-steering. If the vessel heads up to windward, there will be additional wind pressure on the backed staysail, which means more tension on the sheet and accordingly pressure to pull the tiller to windward to make the yacht bear off. Conversely, if the vessel falls off, there is less pressure on the staysail and sheet. The shock cord or hose on the tiller will pull it to leeward so the yacht will head up. In *Self-*

Steering for Sailing Craft, by John Letcher, the author tells about many schemes of sheet-to-tiller arrangements.

A final option is to take an extra crew member along and to dispense with steering devices altogether. If you have three people on board, automatic self-steering is superfluous, for no one has anything to do. Steering by hand will ensure a better lookout, and in no other way do you get such a constant feel of the wind and the sea.

6

~~~~~~

The Anchor Game

When we last visited California, we tied *Whisper* up at a friend's dock in beautiful Newport Beach. Next to us was a sleek, new forty-six-foot New Zealand–built cutter that belonged to Ed Carpenter, who was busy completing the interior. Ed often stopped to look at *Whisper*'s 45-pound CQR plow anchor hanging on the stemhead, the windlass, and the 3/8-inch chain that disappeared inside. One day Ed asked me about an anchor.

"Say, Hal," he said. "If you were fitting out *Matangi*, what kind of ground tackle would you choose? I mean if you were going anywhere. *Matangi* displaces about twelve tons."

"Since *Matangi* is twice the weight of *Whisper*, I would buy a 60-pound plow, 45 fathoms of 7/16-inch chain, and a suitable windlass to handle both," I answered after some thought.

My answer so upset Ed that he went around in a daze for days.

Some time later Ed asked the same question of Al Liggett, who had recently returned from a sailing trip around the world.

"What anchor would you pick?" said Ed.

Al tugged at his beard, eyeballed the long blue hull, and replied, "Well,

Herreshoff-pattern fisherman anchor lashed alongside with the stock in place and ready for use.

if she were mine, I'd find me a 75-pound plow or a nice hefty Danforth anchor and a big hunk of chain to quiet her down. If it gets to blowing some awful night, you don't want to worry."

Again Ed shook his head in disbelief. When he put the question to a third world-cruising sailor and got substantially the same answer, he scratched his head.

"I think you fellows are trying to tell me something," said Ed. "I had no idea you needed such heavy anchors and chain. In southern California we use 15- or 20-pound anchors and nylon, but then we tie up mostly in marinas or use moorings. I guess when you're in a distant land somewhere, your gear needs to be beefy and beyond doubt even if it weighs a quarter of a ton."

Ed's figure of a quarter of a ton wasn't far wrong. Only he forgot to count the other anchors and warps. On *Whisper* our ground tackle is as follows:

(1)	CQR anchor	45	pounds
	35 fathoms 3/8″ chain	315	
	windlass (S-L 500)	90	
(2)	CQR anchor (spare)	45	
	one fathom 1/2″ chain	14	
	45 fathoms 5/8″ nylon		
	Sampson braid	30	
(3)	Fisherman anchor (Herreshoff)	65	
	one fathom 1/2″ chain	14	
	30 fathoms 5/8″ 3-strand nylon	20	
(4)	Danforth Hi-tensile anchor	20	
	one fathom 1/2″ chain	14	
	33 fathoms 5/8″ 3-strand nylon	21	
(5)	Danforth Hi-tensile anchor		
	(spare)	20	
	one fathom 1/2″ chain	14	
	50 fathoms 1/2″ Dacron (spare		
	halyard line but can be used		
	as a warp)	24	
		751	pounds

This equipment gives us five sets of anchors and cables. I carry two spare anchors in case of loss, because it is impossible to replace anchors in remote places. We reckon we can anchor in seven fathoms of water or less with chain with a fair amount of safety. In deeper water we use nylon and chain together. My choice of anchors and cables is worked out

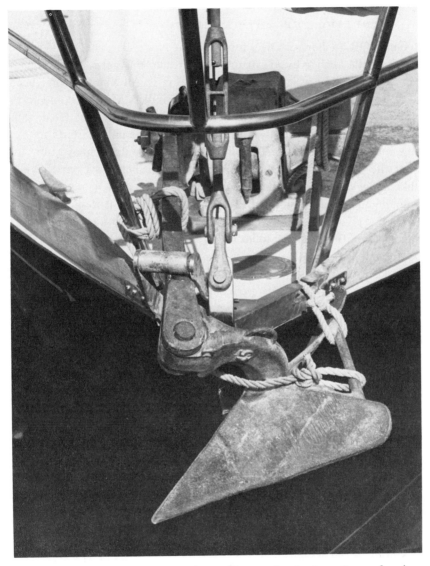

We keep Whisper's *45-pound CQR at the stemhead where the anchor is easy to let go and recover. Two short pieces of ⅜-inch line hold the pivoting fluke tightly against the stem and keep the anchor from rattling around. The short pieces of line go overboard with the anchor.*

on the premise of stout gear to handle the worst conditions; yet I need to handle the ground tackle quickly with a minimum of fuss and wasted energy.

HANDLING THE MAIN ANCHOR

Our CQR anchor runs over a substantial bow roller, which allows the shank of the anchor to go out or come in over the roller so the anchor can be dropped or weighed without touching it. All Margaret or I need to do to recover the anchor is to work the windlass lever back and forth while standing at full height in a comfortable position. The chain falls below—fathom by fathom—until the shank of the anchor starts up the bow roller. If the anchor has been raised with the fluke (plow) upward or at the side, the weight of the fluke rolls the anchor over so that the fluke hangs downward in its proper stowing position. A few more cranks pull the shank of the anchor aft until the widened part of the shank (near the pivot pin) is jammed between the bow roller and a U-shaped metal piece fitted over the roller to keep the chain from jumping off (see photograph).

To keep the fluke of the CQR from banging around, I keep two six-foot pieces of 3/8-inch line permanently tied to the crossbar between the ears of the fluke (these lashings go overboard with the anchor). I take one line to the rope gypsy of the windlass and put a strain on the line, which jams the fluke tightly against the metal stempiece. I lash the second line to the pulpit on the other side. These lines should be as tight as possible.

Not only does this anchor-handling scheme obviate lifting an awkward heavy weight over the lifelines and pulpit, knocking the paint, and getting the anchor man covered with whatever may happen to be on the seabed (often gluey black mud), but the anchor is in position ready to be let go again. During the entire operation I have touched neither the anchor nor the chain. And my back is not wrenched from lifting a big weight at a bad angle. If the cable is muddy, it is a good idea to pull it up slowly and to stop now and then to give the sea a few minutes to flush off some of the mud. We use a brush and buckets of seawater to complete the scrub. Don't stow muddy chain or line below; clean it as it comes on board.

If the chain locker is tall and narrow, the chain will be self-stowing and require no attention below. If the chain locker is wide and flat, a crewman will have to go below to knock down the mound of chain as it builds up. Failure to keep the chain orderly can result in tangles.

Chain lasts for years and years. We end-for-end it occasionally when wear has knocked off much of the galvanizing. Every three years or so we have it hot-dip galvanized, which seems to make the chain like new again.

Contrary to popular fantasy, ordinary anchor recovery with a suitable manual windlass is not a crew-killing job. A lever-action windlass that allows cranking while standing upright is easier to work. Note how the anchor comes aboard without any back-wrenching lifting maneuvers over the pulpit.

To keep track of lengths, we tie several 1-inch wide strips of red cloth at 5 fathoms, white strips at 10 fathoms, and blue strips at 15 fathoms. I then repeat and put red at 20 fathoms, white at 25 fathoms, and finally blue at 30 fathoms. The sequence of red, white, and blue is simple to remember. The strips of cloth are easy to see (and to renew occasionally) when they fly past the windlass gypsy. At night the strips are quite visible with a flashlight.

The anchoring system that I have described has worked perfectly for more than eleven years and thousands of times of anchoring. Margaret and I find the recovery of the chain and anchor not difficult at all. Normally it takes about ten minutes to crank up 20 or 30 fathoms of chain. People are forever telling me how hard the chain is to recover and how tired I must be. Obviously, my observers have never used a good manual windlass. I am perfectly satisfied with my anchoring scheme and see no reason to change it. I certainly don't wish to complicate the yacht with an electric or hydraulic windlass.

When we go to sea, it is necessary to disconnect the chain from the anchor and to plug the navel pipe, the access opening to the chain locker. Otherwise an astonishing amount of water finds its way below. If we are going to windward for several days and do not plug the navel pipe, we have to pump the bilges every few hours. I disconnect the chain and tie its end to a short piece of ⅛-inch diameter line that hangs down from a tapered wooden plug (greased) that seals the navel pipe. The weight of the chain end helps hold the plug in place. Do not drop the chain end into the chain locker without tying a rag or something on the end; otherwise it will be very hard to find. If you don't want to disconnect the chain, you can jam oily rags around the chain or nylon line in the navel pipe.

NYLON

Nylon line is a wonderful material for anchor cable. Its natural stretch evens out shocks and jerks. It doesn't rot or rust, and its strength is unbelievable. It works silently, is easy to recover, and generally comes aboard clean. The line is not heavy and does not cause a weight problem in the ends of a vessel. Nylon, however, is subject to chafe, which makes it dangerous to use in tropical waters, where razor-sharp coral can gnaw through the line insidiously and steadily until the fibers suddenly part. Nylon does not stow itself and is hard to haul by hand because it is slippery and sometimes cuts your hands. Another disadvantage is that in gusty winds a yacht may sheer from side to side when anchored with

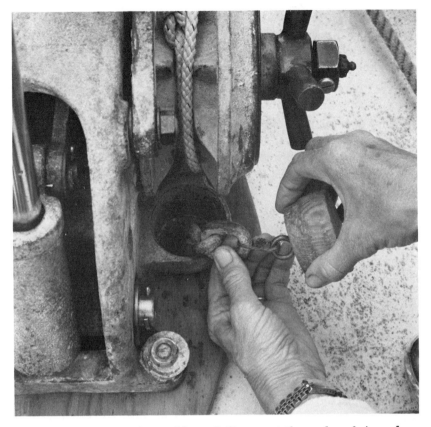

When we go to sea and are offshore, I disconnect the anchor chain and close the navel pipe with a greased wooden plug. Because it is surprisingly difficult to find a chain end in a pile of chain, I keep the chain end handy by tying it to the wooden plug. In addition, the weight of the chain holds the plug in place, and I can recover the chain from on deck. When you disconnect the chain from the anchor, be sure to lash down the anchor first, otherwise . . .

nylon. Chain, on the other hand, is much heavier, hangs in a catenary, and will hold a nervous ship steady. In waters where coral is not a problem, you can use a long piece of chain together with nylon to gain some of the advantages of both. In any case, a short length of chain leading up from the anchor will reduce the chafe of the nylon against the seabed.

Where the nylon comes aboard the yacht, the line must be carefully protected with chafing gear. Although some sailors wrap canvas around the nylon where it passes over a roller or through a chock, there is a problem keeping the canvas in place even if it is carefully tied or sewed. I have had better luck leading the nylon through a piece of heavy red rubber radiator hose two or three feet long whose inside diameter is a snug fit for the nylon. The hose is easy to lash to fittings and protects the nylon yet is reasonably resistant to outside chafe. You can keep the hose in place with pieces of small line tied around the nylon above and below the chafing gear with constrictor knots which will not slip. Metal hose clamps also serve well. But no matter what sort of chafing gear you decide on, it must be inspected every several hours during a storm, because hundreds or perhaps thousands of pounds of pressure are concentrated on one tiny point. If the chafing gear goes, the fiber line goes next. Fortunately, you need to move the line and chafing gear only an inch or two to start afresh.

For the hard usage that anchor warps receive, braided nylon seems superior to three-strand construction, which is often weakened by hockling, an annoying back-twisting in which one or more strands somehow get a reverse twist and stick out laterally from the main body of the line. These unwanted twists diminish the strength of the line and make it hard to handle and to run through blocks.

One of the principal advantages of nylon is its marvelous elasticity; we must not lose this property by using a diameter that is too large. For vessels of twenty-five to fifty-five feet—the concern of this book—nylon of 1-inch diameter is too big; ¾-inch nylon is ample; ⅝-inch nylon is adequate. Captain Irving Johnson anchored his forty-ton ketch *Yankee* for years in European and Mediterranean waters with ⅝-inch nylon with excellent results. The smaller line is also cheaper, lighter, and easier to store.

"I feel certain that you should not use too large a diameter of nylon because if you do it spoils the chance of getting some elasticity," says Captain Johnson. "You will never break a ⅝-inch nylon unless it chafes, and if you get chafe you can break a 2-inch nylon."[4]

The main difficulty with long fiber warps is stowage. It seems that no matter how carefully you coil lines and tie them off, as soon as you turn your back they get into snarls (maybe an invisible ship's cat has begun to play). A small warp can be faked down into a large plastic bucket (with holes in the bottom for drainage). Another stowage scheme is to coil the nylon in a large circle (say a 60-inch diameter or so) and tie the line off with four or five short pieces of marline. Then if half the coil is turned over, you get a figure eight, one coil of which can be pushed over on top of the other to make a small unit. When the warp is to be used,

*This small drum permanently mounted on the afterdeck holds 300 feet
of ⅝-inch diameter line in a compact, neat, easy-to-use, and quickly
available form. The framework is stainless steel. The ends of the drum are
½-inch plywood but might better be made of ⅛-inch aluminum alloy,
which would require no painting. I seize the bitter end of the warp to the
center shaft with a hose clamp. The line runs from the drum through a
block on the opposite quarter and then overboard. If a light anchor is
kept bent to the end of the warp, the anchor can be used at a second's
notice for an emergency brake or a stern anchor. Or if you should go
aground, the anchor can be laid out quickly from a dinghy. You need to
use an anchor warp drum only once to be sold on its handiness.*

you reverse the process. No matter how you stow lines, however, it is
troublesome to get them ready to let go, particularly if you need long
lengths, the vessel is rolling, and there is some urgency.

After fighting the battle of warp stowage for many years, I designed
a stainless steel frame and drum (with plywood sides) that holds 300
feet of ⅝-inch line. We mounted the drum on the port side of the
afterdeck of *Whisper*. We keep a fathom of ½-inch chain and an anchor
shackled to the warp. The anchor is at the stern and is always ready to

drop. In practice this system has worked well. You need to use the anchor warp drum only once to appreciate the ease and speed of both letting go and recovery. The surprising thing is how small 300 feet of line is when it is coiled tightly. The warp drum is only 14½ inches in diameter and 12 inches long and demonstrates that the trick of good stowage is a simple system of even coiling on a readily accessible drum.

THE DIFFERENT TYPES OF ANCHORS

The big three anchors are the CQR, the Danforth, and the fisherman. The first two are burying anchors, while the fisherman is a surface anchor. It is useful to keep these distinctions in mind, because each class of anchor works in a different manner and is better suited for certain conditions.

The CQR (the name is a sort of acronym for *secure*), or plow, was invented by Geoffrey Taylor almost fifty years ago, and is a fiendishly clever design in wide use among cruising yachts. The anchor is made of drop forged steel and consists of a V-shaped plowshare connected to a long H-sectioned shank by a massive pin. The plow or fluke is free to pivot from side to side over a prescribed limit. There is no stock. The anchor is extremely difficult to bend.

In use the CQR falls to the seabed, the tension on the cable straightens out the anchor, turns it on one side or the other, and the plow begins to dig in. In suitable holding ground the fluke digs deeper and deeper as tension on the cable is increased, often burying the entire anchor. If the yacht swings with the tide, the cable will not foul the anchor (as with a fisherman), and a pull from a different direction merely resets the CQR in a new alignment. The CQR is difficult to foul unless you have the bad luck to pick up a tin can with the point of the plow.

The genuine CQR anchor is made by Simpson-Lawrence of Glasgow, Scotland, and is widely distributed. Besides the design, the main feature of the Simpson-Lawrence CQR is that both the H-section shank and the pin and horn (which carries the plow) are made from solid, one-piece drop forged steel. The plow is stamped from heavy plate steel and is welded to the horn. The anchor is then hot-dip-galvanized. Unfortunately, there are many bad copies of the CQR, none of which are recommended. In particular, I have knowledge of a German imitation (which I hope has been improved or withdrawn entirely) that doesn't hold at all and is worse than useless because the counterfeit anchor may give false confidence.

The Danforth anchor is well known and consists of two paddle-shaped flukes arranged side by side with a narrow space between them for the

Veteran sailor Dick Pratt devised this scheme to help with stowage of a large spare CQR anchor so the plow and the shank can be stored and handled separately. The pin connecting the horn and the shank has been replaced with a stout monel fitting held in place with a pin which, in turn, is secured with a shackle. All the pieces are held to the horn with light non-ferrous chain. The anchor can be assembled quickly without any tools at all.

shank. The shank and the flukes are hinged together at one end by the stock, which runs through the end of the shank at right angles and continues across the ends of the flukes and beyond. The crown is built around the pivot point of the shank and flukes, and the crown restricts the shank-fluke pivot angle from exceeding 32 degrees.

If the Danforth initially hits on its side on the sea floor, the stock holds the anchor in an unstable position and it falls over. Tension on the anchor cable causes the flukes to open until they are held at the proper angle by the crown. The pointed steel flukes are forced into the seabed. The harder the pull of the cable, the more the anchor digs in. The Danforth cannot be fouled once it is dug in a little. As with the CQR, a pull from a different direction merely resets the anchor.

One fault with the Danforth is that it is possible to get chain or line between the flukes and the shank (sometimes wrapped around and around). This rarely happens unless the anchor and slack cable are thrown haphazardly into the sea. If cable does get between the flukes and the shank, the anchor is, of course, fouled and will not hold at all. You will know at once because the anchor will drag. If a Danforth is let go slowly with a slight tension on the cable, the anchor will not foul this way. The pivoting flukes of a Danforth can also be jammed open with a small rock or clam shell. When the anchor turns over, the frozen blades will not fall down but will instead skid merrily along the bottom. This is an unusual occurrence but possible. Again you will know because the anchor will drag.

Danforths have been manufactured in all sizes—from 2½ pounds (for dinghies) to 10,000 pounds (for battleships). During World War II thousands were made, mostly of ordinary steel, usually galvanized, but many were constructed of bronze (non-magnetic for minesweepers) and of stainless steel. Various manufacturing techniques have been used— stamping, forging, casting, riveting, and welding. Occasionally you can buy Danforths at a surplus outlet; in the past I have used a superb 33-pound cast Danforth that cost $10. The present Danforth Hi-tensile anchors (which don't cost $10!) are first-rate and are fairly resistant to bending, sometimes a problem in rocks or around mooring cables. The stowage of a Danforth is easy because the anchor lies flat. Again, because of good manufacturing standards, I recommend that you buy only a genuine Danforth anchor, not a copy which may be cheaper but also poorer in quality.

The fisherman is the age-old traditional anchor of the sea and is the pattern that is so often tattooed on the backs of sailors' hands or forearms. I have seen fisherman anchors in many parts of the world—Japan, Chile, and Greece, for example. Though constructional details differed, the design was always the same: two arms fastened to one end of a long shank to make a T-shaped contrivance. The arms are curved slightly toward the opposite end of the shank. The ends of the arms have widened points or flukes to grip the seabed better. A long stock (sometimes of wood) is put through the shank at the opposite end from the arms. The stock is generally removable, which allows the anchor to be lashed flat on deck. When viewed from either end of the shank, the stock and arms are always at right angles to one another. These right-angle protuberances make a fisherman awkward to handle.

A fisherman can be recovered without trouble until it is clear of the water. Then, because sharp iron points stick out on all sides, the anchor becomes a monster that threatens not only to tear off the topside paint but to rip through the hull itself, particularly if the vessel is rolling and pitching as she gets underway. The best thing is to get a line around the crown of the anchor, to bend it to a jib halyard, and to haul away. This will recover the anchor upside down and bring it to the rail or the deck without trouble. The line around the crown can be an anchor buoy line or a special short line eye-spliced around each fluke and allowed to hang down a foot or so (this line goes overboard with the anchor). The line can be picked up with a hook on the hoisting halyard. Paint damage from the metal ends of the stock can be minimized by putting rubber crutch tips over the ends (this also applies to Danforths).

When a fisherman anchor falls to the floor of the sea with tension on the cable, one fluke begins to bite into the seabed at once. If the anchor should fall on its side, the stock upsets the anchor to its proper position. The harder the pull on the chain or line, the more the fluke digs in, until it is buried up to the crown. A drawback to the fisherman pattern is that the other fluke sticks vertically upright. If the ship swings with the tide or drifts in a calm, it is easy for the anchor line to get around the upstanding fluke and to foul the anchor. This problem may require a second anchor, a line ashore, or some close attention.

The fisherman is a surface anchor and is restricted by its stock from digging deeper than the depth of one arm (the distance from the crown to the tip of a fluke). A fisherman relies on considerable weight and an initial grab of the seabed. In soft mud or uncompacted sand a fisherman may well drag; once the anchor lets go and begins to scrape a furrow across the ocean floor, the holding power is gone. In spite of these disadvantages, however, the fisherman is excellent at times. Its flukes are heavy and dig in quickly and hard. On a rocky bottom a CQR and Danforth—burying types—may not work at all, while a fisherman will hold well, particularly on short scope. In sand or shells with a hard crust, and in weed, a fisherman is often the only hope.

On the common fisherman the palm of its fluke is spade-shaped (see drawing). When the yacht swings or drifts in a calm, the anchor line catches on the fluke that sticks ups, hooks under the widest part of the spade, and the anchor is fouled. On the excellent Herreshoff pattern the palm is diamond-shaped and tapers gradually toward both the tip of the fluke and the crown. An anchor line will generally slip up the arm past the palm and not foul the anchor.

You sometimes see fisherman anchors with no palms at all—the arm merely runs out to the fluke in a long tapered point. These anchors are rock picks and are used mostly in halibut boats for fishing purposes and have no place on yachts. A halibut anchor will pull right through most

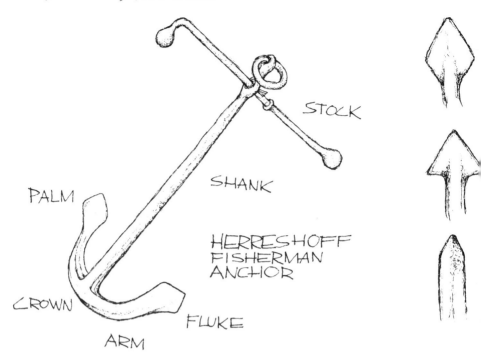

PALM

STOCK

SHANK

HERRESHOFF
FISHERMAN
ANCHOR

CROWN

FLUKE

ARM

types of holding ground, because with no palms there is scarcely any area of resistance.

We have talked about three well-known types of anchors. Which is best? My answer is that like many world cruising people we carry all three because each is good for different conditions. I use a CQR for a basic anchor, the Danforth is ideal for a kedge, and the fisherman is unsurpassed in difficult holding ground. I have found the CQR excellent in 95 percent of the anchorages we have visited. Yet I can easily recall three places—Caleta Morning in Beagle Canal in Tierra del Fuego, a beach anchorage on Isla Española in the Galápagos, and a palm-shaded paradise near the western end of the lagoon of Rangiroa Atoll in the Tuamotus—that were special problems. Each of the three sites had a sand or shell bottom with a hard crust that the CQR would not penetrate even when the anchor was dropped time after time. In two of these places the flukes of a Danforth—kept sharply pointed with a little hand filing from time to time (especially before re-galvanizing)—dug in quickly. At the third place the Danforth skated across the seabed like the CQR, and we tossed over a fisherman, whose heavy flukes penetrated the crust at once. You need all three.

Without question the best fisherman anchors in the United States are manufactured by Paul Luke. The Luke anchors (in weights of 40, 65, 75, 100, 150, and 200 pounds) are close to the original Herreshoff patterns and are made in three pieces for ease of stowage. These anchors are heavy and solid and expensive, but with reasonable luck one will last you a lifetime. In fact, one may extend your lifetime. Merriman-Holbrook, James Bliss, and Wilcox-Crittenden no longer market suitable fisherman anchors.

THE THREE POINTS OF ANCHORING

Although there are a number of refinements—none to be neglected—the three main requirements of successful anchoring are:
1. An anchor of ample weight.
2. Plenty of scope.
3. Suitable holding ground.

The weight of an anchor means a lot. A 20-pound anchor will often skid over a veneer of weed or grass on the sea floor, while a 40- or 60-pound anchor will dig through to sand or shells below. There is no substitute for a heavy, properly dug in anchor. A novice may boast that his yacht was held in a storm by an 8-pound Danforth. This may be perfectly true if the anchor was well dug in. The problem is that the 8-pound anchor may not dig in at all in many types of bottom. It is for this reason I recommend that a twenty-five-foot yacht carry at least one 30-pound burying-type anchor.

With regard to the general weights of anchors, a handy rule for cruising yachts is one pound of anchor for each foot of length. This is for burying types. For fisherman anchors, you should have two pounds for every foot of length. For areas where anchoring is difficult, you may well increase the weights.

Holding power can be improved by sliding a weight part way down the cable. If you hang a 20- or 30-pound pig of lead (or anything handy) on a large bow shackle and ease it down the cable on a light line, the weight will increase the curve of the catenary of the chain or line. When the vessel pulls on the cable, the tension will have to lift the weight and to straighten out the cable before any pull is made on the anchor.

Although a fathom or two of chain is usually employed with an anchor, some very experienced sailors have had good luck using a heavier anchor and bending a nylon line directly to the shank of the anchor, perhaps feeling that the heavier anchor is of more direct benefit than the chain plus an anchor. For example, a 20-pound Danforth and 2

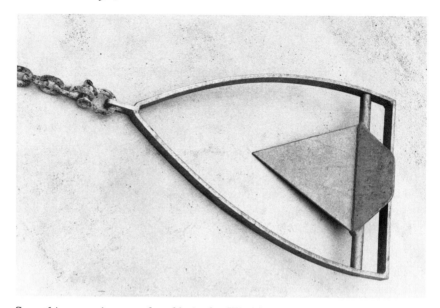

Something new in ground tackle is this Wishbone anchor, which went into
production in Florida in 1976. Designed by Jim Taylor after much
experimentation in the Bahamas, this stockless anchor is quite non-fouling
and appears to dig deeply and firmly in good holding ground. In one series
of tests where Danforths, CQRs, and Wishbones were dragged behind an
automobile on a dirt road, the Wishbone stopped the car every time while
the other anchors dragged merrily along the top of the road. Because the
Wishbone has no stock, it is non-fouling even if the chain is wrapped
around and around the anchor. These new anchors are available in weights
of 7 to 90 pounds (more on special order) and are made from hot-dipped
galvanized steel. The fluke, kickers (fins under the fluke that press against the
frame), and bottom frame piece are made of high-tensile steel. It is too
early to make any big claims for the Wishbone, but Florida sailors haven't
been able to fault the anchor so far. Right off, it appears to have two
advantages over the Danforth: (1) no stock; (2) no possibility of a small
stone or shell fouling the fluke so that when the anchor turns over the fluke
does not fall down. In a check for strength, a 35-pound Wishbone stood up
to 12,000 pounds of pressure before failure. The wishbone frame of the larger
sizes is somewhat bulky and the anchor doesn't stow on anchor rollers like
the CQR or the Danforth (a stowing arrangement can be worked out with a
bowsprit). At first the Wishbone seems a surface anchor, but the thin frame
wishbone appears to dig into soft holding ground. The anchor is impressive
but more testing is needed.

fathoms of ⅜-inch chain weigh 38 pounds. If seabed chafe is not a problem, you might be better off using a 38-pound anchor without chain. Most sailors, however, use a little chain because of the chafe potential and because the heavy chain helps ensure a horizontal pull.

Some people space two anchors along the same cable and claim good results when both anchors have dug in. I feel it is much better to employ two separate cables, each of which can hold the vessel in case one line or chain parts.

The second rule of anchoring is plenty of scope (the ratio of cable to depth), which decreases the angle between the cable and the seabed. The shallower the angle, the more the anchor will dig in. Ideally, the pull on the anchor should be horizontal. *A scope of five to one should be regular practice.* If the holding ground is poor, if there are spring tides, or if the wind is strong, you may have to veer more cable. Conversely, if someone is on board and alert to the vessel's situation, and the weather and water are quiet, less scope is possible. Certainly if you are up a quiet, shallow creek in settled weather, the anchoring requirements are minimal. This, however, is an exception, and for ordinary anchor work *a scope of five to one should be regular practice.* Who can tell when the weather will change? It may change when you're asleep or ashore. I have seen more yachts in trouble from insufficient scope than for any other reason.

A scope of five to one means you will need to veer 20 fathoms of cable in a depth of 4 fathoms. If the water is deeper, say 10 fathoms, you must have 50 fathoms of chain, or part chain and part nylon, to get sufficient scope. Normally, you can anchor in 5 fathoms or less, which means that 25 fathoms of chain or nylon are adequate. It's only rarely that you need longer lines. I recall that Margaret and I bent two warps together to make an 80-fathom length when we anchored in the Society Islands in the lagoon at Bora Bora, which was 16 fathoms deep. In the Chilean channels in Cahuelmó Fiord we lay to a 110-fathom nylon warp in a depth of 22 fathoms during a violent three-day storm. Again, in Puerto Molyneux in the south of Chile, we anchored in 17 fathoms with 100 fathoms of line. Such a long line is wonderfully elastic, and smoothly stretches and shortens as the yacht reacts to blasts of wind.

In tropical waters with coral, however, you must be extremely cautious. The use of several cork or plastic floats will help to keep a fiber line off the bottom, and a stern line to the shore or a stern anchor can keep some tension on the main anchor to keep its line out of mischief. I advise frequent swimming inspections with a face mask. If at all possible, go to a shallower anchorage and *use all chain.*

It's painful to write that every year a dozen or more yachts are wrecked because the owners fail to use all chain in waters where coral grows. Writer after writer has chronicled these misfortunes. Yet some new sailors think that they can ignore the warnings of experience. Fiber line in coral waters means trouble. Typical was the unfortunate experience of David Boyce and Tim Noot in *Amazing Grace* in the Marquesas Islands in 1975. The two men anchored with 30 feet of chain attached to their anchor. Dacron line led up to the yacht from the chain. In the beginning there was enough wind to keep a little tension on the line, which held it above the coral heads growing upward from the seabed. But in time the wind changed. The chain wrapped around and around the coral until the Dacron line was pulled down to the level of the razor-like stone growths. The line chafed through.

Just because you use all chain in coral waters doesn't excuse you from vigilance. It is possible to get slack chain around and around a coral head. The gradually shortened chain silently pulls the yacht closer and closer to the coral until the yacht is directly above the danger, with tight chain leading vertically downward. Then, if a swell lifts the yacht, the taut chain may snap a link. Worse yet, if the coral head is close to the surface, the yacht may be slowly worked up to the hazard with disastrous results. In his book *An Island to Myself*, Tom Neale detailed the loss of Ed Vessey's *Tiburon* at Suvorov Island in the northern Cook Islands because of a broken anchor chain.

The third rule of anchoring is to place your iron hope in suitable holding ground. But what is the nature of the bottom? You find this out by consulting the chart, which may indicate sand, mud, ooze, clay, gravel, shingle, pebbles, stone, rock, shells, oysters, weed, grass, or kelp. Often, however, there is no notation on the chart. You then investigate the bottom yourself by putting a little grease or tallow on the base of the lead on the lead line (arming the lead) and sampling the bottom. The tallow will pick up a little sand and small shells or mud and gravel. Or maybe you will feel separate rocks as you bounce the lead along the bottom.

Smooth rock is the poorest holding ground of all, because on it an anchor is nothing more than a large fishing sinker. *Broken rock* is all or nothing, depending on whether a fluke of the anchor catches on an embedded rock. A heavy fisherman anchor is best; a burying-type anchor may be useless. Sometimes a fluke jams between two rocks or gets stuck in a crack and becomes hopelessly fouled. At other times the anchor may find a crevice and hold well with a pull from one direction;

a wind shift, however—even days later—will change the angle of pull and the anchor may drag. *Pebbles* and *shingle* (coarse gravel) are unpredictable and may jam the flukes of a pivoting fluke–type anchor. The grip of an anchor may suddenly give way in a seabed of small stones. Certainly you should lay out maximum scope. *Gravel* is better, especially for a burying-type anchor. *Mud* is difficult to discuss unless you have some idea of its viscosity, which can vary from a thin and useless *ooze* to the beginnings of *clay*. Certainly a burying-type anchor is best, because it can work its way down where the mud may be stiffer. *Weed* and *grass* are troublesome and require an anchor with enough weight to force its way beneath the growth. *Kelp* is particularly nasty because of its toughness, and you may be better off in deeper water, where there is less growth.

Sand, clay, hard mud, shells, broken shells, and various combinations offer an excellent grip for anchors. The majority of traditional anchorage sites have bottoms of these substances. In considering various bottoms, pay particular attention to any references in a Pilot book that speak of poor holding ground or to such statements as "rock thinly covered with sand" or "a layer of mud over rock." You can be sure that no mention of bad holding ground is made unless some poor mariner has had a hard time.

Unfortunately, the charts that you buy these days tend to omit bottom identification in useful terms and to substitute instead the misleading words *soft, hard,* or *sticky*—words that mean little to sailors. Perhaps the accuracy of the old days is gone because soundings are taken with electronic depth sounders rather than a lead line armed with a bit of tallow to pick up a true sample of the bottom.

UNIFORM STRENGTH

Each part of the anchor gear must be strong and up to the standards of the rest. Take the galvanized shackle that joins the chain to the anchor. The shackle must be stout, of proper test, and the pin should be secured with two or three wraps of galvanized wire tied so that any untwisting motion will pull against the wraps of the safety wire.

If you are using nylon and chain, their strengths should be comparable. For example, it is folly to use $\frac{5}{16}$-inch chain with $\frac{3}{4}$-inch diameter nylon. The chain has a proof load test of 2,618 pounds, while the nylon has strength in excess of 5 tons. A length of $\frac{1}{2}$-inch or $\frac{9}{16}$-inch chain is more suitable.

The bow roller ought to be 6 inches in diameter (but seldom is). If the roller is to be used for chain alone, a groove slightly wider than the diameter of the chain (say $\frac{7}{16}$ inch for $\frac{3}{8}$-inch chain) should be machined around the center of the roller so that the face of every other link will seat itself on the roller, a step that reduces friction enormously.

If the roller is to be used for line alone, it should be smooth with well-rounded edges. Whether for chain or nylon, the sides of the roller housing should be built up so that a pin or a heavy metal strip can be put across above the cable so it can't jump out of position. Chocks or fairleads should be deep, with carefully rounded edges and preferably of closed construction.

If there is no windlass on board, fit a chain pawl at the stem. A chain pawl is a pivoting piece of metal that allows chain to come in when pulled but jams in a link when the chain tries to go out. Save your back by avoiding hard pulling at a bad angle. If necessary, take a nylon line (the anchor warp itself or a short piece of line clapped onto the chain) to a cockpit winch. It is useful to have a snatch block for $\frac{3}{4}$-inch diameter line (The Nicro Corporation makes some superb trunnion snatch blocks) that can be secured around the deck as necessary.

If the anchor cable goes to a bollard or a windlass, the fittings should be through-bolted with backup plates underneath (have you inspected the bolts recently? I hope they're not red brass). If the pawl that keeps the wildcat on the windlass from turning looks suspect, fit a sturdy chain stopper ahead of the windlass to hold the cable. An eye splice in nylon should have half a dozen neat tucks before tapering and should be fitted over smooth, large-diameter metal (not plastic) thimbles that, in turn, are held with shackles of generous size.

In short, go over each part of your ground tackle and try to find its weak point and whether that frailty is less strong than the others.

7

~~~~~~

The Practice of Anchoring

An important part of seamanship is the ability to handle a second anchor. A storm may come up when you are in an anchorage. You may need a stern anchor to keep from swinging near another vessel. You may have to kedge away from a dock if a sudden onshore wind descends in the night. You may go aground and urgently need an anchor to pull you off. A light kedge can keep you at right angles to incoming swells in a rolly anchorage and make the difference between comfort and a night of agony. A second anchor can keep the slack chain of the main anchor from winding around a coral head and causing many problems.

A second anchor is cheap insurance.

The main requirement for putting out an additional anchor is a good rowing dinghy. In it you can easily lay out a nylon or manila warp as follows:

First decide exactly which way you want the warp to run. If there is a handy reference point—a tree, a building, a prominent hill, or a distant light—use it as a rowing target. If someone on the yacht is going to direct

Anchor gear is only as strong as each connecting part. We use stout tested shackles and carefully seize the pins in place with galvanized wire. The safety wire is wrapped aircraft fashion to prevent the pins from starting to open. The twisted wire ends can be poked into the eye of a shackle pin to keep sharp points away from fingers and sails.

you, work out visual signals in advance, because it is impossible to shout to windward in bad weather. Next flake out the entire warp on deck so you don't have to fight tangles when you're in the dinghy. Once in the dinghy, hang the anchor over the stern and lash it in place with a piece of small stuff. Put a knife on the seat beside you. Beginning with the end shackled to the anchor or chain, flake the entire warp—don't coil it— into the after part of the dinghy.

Secure the bitter end of the warp to a mooring cleat or winch on board the yacht and push off, rowing smartly toward your target. Usually the wind is dead against you and the rowing will be hard. As you pull away from the ship, the line will pay out from the dinghy until you come to the end. Row as hard as you can to stretch the warp to its maximum length, quickly grab the knife beside you, cut the small stuff that holds the kedge to the transom of the dinghy, and the anchor will fall into the sea.

One problem of doing this in deeper water is that you lose some of the length of the warp by the time the anchor hits the bottom, turns over, begins to dig in, and someone on board hauls in the slack. I generally extend the length of the warp by bending on a light line 50 or 60 feet long before I lay out the kedge. Then, by the time the anchor is set, I have hauled the light line back on board. This dodge gives me the full length of the kedge warp.

The foregoing description applies to nylon or manila warps. It is not possible to lay out chain from a dinghy because of the weight of the chain. If it must be put out, the only way is for the man in the dinghy to row off with a light line, to anchor securely at the point where the anchor is to be dropped, and to hand-haul the chain across to the dinghy. The man in the dinghy must then shackle the anchor (put on board the dinghy before starting) to the chain, wire the shackle, and finally drop the anchor. The procedure is cumbersome.

When you are in faraway places by yourself, prompt anchor work can mean the difference between routine seamanship and grievous difficulty. One summer, for instance, along the west coast of Vancouver Island in British Columbia, we sought refuge in Clayoquot Sound during an afternoon when the wind began to blow hard from the south. Once inside the large sound, we sailed to Flores Island and anchored in five fathoms in Matilda Inlet, a narrow finger of water whose entrance faced north. We were well protected and put out thirty-five fathoms of chain and lay with the cable taut while the wind whistled across the steep hills and through the tall firs near us. Though the tide was near maximum height, we thought we would have adequate swinging room at low water.

Late that night the wind dropped while we were asleep, and we swung ashore at low water. A sudden lurch told us that we were aground. In a few minutes *Whisper* was tilted to 50 degrees and high and dry on rocks near the shore. If we had done nothing, the incoming tide would have lifted us higher on the rocks. We launched the dinghy and carried out two anchors, both aimed toward deep water. We winched the cables as tight as banjo strings. I passed the night by changing the propeller zinc and scrubbing the bottom with a brush. Finally at 0415 the flood tide began to lift us, and as the ship rose, the taut cables eased us into deeper water.

We had had a night of hard work. My mistake at not allowing enough swinging room or in putting out a second anchor was well imprinted on my mind. What I should have done was to check the swinging room by rowing around the yacht in the dinghy and sounding with a lead line. Our prompt anchor work, however, got us out of a precarious position.

Sooner or later this situation happens to every yacht. You must be prepared to put out an adequate anchor quickly and without fuss.

MY ANCHORING TECHNIQUE

I try to anchor when the yacht is heading slowly downwind or down tide. With headway of, say, 2 knots I drop the anchor at a selected place and rapidly pay out scope. When enough chain is out I snub it, after which the chain will tighten, the anchor will dig in hard, and the vessel will stop and quickly turn around head to wind or tide. If there is a problem with the holding ground, you know it at once.

One difficulty with this scheme is that the chain going aft along the hull may scratch off some topside and bottom paint. If you initially limit the scope of the chain to three times the depth of the water and don't have her going too fast, the chance of paint damage is lessened, because the chain will make an angle from the vertical that will not exceed 71 degrees. Also, as soon as the chain begins to tighten, I give the yacht full opposite rudder to sheer her away from the chain. On *Whisper* the chain runs out on the starboard side, so to sheer the yacht away from the chain I shove the tiller hard to port, which gives right rudder and turns the starboard side of the yacht away from the chain. Of course, if you are using all nylon or nylon and chain, the problem is less. After the vessel has swung, I veer more chain to five times the depth.

It is important not to anchor on the first pass when you are in new waters. Sail slowly through an anchorage once to check the depths, other vessels, to watch out for mooring buoys, fish traps, wreckage, and God

Aground! The helmsman let his mind wander and didn't pay close enough attention to the shore marks and buoys. The 36-foot, steel-hulled, Dutch-built Golden Feather sits on the sands of upper San Francisco Bay while the bored owner waits for the flood tide to lift off the yacht. Note the warp from the anchor laid out toward deeper water. The captain was lucky to ground on a sandbank in protected waters; except for a bruised ego, no damage will normally result.

knows what. If possible, have a lookout at the bow or up the mast. On the second pass you will have a much better notion of the place.

If there is a choice, you should anchor so that the vessel is between her anchor and a danger. This may seem obvious, but if you anchor in a calm or in a contrary breeze or around other vessels that are headed in another direction, it is easy to set your anchor at right angles to a shoal or to aim the fluke(s) away from a danger. If the yacht darts about at anchor and sheers because of the wind, the tide, or her rudder position, the vessel may drag onto the danger before the anchor has reset itself. In a strong wind, of course, there is no choice.

When you drop the anchor, it is best not to have your vessel going too fast. What is needed is a delicate first bite followed by steady, increasing pressure. Too much speed may snatch the anchor out every time it begins to dig in.

The system I have described works well for us nineteen times out of twenty. If, however, there is any doubt about the anchor holding, I use the engine to drag the vessel astern. I feel strongly that the single most useful service an engine can perform is to assist in anchoring. Many times we have sailed into complicated anchorages without using the engine and then have fired up the diesel to pull the yacht hard astern to see if the anchor was really holding. Initially I use low power. When I feel the anchor bite into the seabed, I slowly increase to full power. To check whether we are moving, we look shoreward at a near and far point (one behind another) to see if the relative bearings change. In fog you can use the trick of dropping the lead line vertically over the side until you just touch the bottom. If you drag astern, you can feel the lead bouncing or dragging along.

If you get into a mess while anchoring—and everyone does occasionally, including me—it may be best to pull up everything and to start afresh. If time is not a problem, sail around a little, get your breath, decide what went wrong, and plan your next move. Review in your mind exactly what you are going to do. Explain your plans to the crew. Get everything ready for your next attempt. If you are in a diffcult or dangerous situation, don't be hesitant about asking for advice or help. Anchoring is a great spectator sport, and some very experienced people with local knowledge may be just waiting to assist you. You must, however, evaluate advice from strangers carefully.

Be sure to allow a previously anchored vessel sufficient swinging room. If you anchor too close to someone already at anchor, *it is your responsibility to move,* even if the task is difficult and unpleasant. If a crewman on a previously anchored vessel questions your closeness and asks you to move, don't snap his head off. He may be right. Perhaps you *should* move. Better now than to risk damage or to be disturbed at 0200. Besides, it is impossible to rest properly if you are worried about another vessel slamming into you.

If there are others nearby, don't pay out a ridiculous amount of scope. Think of your neighbors. In normal weather a scope of five to one is adequate. Even this means a swinging circle of 370 feet for a thirty-five-foot vessel in five fathoms. I recall a big fishing boat from Manta, Ecuador, that was anchored at San Cristóbal with an inordinate amount of manila line while the crew was having a run ashore. The swinging room of the fishing boat seemed to take up the whole of Wreck Bay. The vessel—which had become a lethal battering ram—drove all the other fishing boats and yachts wild (Look out! Here she comes again!).

After I anchor, the next job is to take three bearings of prominent stationary points with the main compass or a hand-bearing compass and to write the bearings in the logbook. I can then easily check my position if I think the anchor is dragging. If I like the anchorage, I have the information to locate the exact spot another time (or to tell to someone else). If I should be unlucky and lose the anchor, the bearings will enable me to determine its position for recovery attempts.

You can learn a lot about anchoring by putting on a face mask and swimming out to inspect your iron hook. I was amazed when I first tried it. Once I found a pile of chain with the anchor sitting on top. Another time I discovered a nylon warp wrapped round and round the anchor. Or, on a more pleasant occasion, I looked into the water to see chain disappearing into sand where the anchor had dug in and vanished.

TIDAL CONSIDERATIONS

In an anchorage with wind in opposition to a tidal stream, a vessel that is on a mooring or at anchor may either face the wind or head into the tide, depending on the windage of the craft, her underbody, whether she is on chain or nylon, and whether on long or short scope. A stranger seeking a place to anchor may have to sail through the anchorage a few times to find space that won't be obstructed by a vessel that seems to be anchored over one spot but is actually at the end of her cable elsewhere. An inviting place in a crowded anchorage may actually be covered by two vessels, each temporarily off station in opposite directions—one pushed by the wind and the other by the tide. Pay attention to the direction of anchor or mooring cables leading into the water from the bows of vessels in the anchorage.

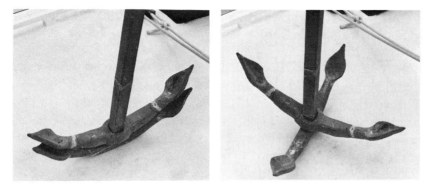

This small grapnel has its movable flukes and crown made with a square mounting hole. To assemble the anchor, the removable fluke section is lifted off the square shank, turned a quarter of a turn, and then dropped down again. Maker unknown.

If you arrive in an area with a sizable tidal range and wish to anchor, you will have to work out the state of the tide and whether it is flooding or ebbing so you can calculate the depths at low water. If there is any choice, it is best to arrive at low water so you can see if there are any wrecks, sandbanks, or underwater obstructions that cover with the flood. Secondly, if you should be unfortunate and run aground, the rising water will float you off. With tide tables and accurate large-scale charts of a harbor, you can make precise calculations of the water depths at low water so you won't go aground. The English are particularly expert at this, and their east coast sailors can tell you to a fraction of an inch how much water you will find over a certain bar or shoal.

Unfortunately, different countries use various datum levels on their charts; the terminology used to describe the tidal heights is confusing. I suggest the easiest scheme is to follow the directions in whatever tide tables you have on board.

As a practical matter, you often don't have pertinent tidal tables or large-scale harbor charts when you are in remote places. You may have a small-scale chart with a few soundings, and tidal calculations based on a port or river many miles away. A persistent wind sometimes makes substantial differences in predicted tidal heights. In these cases, I sail in cautiously, in daylight, noting the depths with an echo sounder or lead line and comparing what I find with the charted soundings. I try to tell from the currents in narrow places whether the stream is ebbing or flooding, and from the shoreline whether the tide is high or low. I look to see where other vessels are anchored and try to anchor with a fathom or two or three beneath my keel at low water.

MOORING

Riding to a single anchor demands a fair amount of swinging room. If this is a problem, you should *moor* with two anchors. If there is a tidal flow, one anchor should go in the direction of the ebb, the second should head toward the flood. The heavier anchor should be laid in the direction of the greater expected strain.

You can moor under sail by dropping the first anchor while you have way on the vessel. Or if there is a strong tide, you can hand all sail and let the tidal stream carry you along after you have dropped anchor No. 1. Veer twice the amount of chain—to ten times the depth—and wait until the anchor is well set. Then drop a second anchor and heave in one-half of the chain of the first anchor so that the yacht is midway between the two anchors. Secure the two cables together and lead them over the bow. The vessel will then swing with the wind or tide over one point above the sea floor.

If such mooring is impossible because of traffic or restricted space, it may be easier to drop the main anchor and to carry out the second anchor in the dinghy (also less chain heaving). The kedge warp can be tied or shackled to the main cable and a little additional chain let out so that the join is below the level of the keel. It may be necessary to put a heavy swivel in the chain below the stem to keep from twisting and kinking the cable, especially if you are going to be moored for some days.

Mooring is often preferable to anchoring with bow and stern anchors, because the yacht can swing in any direction. With bow and stern anchors and a beam wind, heavy loads are put on the ground tackle, loads that are significantly reduced when the yacht can swing head to wind.

BUOYING THE ANCHOR

If you suspect that an anchorage has debris on the bottom, the best plan is to buoy the anchor. You lead a light line from a float to the crown of the anchor and toss the float and line overboard when you drop the anchor. The line should be just long enough to reach the surface at high water, or perhaps a few feet more if there is a strong tidal stream. Try to keep the buoy line as short as possible, because a long line can lead to many difficulties. A CQR has an eye forward of the pivot pin; on a Danforth you can thread a buoy line through or around the crown. Then, if the anchor gets fouled, you need only row out to the buoy and haul in on its line, which will upset the anchor, and recover it upside down. An anchor buoy is especially handy when you have two anchors out and want to recover one.

An anchor buoy also marks the position of your anchor to other vessels. Once, however, another yacht picked up our anchor buoy and tried to lay to it as if it were a mooring. We tried to explain what the buoy was, but all we got in return was a torrent of foul language. (People seem to be particularly sensitive if you question their anchoring techniques.) We had no choice except to winch up the anchor, recover our buoy, and move elsewhere.

There are a number of problems with an anchor buoy: (1) it is one more thing to do when you are busy sailing into a strange anchorage; (2) if the buoy line is long enough to reach to the surface at high water, the line may be slack enough at low water to foul your rudder or propeller; (3) the curse of buoyed anchors is power vessels, which often buzz around anchored sailing yachts like unwanted bluebottle flies. The propeller of a passing motor vessel may sever the buoy line. If the motor vessel doesn't cut the line and instead wraps it up and fouls her propeller, the momentum of the motor vessel may pluck your anchor from the bottom. Suddenly you may be towed away by a vessel that may not wish to be a tug; her master may even direct a few unkind words at his unwanted tow.

Sailors have used various schemes to keep an anchor buoy from fouling a propeller or rudder, but none are simple and foolproof. In any case, *never* use floating line. Put a small lead weight eight or ten feet down the line, so the buoy line will hang down vertically below the float and not drift out horizontally waiting for a propeller to come along.

The safest anchor buoy arrangement that I know of is to use a dan buoy, a float with a slim, six-foot (or whatever) vertical pole above and below the float (a total of 12 feet), similar to a man-overboard pole. The bottom of the pole is held down with a lead weight, and the top of the pole can have a small flag, perhaps with the name of the yacht, the word "anchor," or its symbol. The idea is that the anchor buoy line will be fastened to the end of the submerged part, which should be long enough to clear any expected propellers or other problems. If a fishing boat or ferry hits the dan buoy, the force will merely push the buoy aside. In use the anchor dan buoy can be taken apart at the float in the middle and its two halves lashed on the coach roof. Before anchoring, the buoy can be assembled and placed outside the lifelines ready for dropping with the anchor.

There is one other time to buoy anchor gear. If you have to clear out of

A 65-pound Herreshoff-pattern fisherman anchor made by Paul Luke of East Boothbay, Maine. This anchor is made to high standards and is extremely strong. It disassembles into three pieces, which are easy to store in out-of-the-way places. These anchors are available in weights of 40, 65, 75, 100, 150, and 200 pounds.

an anchorage in a hurry with no time to recover your ground tackle, you buoy it before you leave it behind. You bend a light line—whose length is at least equivalent to the depth of the water at high tide—to the bitter end of the chain or warp. Tie a float or two to the other end of the light line before you slip the cable. Then, when the weather moderates, you can sail back, find the floats, and recover your cable and anchor. To simplify slipping the anchor, it is a good idea to fasten the bitter end of the chain to the ship with a strong line that reaches the deck via the navel pipe. Then you can cut loose the anchor and cable without going below.

FREEING FOULED ANCHORS

Once in a while when you start to recover the anchor, you find that it is fouled on a mooring chain or hooked under a rock. If a non–fisherman-type anchor is hooked on a chain or an old wire cable, you may be able to slip the anchor out by lifting the offending cable a dozen feet or so and then *suddenly* releasing the warp or chain on the yacht. A Danforth or CQR will tend to fly out from under the obstruction.

If you have a powerful windlass on board, you may be able to lift the offending chain (or whatever) to the stemhead, where you can hold it with a second line while you extricate the anchor. Or if this is not possible, you can drop a second small anchor or grapnel (buoyed, of course) to hook and hold the offending cable while you release and recover the main anchor. You can then slack off the line to the second anchor and recover it by hauling on its buoy line to the crown. A single fluke anchor can sometimes be released by sailing or motoring right over it on short scope. This may succeed in turning it over. If that doesn't work, try letting out all the cable (and even bending on more) and sailing in various directions.

In all these operations you must be careful to keep your hands and fingers and feet away from the surging chain, because the forces involved can be thousands of pounds. If you get in a situation with jammed line or chain on a cleat or bollard, you may be able to take the strain off by securing a second line to the cable with a rolling hitch and leading the line to a cockpit winch. It may be wiser to cut away a few feet of jammed line or chain than to risk severe injury. Be careful!

Another way to clear a fouled Danforth or CQR (not a fisherman) is to pull the cable tight enough so that the chain is vertically above the anchor. Then carefully lower a separate chain loop (about 10 inches in diameter) down the cable on a light trip line until the loop falls to the lower end of the shank of the anchor. You can feel the chain loop passing the anchor shackle and slipping down on the metal shank. From this point on there are two variations. The first is to ease the main anchor cable so the shank falls from a vertical to a horizontal position. Then haul away smartly on the tripping line and hope that the chain loop will pull the fluke away from the obstruction. If this doesn't work, start all over again and get the chain loop at the lower end of the shank as before. Then get into a dinghy with the trip line and row a long distance away while paying out the trip line. Now have someone on board the yacht ease the main anchor cable a bit. If you heave on the trip line (you will have to anchor the dingy or do it from shore), you may be able to pull the fluke away from its impediment.

I have also had some luck in freeing fouled anchors by pulling myself down an almost taut anchor chain. I am a poor swimmer but in desperation have put on a face mask and old gloves and hauled myself quickly down the chain and unhooked an anchor fluke from a cable on the seabed. Three or four fathoms is my limit.

SAILING OUT THE ANCHOR

If you have no engine and an onshore wind comes up when you are anchored near land and you want to take your anchor with you, the best thing is to sail the anchor out. You put up the sails, haul the sheets in hard, and back a headsail or shove the main boom to one side to get moving. The ship will sail rapidly toward the anchor (while you quickly pull in chain). Then you shift to the other tack (still hauling in chain). After a few boards you should be over the anchor and moving fast enough to snatch it out as you pass above. This maneuver leaves you sailing close-hauled into the onshore wind and away from the lee shore. Be careful to keep your fingers out from under the chain as it tightens when you change tacks. I have always done this operation with two people, but I suppose a singlehander could do it with some fast deck work. Before starting, decide in advance exactly what you are going to do, use moderate sail area, and shorten up the anchor cable as much as possible.

STORM CONDITIONS

I believe you should keep all anchors and warps on deck when the conditions are nasty-looking or you think that the weather will worsen. When you are anchored, there should always be a *second anchor ready to go* (with the bitter end secured). When you want an anchor, you need it at once; there is no time to go burrowing in lockers for a tangled warp, for hunting under the cabin sole for an anchor that may not have been out in years, or searching for a shackle or a piece of wire to seize a shackle pin. In bad weather a storm anchor belongs on deck with its line or chain ready for use. In any case, before you enter an anchorage you should have two anchors out and ready.

The windage of sailing yachts is considerable and escalates rapidly with increasing winds. A sleek sailing hull may appear to have little windage, but her wide and tall mast and mass of wires and lines going aloft add up to a substantial total. When the wind speed doubles, its force is cubed. In a 25-knot wind, for example, each square foot of frontal area receives 2¼ pounds of force. With 50 knots the figure is 8 pounds, which means that a mast 6 inches wide and 50 feet high will receive 200 pounds of wind pressure alone. Total wind forces on the hull, coach roof, deck structures, mast, and rigging put a great strain on the ground tackle. In severe storms the windage can be reduced by taking down awnings, flags, poles, antennas, and radar reflectors. Sails and loose gear can go below. Halyards, lifts, and downhauls can be unreeved. In survival conditions we must do everything to help our cause. Get those singing lines down!

In addition to windage, shock loading is another factor. Gusts and

A nylon anchor spring can be connected to chain with a chain hook, a piece of iron that every farm boy knows but few sailors are acquainted with. The nylon must be protected from wear by a large metal thimble and adequate chafing gear.

squalls above the level of the storm can impose severe side-to-side sheering loads. A third factor is that substantial jerking strains can come from unusual swells. The combination of windage, sheering loads, and jerking strains may overpower the ground tackle. Or an unexpected current from a spring runoff in a large river plus a heavy ebb tide can be the cause of anchor misdeeds. One study concluded that a thirty- to forty-foot yacht anchored in Force 12 winds can generate surge loads up to 3,000 pounds. All is not lost, however, because a 50-pound burying anchor on a very long scope in good holding ground can withstand such strains.[5]

When you are anchored in sheltered water during gale force conditions, the ship will often jerk hard against her chain in violent gusts. The snubbing may damage the anchor windlass, the samson post, the bow roller, the chain stopper, or even break the cable. The terrible jerking can be eased by fitting a nylon spring. I use 30 feet of ½-inch three-strand nylon. One end is eye-spliced to a chain hook that clips around a link of chain. I belay the other end of the nylon line to a bow mooring cleat and let out chain until the nylon takes the full strain of the ship pulling against her anchor. In other words, we use a stretchy piece of light nylon as a rubber band between two parts of the chain to ease the snubbing. The chain is still hooked up, and if the nylon breaks or chafes through, the chain is there to hold the vessel. It is important to put the nylon through scrap pieces of soft hose to prevent chafe whenever the nylon is near anything, and to inspect the line from time to time to keep it from rubbing itself to destruction.

A few years ago in Honolulu, I learned about a different type of anchor spring from my friend Keane Gau, which he used when he anchored his forty-six-foot steel ketch *Bluejacket* off both Pitcairn and Easter islands in 1970. (Actually, the islands have no suitable anchorages, but in settled weather you can put down a hook on nearby sandy patches.) Keane, a superb seaman, lowered a heavy anchor with plenty of scope and led the cable to a 24-inch diameter spherical Norwegian fishing float-cum-bumper made of plastic. Keane secured the cable to the float with a short piece of chain (nylon would serve equally well) and then veered another 100 feet of cable, which led from the bow of *Bluejacket* in the usual way.

When the wind was light, the yacht merely ranged around the big red buoy, riding lightly to what was in effect a 100-foot mooring line. If the wind started to blow, the yacht tugged at the float, but before there was any substantial pull on the anchor, the buoy had to be dragged under and submerged, something the large float resisted mightily. From high on the island, some distance away, Keane glanced out at *Bluejacket* occasionally. As long as he was able to see the red buoy on the same bearing, everything was OK. I believe this technique might be extended to storm anchoring.

If you enter a bay where the depths increase rapidly close to the shore and the wind is coming from the land, you may have to take a line ashore to keep the vessel from blowing into deep water. If the wind is strong, the best scheme may be to go very close to the shore and to use a dinghy to take a line from the bow to the land. (Don't let go of the yacht until you have the oars in position and are ready to row.) Once back on board, you can ease the line to twice (or whatever) the distance you want to be from land, drop a stern anchor to keep from swinging, and then take up on the bow line until the stern anchor is set and the bow line is adjusted to your satisfaction. A good rowing dinghy is invaluable in these maneuvers.

Do not overlook the advantages of lines ashore to stout trees or docks or anything else. If there is nothing to tie to, carry an anchor ashore and dig it into the earth. As long as the wind is not blowing toward the land, you will be quite safe. There is no possibility of dragging if you are tied ashore. Of course, if the sea conditions become unfavorable, you will have to move. In the Chilean channels, where the depths are great and the winds are supremely violent, big and little ships alike regularly take lines ashore. Not one, but several.

When we were in the South Pacific, I recall talking with Andy Thomson, the famous schooner captain of the Cook Islands. Andy told us that he once bested a frightful hurricane from the north at Rarotonga by putting his vessel in a narrow opening in the reef and anchoring and tying to the reef on each side with twenty or more lines. The ship faced the wind and seas and rose and fell as the blasts of the storm passd. "We put out everything but my shoelaces," said Andy. "Warps, spare line, cargo nets, halyards, sheets, chain, cable borrowed from on shore—everything. We had the life of the ship to gain and nothing to lose by doubling and redoubling the lines. If she had been wrecked, what good would the lines have been anyway? After the storm it took us days to sort everything out and to recover our anchors. It was a hell of an experience, but we saved her."

In storms it may well be necessary to keep an anchor watch around the clock until conditions improve. This means that one person must be awake and dressed, alert to the yacht's position, and capable of getting the vessel under way at once. If there is a chance that other vessels may drag down on you, if the wind is strong and changeable, or if the holding ground is abysmal, one crewman has got to keep watch. Even if an anchorage is poor, it may be better than going to sea under some circumstances. A person may be desperately tired or sick or you may need to make critical repairs. With care and attention you may be able to nurse the yacht through a storm in a bad anchorage.

If you are dragging and trapped in an anchorage or on a lee shore, an engine can be extremely useful. Many small and large ships have been saved by firing up and putting the machinery in gear at low revolutions ahead, standing regular watches, and hoping to go nowhere. Often the winds of a severe storm change soon after their maximum velocity. Three or four hours of engine work may get you through a crisis. Or a lull in a storm may allow you to motor ahead or to one side enough to get out an additional anchor.

A FINAL WORD

To summarize this long discussion of anchoring, let's start from the beginning. When we anchor, we look for a place sheltered from the ocean's swells. Quiet water is more important than protection from

Here famed singlehander Al Petersen demonstrates how to hank on a jib aboard his 33-foot gaff cutter Stornoway. Note the foot ropes leading to the end of the bowsprit and how the staysail boom is tied off to a shroud to keep the boom out of mischief. The key to successful short-handed sailing is scrupulous attention to detail. Petersen was awarded the Blue Water Medal of the Cruising Club of America in 1952 for a notable circumnavigation. Later married, he and his wife, Marjorie, have continued to make extensive cruises aboard their lovely double-ender designed by Albert Strange and built in 1926.

the wind, although we would hope for that too. We hunt on the chart for a bay within a bay, a hook of land that curves to form a shield from the sea, a series of close offshore islands that serve as a barrier between us and the ocean. Can we slip up a river a few miles? Why not go behind that big breakwater or sandbank? Will there be reasonable access to the shore? A safe place to leave the dinghy?

Pay attention to the scale of the chart. Work it out it cables (tenths of a mile) which you can estimate. Sometimes a small-scale chart will have excellent coves for anchoring which are hardly visible on the tiny drawing. It may help to examine the chart with a magnifying glass.

What is the prevailing wind? Will the anchorage be safe from all winds? Will nearby canyons and mountains and deeply indented hills cause squalls to funnel down into the anchorage? What does the Pilot book say? If the wind shifts when we are in the anchorage, is there an alternate place of refuge or must we clear out? What do the local fishermen advise? Go and ask them. Do their words make sense? Where and how do the fishermen keep their boats? If the fishermen winch their boats up a cliff or pull them up on a beach, look out.

Can we get out of the anchorage in the night if the wind shifts? If we clear out, what will the compass course be? Write it down and work out during daylight hours any special strategy with regard to rocks, reefs, or a darkened shore at night. If things look chancy but you are very tired and need rest, you have three choices: (1) go out to sea and heave to on the offshore tack; (2) continue sailing to a better anchorage; or (3) try the marginal anchorage. Choice No. 3 may be satisfactory, but by all means be ready to clear out. Tie a reef in the mainsail and hank on a small jib. Work out the course, tidy up the lines and gear, and *then* sleep.

"When a Vessel comes to an Anchor," advises *Lever's Young Sea Officer's Sheet Anchor* of 1813, "it is always prudent to take three Reefs in the Topsails before they are handed, as they would be ready, should a sudden gale arise, if there be a necessity for running out to sea."

But back to the new anchorage. What is the nature of the holding ground? Is the depth moderate? Is the swinging room adequate? Does the chart indicate submarine cables, permanent moorings, commercial oyster beds, or current eddies? Is the tidal stream from a nearby river a problem? Will it cause a mean or dangerous condition with the wind across the tide? Dinghy work may be safe only at slack water or with the flood or maybe not at all.

Is it likely that those pleasure boats with the light anchors will drag down on you, or are the other vessels on substantial moorings? If you drag, where will you go? One hates to think negatively, but if you have the choice of anchoring in front of a smooth beach or a mass of rocks, the choice is obvious.

Are there traffic problems in the anchorage? Will you have to move for the evening ferryboat? Do the fishing boats go out at 0230? Will you be prey for all the bumboats on the island? Will clouds of mosquitoes and gnats descend on the ship when the onshore breeze dies? Are there glue factories or sewer outlets or cement plants to windward? Or—worse yet—military firing ranges (more common than you think)?

These problems don't arise often, and very seldom in combination, thank goodness, and dropping a single anchor is usually simplicity itself. It is good, nevertheless, to review all the contingencies. Just as the captain of an airliner scans the ground for a dozen telltale signs before he lands, so should the master of a ship look carefully before he puts his faith in an odd-shaped piece of iron that ties him to the earth.

Collecting and writing and thinking about all the foregoing points concerning anchoring has been a tedious business. The task has taught me how little I really know, and that a seaman's schooling is never done. Few statements stand unchallenged, and you are forever learning. Like navigation, anchoring is 60 percent the science of hard facts, 35 percent practice and judgment, and 5 percent luck.

If the cook makes morning coffee directly into a thermos jug, the coffee will stay fresh and hot for hours.

8

~~~~~~

Heat and Cooking

It was a cold day in February when *Whisper* was launched in Vancouver, British Columbia. An icy blast of subzero wind screeched across False Creek, and Margaret and I almost perished from the cold. We knew that we would need heat on board at 49 degrees north latitude, so we had installed an expensive diesel stove from the United States. But we had problems with the draft. The stove wheezed and bucked, and dense clouds of oily soot descended on our beautiful new decks and sails. Each particle of soot deposited a whorl of carbon that was soon smeared into a broad band of greasy black.

It was desperately cold. We needed heat. Every new snowstorm forced us into greater efforts below. We changed the oil control settings. We adjusted the draft. We tried a stove stack with a different head. We even tried burning costly stove oil. But it was no use. Soot belched upward, outward, and downward. The fresh snow on the coach roof was measled with black, and it wasn't long before broad tracks of soot led along the deck, across the cockpit, and below to the cabin sole. The vessel was a mess. Our spirits were even messier.

We had learned to like the steady heat from the diesel stove which kept the yacht dry and warm. The stove was excellent for cooking, with its wide top and tidy oven. But even if we had had a chimney sweep in the crew, it was quite impossible to live with the soot. When we had bought the stove, the manufacturer had told us that we would need no blower; now the Washington Stove Works informed us that we would need to install an electric fan if we wanted cleaner burning. Since we could neither afford the twenty-four-hour-a-day battery drain nor stand the noise of the blower, we chucked out the cast-iron monster.

Our next stove was a Taylors Para-Fin cooker from England. This was a cooking stove and gave off only a little heat. The compact two-burner stove was made of enameled iron and used Swedish Primus burners, which were fed kerosene under pressure from a special two-gallon tank that we had fabricated to fit in a corner of the galley. We kept up air pressure in the tank with a small bicycle tire pump. Though we seemed to use the stove a lot and were forever making tea and coffee, one tank filling lasted three weeks.

Underneath the two burners the stove had a small warming oven that was good for taking the chill off plates, for keeping food warm, or for heating rolls. For baking bread, we bought a stainless steel folding oven that rested on top of the stove and was heated directly by one of the Primus burners.

We mounted the long dimension of the stove fore and aft, but the pivots of the pillar gimbals that came with the stove were much too high. At sea the stove swung so violently that pots were sometimes hurled across the cabin. I made new gimbal brackets with pivots six inches lower—level with the top of the stove. I bolted a ten-pound slab of lead underneath the stove, and Margaret stowed a heavy iron frying pan in the bottom of the warming oven. The lower pivots and weights helped materially, and we were able to cook in fairly violent weather. Better yet, we had a flat, always horizontal stove on which to set hot cups of coffee or soup or whatever. In severe storms at sea we found that gimbaling was not possible, and we were obliged to lash the stove in place to keep it from beating itself to death.

As good as the cooking stove was, it did not heat the cabin. We considered various heating schemes and rejected coal and wood and charcoal. The problems of stowing enough fuel for extensive use seemed insoluble unless *Whisper* towed a barge laden with anthracite, fagots of pitch pine, logs of pressed sawdust, or sacks of charcoal. We knew these fuel sources were dirty, often unobtainable or hard to get, and not really suitable for long-term daily use. We had sometimes enjoyed a charcoal fire on a friend's yacht, but such a fire was an *occasional* proposition, not a day-after-day necessity. One-third of a bag of charcoal for a single stove loading was costly. I wondered how many bags could be carried. Besides, the heat was hard to control, and there was a mess to clean up.

A *Taylors kerosene heating stove is simply a cylindrical can containing ceramic elements which are heated by a Primus burner underneath. A 25 mm copper flue at the top leads outside.*

Trying to light a solid-fuel fire at sea when the vessel was rolling heavily seemed horrendous.

We elected to continue with the world voyagers' favorite fuel—kerosene—which is cheap, widely available, and easy to store. Kerosene gives a hot, controllable fire from a very small amount of fuel when run through suitable burners.

For cabin heating we purchased another Taylors stove. This model had six ceramic elements that fitted inside a cylindrical brass can 11 inches high and 7 inches in diameter. A single Primus burner mounted underneath heated the ceramic elements, which soon glowed red and radiated heat in all directions. The fumes from the stove were conducted outside by a 1-inch copper pipe topped with a miniature stove stack, or Charlie Noble. The stove was neat, compact, reasonably clean, and, for nights that didn't fall below 25 or 30 degrees, the unit put out ample heat for *Whisper's* living area, which very roughly measures 8 by 23 feet. We mounted the stove as low as possible to ensure warmth at foot level.

The heat was adequate for winters at 40 degrees north latitude and for summers up to 56 degrees (our farthest north). However, we often used the stove nearer the tropics during chilly periods. At sea the stove burned at any angle of heel. Pitching never bothered it. We had trouble

To keep solid water from going down the flue of the Taylor's heating stove, I glued a scrap of large diameter PVC plumbing pipe around the stack outlet. The plastic shield (with two drain holes at the bottom) acts as a barrier to water but still allows an air space for the cabin fumes to escape. It is imperative not to cover the flue with a sail bag or to restrict the outlet in any way.

with green water occasionally getting into the stove flue, but we solved this problem by surrounding the outside part of the stack with a scrap of PVC plastic plumbing pipe slightly higher than the stack itself. The inside diameter of the plastic pipe was about ½ inch larger than the diameter of the stack to ensure ample breathing space for escaping fumes. In effect, we had a surrounding guard of plastic pipe (cemented to the coach roof) around the stack to stop green water. In the tropics or during the summer we taped a plastic cover over the outside of the flue.

(I must emphasize that nothing must interfere with the exit of the fumes, whether it be a sail bag accidentally piled on top of the stack, a misaligned asbestos gasket, or anything else. The stack must be free for easy outflow; otherwise the crew is liable to be overcome by carbon monoxide poisoning.)

I can hardly tell you the feeling of warmth and comfort we obtained from the permanent installation of a stove that was easy to use. For years we lighted the Taylors heating stove every night and morning during the cold months. We came to know and to welcome the familiar hiss of its Primus burner.

So often visitors came to *Whisper* for dinner during the winter. Our guests would arrive wearing layers of woolens and be ready for an evening of freezing. But once they were aboard, we invariably got the same response:

We keep this single-burner Tilley stove mounted on gimbals next to our diesel stove. The brass tank holds more than one liter of kerosene, so the stove runs many hours on a single filling. We have a big slab of lead underneath the circular tank to counterbalance the weight of a heavy pot. We added the retaining metal fingers at the top. This is a wonderful, simple stove and I can't imagine sailing without it. Unfortunately, it is no longer made, but sometimes you can find a used one.

"Gosh, it's pleasant down here. You're quite warm and snug. I had no idea . . ." And off would come the sweaters and the expressions of uncertainty.

At sea a source of dry heat can make the difference between a wet and unpleasant passage and a dry and tolerable trip. We put a few brass hooks on the overhead above the stove, and many times we have had a line of gloves or woolen socks or a sweater drying. Margaret and I can't think of anything more horrid than a long trip in cold weather without a dependable source of dry heat.

To use kerosene appliances you must understand the burners. To my knowledge, there are two types: the Swedish Primus (similar burners are made by other manufacturers) and the Tilley burner produced in Northern Ireland. Both work on the principle of firing the vapor of superheated kerosene in a special burner. To light the burner, you prime it by burning a small amount of alcohol, which heats the burner enough to vaporize the kerosene. The procedure is to pour a little alcohol into a priming cup underneath the burner, or you can saturate a Tilley wick (see page 182) with alcohol and clip it around the burner. We use the Tilley wick system, which gives a measured amount of alcohol and a burning scheme *that cannot backfire into a container of alcohol.*

Once the burner is lighted properly, it will continue to vaporize the fuel and to burn with an extremely hot flame. Since a Primus fire tends to be all or nothing, it is often helpful to insert a metal flame-tamer between the pot and the fire if you need low heat.

The three requirements for successful operation are (1) clean burners, (2) filtered fuel of reasonable quality, and (3) adequate priming.

The combustion of kerosene eventually builds up tiny deposits of carbon in the metering jet of the burner. These deposits interfere with proper combustion and must be removed. Both the Primus and Tilley units have self-pricking burners in which the control knob is turned backwards to force a tiny cleaning wire through the jet. This takes only a second and can be done while the burner is alight. In other models of Primus burners you use a small pricking tool to force a thin piece of wire into the jet to clear it.

We pour our kerosene through a piece of thick felt in the bottom of a funnel to filter out water and impurities. No. 1 diesel oil (the light, non-brown, clear grade) often works well in kerosene appliances and costs less. If you can use the same oil in the engine, the fuels can be interchangeable. Diesel fuel varies in quality, and it is best to sample a little. In western Canada, for instance, the oil characteristics are modified seasonally. Most world cruising yachts that use kerosene carry at least ten gallons, which lasts for a very long time.

The main trouble with Primus and Tilley kerosene burners is caused by inadequate priming. *Owners who fail to heat the burners adequately during lighting attempts will never have any success.* If kerosene under pressure floods into a cold burner, the kerosene will burn in its natural, unvaporized state and will vomit up with a great hissing and a huge smoking yellow flame. No amount of swearing, praying, kicking, spitting, pounding on the floor, or other violent exorcisms will take the place of adequate priming. If a burner flares up, the cause is simply that it is not hot enough to vaporize the fuel. You need to re-prime or to prime more in the first place. *There is no other way.* Shut off the burner and start again.

This all takes much longer to describe than to do. In practice you can usually cook dozens of meals without fiddling with the stove burners. In eleven years of living aboard, Margaret has cooked over 10,000 meals on *Whisper*. She rarely has trouble with the Primus stoves. Some people complain that kerosene smells, but with everything kept clean and tight there is little odor. If you are cleaning a paintbrush and spill turpentine, there will be a pungent smell from it too. Or coffee or wine or cleaning fluid, for that matter. A minor disadvantage of kerosene burners is that you need a small amount of alcohol for priming. This is perhaps offset by the possibility of using kerosene in a diesel engine in a pinch.

An alcohol Primus stove works exactly like a kerosene stove, although the burner is slightly different. The disadvantage is that the fuel is often very expensive or unobtainable. I recall that in Papeete—the largest city in the central South Pacific and the only source for thousands of miles— we watched the owners of one yacht purchase alcohol from a local pharmacy at staggering prices. We saw the same problem in northern Brazil.

In most countries alcohol is markedly more expensive than kerosene (paraffin), and because it is less generally useful finding places that sell it is harder. In terms of heat production it is the coolest of the fuels under discussion, with its flame producing 2,500 to 3,000 Btu's per hour. Kerosene makes 3,5000 to 4,000 Btu's. The liquid petroleum gases—butane or propane—make 5,000 to 6,000 Btu's per hour. In more useful terms, I have found that it takes a Tilley kerosene stove 7¾ minutes to bring one quart of cold water to a furious boil. An alcohol stove takes 8¾ minutes—or 13 percent more—to do the same job.[6]

The flash point of alcohol is about 70 degrees Fahrenheit while the flash point of kerosene is 160 degrees F. This means that alcohol is about four times more flammable. Water will readily put out an alcohol fire but not until the alcohol has mixed well with the water. Alcohol has a low surface tension and spreads rapidly over counters and stove tops, which allows a flash spread of alcohol fires. Kerosene, however, does not vaporize readily and has a higher surface tension. In fact, you can plunge a match into a cup of kerosene without lighting it.

Many people use butane or propane stoves, but after having personally watched two vessels get blown into a million pieces—including their owners, who were carried past *Whisper* on bloody stretchers—I refuse to have appliances that use bottled gas on board. I note that when the proponents of bottled-gas stoves write articles, there is always mention of several ghastly explosions, together with various schemes that the authors have devised to overcome the explosions. If this type of cooking and heating has such inherent dangers, why have it at all? Also, bottled-gas cylinders are by no means easy to refill in many places, and it is necessary to carry various types of adapters and connections, especially in foreign ports. If you should decide on butane or propane, by all means have good-quality stoves and fittings installed by a first-class professional. Have a gas detection unit put in to keep track of any leaks. And finally, get an engineer to inspect the whole system, including the installation, the stoves, and the detection unit.

A boating fuel for the future may be compressed natural gas (CNG), the same stuff that is piped into houses for cooking. CNG, unlike propane or butane, is lighter than air and will not collect in the bilge of a yacht. At present, however, CNG is available only at fuel docks in California.

Comfort on a small vessel in cold weather requires a combination of dry heat, thorough ventilation, and insulation. All are important. On *Whisper*, which has a fiberglass hull, we carefully insulated the entire interior of the yacht with two layers of ¼-inch indoor-outdoor carpet (Ozite) tacked on with contact cement. The job was tedious, because each piece of carpet had to be cut and fitted. In addition, we drilled dozens of ¾-inch ventilation holes through various lockers and bulkheads, and we installed six vents and eight opening portlights. Dead, damp air is conducive to mildew; dry, warm, moving air is what you need for comfort.

We were quite content with our kerosene cooking and heating stoves until we spent an additional winter in British Columbia several years later, a winter that was exceptionally cold. The Taylors heating stove performed valiantly, but it couldn't combat the rigors of snow and ice on deck and the frigid drafts that sometimes raced down the hatch.

Since we spend considerable time in the higher latitudes, we made another drastic change. We installed a Dickinson diesel stove, a Vancouver product that uses a special pot burner that requires no blower and which is quite clean-burning. We had seen these stoves on many fishing vessels and yachts in Canada and discovered that hundreds of owners ran them for as long as six months without shutting them off. The fuel consumption is about one gallon of oil for each twenty-four hours of operation.

We bought the Pacific model, made of iron and stainless steel with a

The danger of using butane or propane gas aboard a yacht is that a leak can cause a catastrophic explosion. The captain of this vessel claimed that he was careful; yet something went wrong. The owner's wife—who was aboard at the time of the explosion—was fortunate not to have been killed. The wreckage of the yacht went out with the next tide, and a few hours later there was nothing to be seen except four mooring lines drooping forlornly into the water. Certainly if you choose gas for cooking or heating, you should install reliable gas detection alarms and keep them in good order. The violence of a gas explosion is incredible. When this yacht blew up, the noise was audible two miles away.

The Dickinson stove has a heavy metal top, an oven large enough for four bread pans, and is a good source of warmth in cold weather. The stove requires a 125 mm diameter stack. In the tropics we set a two-burner Primus stove on top.

nickel alloy top. The stove weighs 120 pounds and measures 18 inches wide, 22 inches long, and 23 inches high. Normally we cook on the top, which has fiddle rails, rods, and clamps to keep pots from dancing off (it is not practical to gimbal such a big stove). The oven, with thermometer, measures 10½ x 10½ x 13 inches deep, quite enough for four bread pans. The stove is well made to professional oceangoing standards and should last twenty years or more. The controls are inside. The Dickinson catalogue lists six other models, including a cylindrical heating stove 23 inches high and 11 inches in diameter that weighs 39 pounds.

The secret of the Dickinson stove is its natural-draft pot burner, which requires a 5-inch diameter flue with as straight a run as possible. Several 30- or 45-degree bends in the flue are tolerable, but 90-degree elbows are not. We have a stack length of 5½ feet on *Whisper* and use a Breidert top as recommended. We also have a 12-volt fan for fast warm-ups, but a fan is not necessary for operation. The stove uses No. 1 or No. 2 diesel, stove oil, or kerosene. The lighter oils are cleaner-burning, but with a suitable stack No. 2 diesel oil works perfectly well. There is no soot, and it is an advantage to use the same fuel as is used for the engine. The stove is silent in operation, and we have run it for as long as ten days at sea with no problems.

Fuel can be pumped to the stove from a bilge tank with a tiny electric auto-pulse pump (the type used in Jaguar automobiles). A better and non-electric arrangement, however, is a gravity tank. We have a 12-gallon stainless steel tank mounted under the deck aft and outboard of the

Margaret occasionally uses her Tilley kerosene iron to touch up a shirt or blouse. She irons on a small sleeve board or on the saloon table padded with a towel and a folded sheet. The Tilley iron is a little bulky, but it is surprisingly efficient and is good for ordinary ironing, applying iron-on trouser patches, or for drying out dollar bills when the captain fell in.

stove. We can fill the tank from a deck pipe or from the engine bilge tank by means of a small hand pump.

To light the stove, we open the oil feed valve to allow a little oil to run into the pot and then drop a lighted square of toilet paper into the oil (a 24-inch mechanical finger is helpful). Michael DeRidder taught us another scheme, which is to pour a tablespoonful of priming alcohol on top of a little oil in the pot and then to light the alcohol with a match held at the end of a long wire or mechanical finger. The stove has plenty of heat potential, and we generally use the lowest possible setting. If the stove were turned up, we could melt scrap iron.

The installation of the stove was a big job. Not only did the unit require a substantial bolt-down mount, but I had to fight the battle of the tank, the flue, and the plumbing. Once the stove is set up, however, there is almost no maintenance except for routine cleaning.

During cold weather in port we generally use the stove only during the hours we are up, preferring to shut it off at night. If the weather is especially cold, of course, we let the stove run all night. The stove keeps the yacht warm and dry, there is no danger from fumes, and we always have hot water by putting a kettle on the back of the stove. Margaret can bake fish or an occasional roast, and she can simmer sauces and soups to her heart's content.

Since the new diesel stove was large and we were short of space—small ship owners are always short of space—we substituted a permanently mounted one-burner Primus for the Taylors cooking stove. This means that we normally have two stoves in the galley: the diesel stove for general cooking and heating, and a one-burner Primus for casual use or during rough weather. In the tropics and during the summertime in the high latitudes we shut off the oil stove and place a second small Primus stove on top. We have, however, baked bread, pies, cakes, and cookies in the diesel stove oven near the equator many times.

This account may sound as if we have a hobby of changing stoves, because we have come almost full circle. It's true that in many years of living on our yacht we have added and subtracted. But not from choice. Only by learning more and crystallizing our sailing objectives. One thing is certain: in a chilly, watery environment we can't make it without warmth and plenty of hot food.

9

~~~~~~

Planning the Trip

The sternest test that a small vessel will find is to encounter a severe storm at sea. Newcomers to sailing sometimes secretly hope—as did Thurber's Walter Mitty—to weather a typhoon to prove themselves and their ships, but this is arrant nonsense. In prolonged winds of 60 or 75 knots a yacht will be lucky to survive. Even if she weathers the seas and the winds and has enough maneuvering room to avoid being driven ashore, she may suffer severe damage. Her crew may be injured and terrified and her passage time will be slow and unpleasant.

Fortunately, the habits of hurricanes, typhoons, tropical storms, and severe winter gales have been studied and charted for a long time. With care in the planning of an ocean crossing the chances are excellent that you can avoid such tempests. Or at least diminish the risk of unexpected meetings. Of course, if you continue to sail on the oceans of the world, sooner or later you will get a blast of heavy weather. But careful planning can minimize severe drubbings by monstrous seas and winds.

Cataloguing the charts for a long sailing trip is a tedious and time-consuming chore. You need enough charts to cover your route, plus a reasonable number of alternate stops, but you can't afford the expense, the bulk, and the weight of too many plans. Yet you must not have any omissions. Planning demands many small decisions after you have decided on a general route.

Management of a vessel in hard going is an important part of seamanship; a more fundamental discipline is to try to avoid storms in the first place.

A basic source of planning and scheduling information is *Ocean Passages of the World*, a hefty British Admiralty publication that makes hundreds of recommendations for long voyages. My edition is dated 1950 and is out of print, but a new edition has recently been released. The book is written in telegraphic style, and a Spartan text tells about routes, courses, dangers, special problems, and likely winds and weather. The book is somewhat general, however, and is more a telephone directory of routes than a reading book of ocean highway information. My edition has 27 pages on wind and weather, 190 pages on steamship routes, 118 pages on sailing ship routes, and 30 pages of general notes and cautions.

The appendix of *Ocean Passages* has eight foldout charts that show climate, currents, and sailing and steamship routes. No potential round-the-world sailor will fail to be enthralled by Chart 7 (Admiralty Chart 5308), "The World—Sailing Ship Routes," a sketch map on which pink, gray, yellow, and brown bands flow artery-like across the oceans of the world to suggest routes in various directions for certain times of the year. The colorful tracks are based on the experiences of thousands of large commercial sailing vessels over a century or more.

Some of the routes have limited suitability for yachts. Not many small vessels, for example, run down their easting in the gale-swept Southern Ocean. Nevertheless, *Ocean Passages* is a good place to start. The book's warnings are well worth strict attention. Instead of buying this bulky book, however, it might be easier to borrow a copy and to type out the few paragraphs you need.

You will find more detailed information about weather and winds and regional storms (along with masses of material about local ports and conditions) in Sailing Directions. These volumes—generally called Pilots —tell of sailing conditions in every part of the world. Although many countries publish regional information, the main Pilots are from the United States and Great Britain. There are 98 volumes of U.S. Pilots and 73 volumes of Admiralty Pilots. Of course, you only need books for the part of the world you plan to visit—generally two or three volumes. These are of inestimable value to mariners, and you should purchase new volumes—together with the latest supplements—to cover your itinerary. Although there is almost universal interchangeability, U.S. Pilots are written with U.S. charts in mind. Admiralty Pilots have many U.K. chart references. So if there is any choice, you should purchase Pilots and charts from the same country.

Each U.S. Pilot has some 250 loose-leaf pages (about 8 x 10 inches) that fit into a heavy and bulky binder (whose metal parts soon rust). Replacement pages are issued every few years to update the text. Though the Pilots are prepared for all mariners, the emphasis is on large commercial vessels; in recent years the tendency has been to bypass smaller places and to deal more with major ports.

Admiralty Pilots are permanently bound volumes that measure 6 x 9½ inches or 8½ x 12 inches and are easier to store than the bulky U.S. Pilots. Supplements are issued from time to time, and every eight or ten years each volume is reprinted. Like their U.S. counterparts, the Admiralty books are packed with information about a particular area and include a chapter on regional weather. The writing is clear and pithy but decidedly pessimistic and negative, as such books must be that describe every bad current, every treacherous rock, and every hazard.

According to a recent article in *Yachting Monthly*, some 89,000 Admiralty Pilots are sold each year, up from 57,000 copies a few years ago. A surprising thing about these volumes is that the writing staff is the same size as it was in 1907, just three naval assistants and one clerk, supplemented by eighteen retired naval officers who work at home as revisers. "The terse, clipped, informative style of these volumes is familiar to yachtsmen," writes John Brown. "Verbiage and time-wasting and wooly conceptions are rigidly excluded."[7]

Many are the seamen who have constructed a crude harbor chart based on these sentences alone when a needed large-scale chart was suddenly found to be missing.

A special kind of Pilot that is sometimes available is a yachtsmen's guide prepared by a sailing group, a knowledgeable author, or local authorities. The Clyde Cruising Club publishes an excellent and up-to-date Pilot for Scottish waters, for example. *A Cruising Guide to the New England Coast,* by Roger Duncan and John Ware, is superb. There are several useful yachtsmen's Pilots for the West Indies. In the Galápagos a local charter-boat captain wrote a handy little guide. These books need to be used with caution depending on the publication date and the authority, but generally they are well worth having even if you only pick up a single useful point. Note that I am speaking of guides prepared by experienced seamen, not publicity handouts put out by tourist bureaus.

The third type of planning guide is Pilot charts, which are general ocean charts with detailed data on winds, calms, fog, severe storms, gales, water and atmospheric temperatures, magnetic variation, currents, ice, barometric pressure, and a weather summary. Pilot charts are generally issued for each month, and the information is expressed by different symbols and colors. To find out about the conditions in a certain area, it's best to purchase Pilot charts for one calendar year so you can follow seasonal weather patterns. These road maps of the sea, with their neat wind roses and curving colored lines, are fascinating documents. The Pilot charts aren't infallible, however, and it's possible to encounter other conditions than the stated figures, which are *averages*, not *certainties*. Yet by and large these charts are a marvelous planning aid.

So we have three basic guides to help us avoid severe storms, which —as we have discussed—are the primary hazard in ocean trips. The guides are also the key to fair winds, the No. 2 planning concern.

To explain the use of these books and charts, let me tell about a Pacific trip that Margaret and I made several years ago. Our goal was an extended voyage around the major part of the Pacific basin. When we studied the planning guides, we soon discovered that we faced three main problems: the South Pacific hurricane season, typhoons off the coast of Japan, and a high gale and fog frequency around the Aleutian Islands. The problem was to juggle dates so that we would minimize our exposure to these hazards. In addition, we hoped to stay in the belts of running or reaching winds, to sail with favorable currents, and to maintain a reasonable schedule.

Margaret and I pulled a figure of eighteen months out of the air, and we started sticking pins with date flags into a general Pacific chart. Reading in *Ocean Passages* and various Pacific Pilots and studying the Pilot charts along with accounts of other voyages told us that we should sail north from Samoa by November to miss the South Pacific hurricane season. Similar reading about the east coast of Japan suggested that we should be away to the north and east before July. In the Aleutians we had no season of severe storms, but we had a winter gale frequency of up to 20 percent (a Force 8 or more storm every six days on the average). We changed dates and moved the schedule backwards and forwards and decided to leave Japan in midsummer so that we would be in the North Pacific when the gale frequency was not so severe. As expected, we encountered some fog, but the August gale frequency in the Aleutians varied from 1 to 7 percent, suggesting that summer was the time for a visit.

In other words, we tried to play the averages to have as storm-free a trip as possible. This could have meant staying in a protected harbor during a bad season or hurrying to cross a dangerous area to minimize exposure to severe hazards.

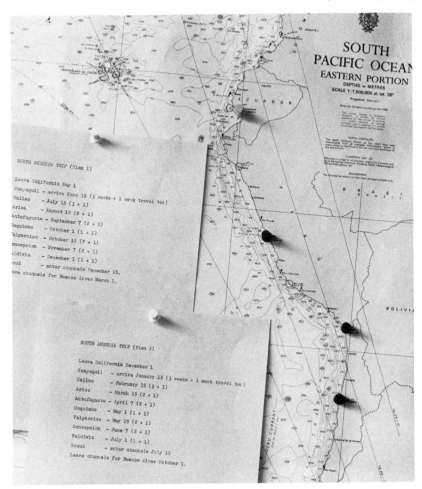

Rough schedules are a good first step in trip planning. As a project develops, there will be many changes. One method of visualizing routes is to use small-scale charts and colored pushpins.

We also talked with several friends—merchant ship officers—who made useful suggestions about routes and places. We have found that big ship people are often intensely interested in small sailing vessels and will go out of their way to help you. The captain and mates will sometimes give you extra charts and pass on all sorts of good ideas and advice. If it seems convenient for them, Margaret and I always try to pay courtesy calls on the captains of nearby big ships when we are in foreign ports. We have made some wonderful friends.

To learn about the winds and currents along a proposed route, you study *Ocean Passages* and the Pilots for general information and Pilot charts for specific recommendations. The long way around is often shorter if the detour takes you away from strong head winds and adverse currents. For example, we know about a yacht owner who repeatedly tried to go northeastward into the Caribbean toward Venezuela from Cartagena, Colombia. The month was April and the trades blew strongly; according to the Pilot chart, the prevailing wind was Force 6 from the northeast plus 28 miles of adverse current per day. Though the captain was determined and the ketch was powerful, she could make no easting until the owner abandoned his head-on approach. He finally made his easting via long reaching legs to the northward into an area where the wind and current were more favorable to him.

Ocean Passages does not recommend the direct route between Hawaii and San Francisco, because a sailing vessel would be thrashing to windward for hundreds of miles and beating back and forth trying to make mileage to the northeast—directly into the trade wind and contrary current. The suggested route is roughly northward, close-hauled or almost close-hauled on the starboard tack, until you pass above the northeast trades into the westerlies, whose latitude varies somewhat with the month, depending on the location of the North Pacific high-pressure area.

In time you learn a few wrinkles. For example, if you are going to sail through an island group, it is helpful to arrive at the windward end so you will have a free wind from island to island. . . . In the Tuamotus there are often extensive underwater reefs running far out from the south and southeast sides of the atolls—the coral grows toward its nutrients, which flow from the southeast trade wind, I am told—and a mariner is advised to sail around the *north* rather than the south side of an island. . . . You may wish to delay a passage through a hazardous area until you have a full moon to help you see at night. . . . In going northward from Rio de Janeiro against the Brazil Current, it may be wise to wait until the northeast monsoon (so called locally) has eased. A week in port may be a week gained. . . . The weather systems around Vancouver Island come from the northwest or southeast. Depending on your direction of sailing, it will pay you to wait for a fair wind. . . . And so on.

A sound investment for safety and peace of mind is a great stack of up-to-date charts before you set out on a long trip. If you are in doubt about a certain chart, *buy it*. You need small-scale charts for planning and navigational use, medium-scale for the approaches to islands and coastlines, and large-scale detailed drawings to guide you into harbors and through intricate passages. Not only must a prudent mariner have adequate information about intended ports, but he ought to have limited coverage of contingency stops. If you have a problem along the way and decide to run off to a convenient port to leeward, you will need the chart. If you haven't room for all the charts when you set out, or are unsure whether you will continue after the first long jump, arrange to have a batch of charts sent to you.

Unfortunately, the cost of charts has risen astronomically. I have a 1921 U.S. chart of the Chilean channels (currently being sold) with stamped prices of 15¢, 25¢, $1, $2.60, and $3.50 on its lower margin. I think these prices are outrageous and quite unfair, but there seems little we can do except to protest to the authorities. World cruising sailors often trade charts, and I am sure this practice will spread. A World Chart Trading Center might be a good business enterprise for a retired sailor or an armchair aficionado. Sometimes, when a cruise is completed or called off or postponed, it is possible to purchase a roll of charts cheaply. In the eastern Carolines I salvaged an enormous roll of Southeast Asian and Japanese charts from a wrecked tuna boat. Last year Margaret and I met the Norwegian yacht *Preciosa*, whose crew was given a set of charts for almost the entire world by a friendly shipping company. I have also heard of small boat sailors buying charts from shipping companies (sometimes through large chart agents), which periodically replace their charts. While I am not a fan of outdated charts, which can be dangerous to use, an old chart is certainly better than no chart. And charts can be brought up to date by consulting suitable Notices to Mariners.

At the moment we have about two hundred charts on *Whisper*, plus eight volumes of Pilots, *Ocean Passages*, and two dozen assorted Pilot charts. Each chart is folded in half (with the drawing outside so I can see what it is) and is then stowed flat. Several dozen charts are in a drawer under the chart table. The rest are either in a special flat box (4 x 26 x 40 inches) mounted under the forepeak overhead or stored away in several big rolls. Margaret keeps a record book that lists all the charts on board by name, number, latitude and longitude, and owner (in case of borrowed charts).

Half of our charts are from the United States, but we often buy Admiralty charts directly from a British agent. I find the Admiralty small-scale charts especially good for planning purposes and in general prefer the English plans because of more information and better draftsmanship. We try to use the charts of the country through which we plan to travel (Canadian charts for Canada, New Zealand for the Cook Islands, Japan for its islands, etc.). If your sights are on French Polynesia, by all means

Whisper *tied up to* Gaucho *at the Yacht Club Argentino facility at San Fernando, in Buenos Aires, Argentina. We had last seen* Gaucho *in San Francisco. She traveled to far-off Argentina by way of Panama, the Azores, and Brazil; we had come via Peru and Chile. Now we were together again and busy comparing notes and gossip.*

get French charts (Service Hydrographique et Océanographique de la Marine, route du Bergot—29283, Brest, Cedex, France).

Don't forget suitable tidal current and height tables, light lists, and traverse tables. You will need to order a new Nautical Almanac well before the end of the year and arrange for its delivery. I'm not much on the use of radio aids, because they are often so useless, but I find that the Admiralty List of Radio Signals—a blue paperback—is a handy guide, because in one volume you have an easily usable list of every beacon in the world.

When you go foreign, it's hard to decide where to stop. Some ports are famous and you want to see them. Tahiti and Moorea are easy choices, but shall you go to Kapingamarangi or Pingelap? To Suvorov or Rakahanga? To Abemama or Tabiteuea? You make some stops because of your reading or from recommendations, because of protected anchorages, because you are tired and want to rest, or simply because you are intrigued with the name. Margaret and I prefer to make fewer stops but to stay at new ports for longer times.

Another planning consideration—at least in the areas of the world with low and dangerous islands—is a clear and uncluttered route. It is best to go out of your way to avoid unlighted islands at night. Not only will your passage be simpler in deep waters where the currents may not be so variable, but you can relax and enjoy the passage instead of dying a thousand navigational deaths. Commercial shipping lanes mean constant vigilance and worry; if you can arrange to cross shipping lanes at right angles and to leave them far behind, all the better.

Ocean cruising isn't the only kind of sailing that should have careful planning. Coastal passages and lake trips are much easier, quicker, more satisfying, and safer if they are prepared for by checking into prevailing winds, storm patterns, times of calms, land breezes, and so forth. While genuine local knowledge is helpful, waterfront gossip sometimes has little value; the loudest talkers may never have left the harbor. You may be astonished at what a little study of books and charts will reveal.

A voyaging sailor's schedule shouldn't be too detailed and structured. In the first place, you are almost never on time. You are behind schedule because of maintenance on the yacht (the parts didn't come), and because you have found a new place and new friends that you like. When you sail on the oceans of the world, you need to throw away the calendar.

Whisper's masthead light is this tricolor fixture mounted at the best of all places. The light uses a vertical filament bulb, which shines through thin edge-glued acrylic filters of white, red, and green to give sharp dividing lines of color. This fixture is made by the German firm of Ahlemann & Schlatter of Bremen and is marketed under the name Aqua Signal. Other high quality lights, such as Marinaspec, are available or you can make your own. I see that the stainless steel shackle of the block for the spare jib halyard has worn into the bronze eyebolt for the spinnaker halyard block. Since I do not use a spinnaker, a better fitting for the spare jib halyard block would be a separate tang hanging downward. I must add this job to my list of projects.

10

~~~~~~

Can You Be Seen at Night?

At night the greatest hazard to small and large vessels is the risk of collision. All ships carry navigation lights to call attention to one another and to define each ship's right of way. Because lights are so important, they should be powerful, easily seen, and mounted according to international regulations. Unfortunately, however, the lights on today's small sailing vessels often have gross deficiencies, both making them illegal with regard to the rules, and putting their owners in grave danger from big ships and one another.

The problem areas are as follows:

1. The electric bulbs are entirely too small. The fittings are ill-designed and flimsy. Kerosene lamps in yacht sizes are hopeless.

2. The lights are badly placed, are obscured by sails, poles, or cabin structures, and are often mounted at wrong angles on bow pulpits, which makes it impossible to judge course changes on approaching vessels.

3. Battery power is limited and wire sizes are too small, resulting in a marked voltage drop at the light.

4. Salt spray interferes with the lights, the wiring and fixtures, and general efficiency.

5. The light loss through red and green glass or thick plastic filters can be as much as 88 percent. At a distance of a mile or more the colors may not be distinguishable at all.

According to the International Regulations for Preventing Collisions at sea, sailing craft under way must exhibit a red sidelight whose sector goes from directly forward to 112.5 degrees (ten points) to port. The green sector is from forward to 112.5 degrees to starboard. The stern light must extend rearwards for 135 degrees. The sectors of the three lights total 360 degrees and are the primary means of identifying the intentions of the vessel in question. The rules specify that sailing vessels over thirty-eight feet in length must carry sidelights that are visible for two miles. Sailing yachts under thirty-eight feet can carry either separate sidelights, a combined port and starboard lantern that is visible at least one mile, or a single masthead fixture that combines the sidelights and stern light. These distance figures are *minimums*, and a concerned seaman might well increase the power of his navigation lights.

So, because of legal requirements and for common sense (the reason the rules were made), you need to carry lights that can be seen and recognized at a distance of several miles. Bulbs suitable for flashlights, and fixtures built for model yachts in a park pond, are less than useless in situations where people's lives are concerned. I would hate to have my life depend on seeing a No. 90, 6-candlepower (75 lumens) bulb—a typical size—at two miles after it was filtered through thick colored glass. In my judgment, the Mickey Mouse lights and fittings supplied by most chandlers are little short of criminal. Many of the lights I have examined remind me of Christmas-tree ornaments, which are visually sparkling but functionally useless. The main difference is chrome plating instead of tinsel. Not only are the skimpy little lights inadequate for illumination, but the manufacturing standards are so shoddy that salt-water damage often reduces their paltry efficiency even more. Instead of emphasis on broad areas of intense illumination, filters that transmit the proper colors without significant light losses, and robust construction resistant to salt spray, the advertisements blandly speak of chrome plating, and light to "yachting bureau standards" (whatever that means). A fifty-foot yacht may easily have $5,000 worth of winches, but her navigation lights are usually the same as found on a twenty-five-foot vessel (a catalogue in front of me lists a pair for $11.95).

The operative question seems to be "How little can I get away with?" instead of "How can I best show the position of my vessel at night to safeguard both myself and others?" The reason is, of course, that most yacht owners sail very little and often not at all at night. The inadequacy is because the yacht owners do not demand suitable lights from the builders.

Oceangoing sailors who have experienced heavy ship traffic and are

*How ridiculous can you get? The maker of this tiny and widely sold fixture
claims that it puts out enough red and green light to be seen at two miles. In
my judgment, however, the light is not much better than a flashlight, and
I would hate to trust my life to such a paltry scrap of hardware. If this light
passed Coast Guard tests as stated, the inspector must have been watching
the light with a telescope. Not only is the fixture inadequate for safety and
common sense, but the location means that a sail on deck, a sailor's foot,
the rigging, or even a piece of line can mask the light. This small yacht needs
larger and better placed navigation lights. On looking around, we also see
that the forestay turnbuckle lacks both locking cotter pins.*

familiar with the Dover Strait in the English Channel, for example, don't
have to be told that their lights may well mean life itself. In sailing
south from Kobe, Japan, one night in May 1968, my wife and I counted
the bright lights on sixty-three large and small commercial vessels heading in and out of Osaka Wan. As we we watched, each coastal vessel and
fishing boat and tanker and cargo ship maneuvered according to the
Rules of the Road. The ship traffic flowed like automobiles on a well-
ordered freeway. In such a situation our lights were crucial.

In the 1976 Observer Singlehanded Transatlantic Race, 30 to 40
percent of the entrants used the superb new Ahlemann & Schlatter
masthead lights (Aqua Signal), which although relatively new, have

been quickly adopted by serious oceangoers because the lights are brighter and more easily seen. In spite of all this salty talk about oceans and far places, however, you can be run down in Long Island Sound or in San Francisco Bay. A weekend sailor needs good lights too.

In my opinion small oil lamps are worthless for yachts. To get reasonable light you need a ⅝- or ¾-inch wick, which means a 16-inch kerosene lantern. Three 16-inch Davey oil lamps make excellent navigation lights but take up a great deal of space. In the usual 12-volt electrical systems, automobile-type bulbs are employed, which are designed to accept up to 14 volts because of surges in automotive electrical generating systems. The lead-acid storage battery suffers a voltage drop when partially discharged and may only put out 10.5 volts. At this voltage a 12-watt bulb, for example, emits only 5.5 candelas through clear glass and 0.7 candelas through colored glass.[8]

There have been various schemes to increase the light from a single source. One idea is to use silvered electric bulbs to collect and focus the light from a small filament. In practice the center portion of a silvered bulb's output is high, but there is a severe falloff of light at the edges. Since each sidelight is required to be spread over 112.5 degrees, the silvered-bulb idea is useless. Reflectors and mirrors behind the bulbs are likewise no good.

Because sailing vessels are usually heeled (and pitching as well), the use of magnifying lens systems is impossible. The only hope in this direction is for someone to make a double-gimbaled, dampened-motion lantern and to use a dioptric lens around a light source.

Variations of these schemes appear and reappear from time to time, but since there are no performance standards to meet, the manufacturers have no goals except sales volume. I believe the only realistic approach is for the U.S. Coast Guard to begin to test and certify the intensity of navigation lights for all small vessels—including fishing boats and power yachts. Certainly navigation lights are as important as life jackets and fire extinguishers. The Royal Ocean Racing Club has instituted the Offshore Racing Council rule that sidelight bulbs must be 10 watts or give 1.5 candelas *outside* the lantern; the German Hydrographic Office regularly tests and certifies lighting equipment for small vessels. The French government is looking into the problem, and I feel it is only a question of time until absolute international illumination standards are established.

Inadequate lights lead to a false sense of security. Novice sailors often have a naïve belief that their lights (of whatever strength) will not only be seen by others but that the other vessels will take prompt evasive

The starboard light hidden beneath the toe rail of this Hinckley yacht is typical of inadequate navigation lights. Such a light is also hidden from the eyes of any seamen on large ships that might be approaching from ahead. Lights must be visible above as well as ahead. If navigation lights are going to be hidden, why have them at all? Night sailing would be a lot safer if the lights got as much attention as the fancy ventilator. Fortunately, Hinckley has begun to use the Ahlemann & Schlatter lights on some of its new yachts.

action. This may be a welcome thought, but it is nonsense. A parallel situation is a radio operator listening to Morse code. If you turn down the volume until the operator can no longer hear the code, he is not going to get the message no matter what is transmitted.

What we need are strong light sources in large port and starboard fixtures with sizable areas of thin colored glass or plastic. The white stern light is not such a problem, because the bulb is not so severely filtered. If we had unlimited battery power like big ships, we could simply put a 60-watt bulb in each of three large lanterns and forget about the problem. With a 12-volt system such bulbs consume 5 amps each, however, and the three together would draw 120 amps during an eight-hour night, an electrical demand impossible for a sailing yacht. Three 25-watt bulbs would consume 50 amps in the same period. Three 10-watt bulbs would require 20 amps. A 10-watt bulb shielded by thin colored acrylic gives a fair light at one mile; 25 watts is better and can be seen well at two miles if unobstructed and above the water a bit. But the power taken by three 25-watt bulbs is staggering for a small sailing yacht. A further point is the necessity for a good shielding arrangement or an optical system to prevent the overlap of colors.

It doesn't take much study to realize that the best possible place for navigation lights is at the top of the mast, where they are high, unobstructed by the sails or anything else, and are away from salt spray. For this reason I bought an English masthead fluorescent lighting fixture some years ago. The light from a 12-inch vertically mounted lighting tube was split into red, green, and white sectors by a colored plastic housing. For a drain of only .8 amp (6.4 amps for our 8-hour night) I got light equivalent to a 40-watt incandescent bulb. The stern sector of the light was bright enough to require a shield to keep the light from the helmsman's eyes. The appeal, of course, was three lights from a single bulb and the reduced amperage draw of the fluorescent unit.

This masthead light was much better than anything I had seen before, and my sailing friends all commented on its excellent visibility. The colors were a bit milky, however, and tended to merge at a distance. The color separation from the red to the green was only fair. At two miles I could see a blob of color but not distinct bands of vivid red and green.

Bernard Hayman, the editor of the English magazine *Yachting World*, has long campaigned for improved yacht lighting. It was in the pages of his magazine (January 1971) that I first read about a vertical filament tungsten bulb and the importance of using a bulb with a point source of light rather than a broad source like a fluorescent bulb. Hayman discovered that in a combined port and starboard lighting unit the width of the centerline dividing support pillar was critical. The metal divider between the red and green sectors on one commercial fixture caused a blind or ambiguous zone of 15 degrees. Later, by edge-gluing suitably colored acrylic, Hayman reduced the angle of confusion to less than 2 degrees.

This Swedish-built yacht has her bi-color green and red Ahlemann & Schlatter navigation light mounted on a horizontal bar at the foot of the bow pulpit. With the fixture mounted forward of the headstay, the red and green lights cannot be cut off by sails. The light does get a great deal of spray, however, and must be strong enough to withstand green water and occasional knocks from anchoring and berthing maneuvers. Compare this light to the one shown on page 153.

In February 1974 the German firm of Ahlemann & Schlatter in Bremen announced a high-quality line of new lighting fixtures with vertical filament bulbs. The casings are made of polished non-magnetic stainless steel. The lenses are fabricated of solid acrylic glass, edge-glued in cases of contiguous colors, and the bulbs are carefully positioned at the optical center of the cylindrical unit. Bulbs of either 10 or 25 watts are offered for 6, 12, and 24 volts. The lights are available in single colors of red, green, or white, in combined red and green, and in combined red, green, and white.

I was in Buenos Aires at the time and sent for a one-bulb masthead light that combined the port, starboard, and stern lights in a single unit. One night on the grounds of the Yacht Club Argentino, Margaret and I compared the Ahlemann & Schlatter lantern (with a 25-watt vertical filament bulb) with the fluorescent light at *Whisper's* masthead. The color saturation and the brightness of the new light were outstanding; it was superior close up and at distances of one and two miles. The cutoff between the different colors was sharp and decisive. The brightness was surprisingly good with a 10-watt bulb also. I junked my masthead fluorescent unit at once and have sailed since with the new German fixture. I feel that my navigation lights are a hundredfold better than the toy fixtures on the bow pulpit that I once had. The amperage draw for the 25-watt bulb is 2 amps, or 16 amps for an eight-hour night. The 10-watt bulb draws about 7 amps for the same period.

I note that such well-known builders as Camper & Nicholson in England, Nautor of Finland, and Hinkley of Maine have adopted the new lights, but what is more significant is the number of these excellent lights on the ocean-racing fleets and on the vessels of singlehanders and cruising families. The Ahlemann & Schlatter lights are distributed in the United States by the Nicro Corporation.

When an auxiliary sailing yacht is under power at night, she must show the same lights as a power vessel, which means the usual sidelights and stern light plus a white 225-degree (20 point) masthead light (formerly called a steaming light). The masthead light must be one meter or more (Annex I) above the running lights. Most auxiliary yachts already comply with this rule. If an auxiliary sailing yacht thirty-eight-feet long or less elects to use a tricolor masthead lamp for sailing, the old lights should be retained for powering. A yacht between thirty-eight- and sixty-five-feet cannot use a tricolor masthead light but can elect combined sidelights if the owner chooses.

Some ocean voyagers feel that a single white all-around masthead light is best for visibility at sea. In the absence of any other, I certainly agree. Any light is better than no light. The use of a low-amperage tricolor light for yachts of thirty-eight feet or less, or combined side-lights and a separate stern light for yachts up to sixty-five feet, however, indicates a vessel's position and intent. A singlehander who is asleep should properly show one all-around red light six feet or more above a second to indicate "not under command" (Rule 4).

The problem of lights at sea for small vessels on long voyages is simply one of battery power. In shipping lanes or along busy coastal regions we need lots of luck plus powerful lights. In the solitary reaches of deserted oceans the lights are not as important. The crews of many single- and doublehanded yachts often get a high percentage of their sleep during the day and stay awake at night. An alert crewman can see the lights of a big ship long before the ship can see the weak lights of the yacht.

For potential collision situations the best thing is a white rocket flare, which is permitted and encouraged (Rule 36) as an attention-getting signal. A second signaling device is an Aldis lamp, which is an extremely powerful mirror-reflecting device whose light can be directed on the sails or at an approaching ship. The single-letter signals "D" (Keep clear of me; I am maneuvering with difficulty), "E" (I am altering my course to starboard), or "I" (I am altering my course to port) can easily be sent. On *Whisper* we have used a 12-volt Aldis lamp for years for signaling situations both at night and in bright daylight. The Aldis lamp has a crude gunsight at the top which allows the light to be directed accurately. Depending on wave height and the height of the operator, an Aldis lamp signal can easily be seen five miles.

A new type of attention-getting device is a masthead strobe light, which is the same sort of winking anti-collision light that we see on private and commercial aircraft and on man-overboard lights. This light is based on the ionization of gas in a xenon-filled flashtube which produces a blue-white flash whenever the electrical energy in a capacitor is discharged. Earlier in the chapter we mentioned the common usage of a No. 90 6-candlepower bulb in many yacht lighting fixtures. This small bulb puts out 75 lumens. The xenon tube, by constrast, emits from 200,000 to 1,000,000 lumens at its peak output, depending on the unit. This extreme brightness together with the pulsating nature of the light makes an eye-catching attraction. Though the light flashes are extremely powerful, their duration is only a fraction of a second, and the light is set to flash only once or twice or three times every minute. This means that the power requirements are modest and can be supplied by a dry battery.[9]

I am impressed by the brilliance and attention-grabbing qualities of these units and judge the xenon flashers to be excellent for emergency use when you need to show your position to others at sea. I feel strongly, however, that masthead xenon lights should be used only in emergency situations, not for routine sailing and attention-getting in harbors by show-offs and exhibitionists. If xenon flashers are used as daily playthings, who will pay attention in an emergency?

Xenon flashers are a long way from wick-type oil lamps. Maybe in the future we will use laser-powered running lights at night. In fog we may switch on powerful transponders to register unmistakable pips on big ships' radar sets to reduce the hazards of collision even more. Perhaps a simple amplified sound detection device will alert us to the noise of approaching propellers on ships or of waves dashing on rocks or shorelines when we can't see such hidden dangers with our eyes. But whatever we find in the future, there is no substitute for a rested and wide-awake person on watch.

11

~~~~~~

Managing without Refrigeration

We do not have refrigeration on *Whisper* because I refuse to put up with the mechanical complications of a cold-making device and the daily noise and smell of an engine to drive it. A butane refrigerator is out of the question for us because of the explosion risk and the bother of refilling tanks and dealing with piping and valves. On the tropical islands of the South Pacific we saw dozens of excellent kerosene refrigerators in houses ashore, but the Swedish Electrolux company explicitly warns of fire danger if their appliances are subjected to the unpredictable motions of a ship. We could use an icebox, but if we can buy ice it means that we are anchored or tied up at a village or city, where it seems more logical to shop daily for a piece of fish or a couple of pork chops than to haul ice. It may be a painful truth, but most cruising yachts spend 95 percent of their lives rocking gently on a mooring or tied to a dock in the shadow of city buildings somewhere.

"Then we have the same food as people with refrigeration," says Margaret. "Depending on the climate, we go to the store every day or two for meat and crispy vegetables—the most perishable items. For butter and cheese and fruit we shop every four or five days. Instead of frozen orange juice we squeeze fresh oranges, which make a much tastier

Out they come! Three loaves of freshly baked bread from the galley oven.

and more healthful drink. The extra time we spend shopping is probably less than that devoted to the expense, maintenance, and repair of a refrigeration unit. In addition, the cook doesn't have her galley torn apart at regular intervals and her ears bruised by swearing mechanics. I believe we're more popular with our neighbors because we don't run the engine."

You can elect to use an icebox if block ice is available. With a top-loading box insulated with three or four inches of polyurethane foam, a suitable vapor barrier of gelcoat or stainless steel, and a policy of opening the box as infrequently as possible, the ice will keep a week or more. The catch is the block ice. In the West Indies, the United States, and some parts of Europe you can generally buy block ice, and the icebox arrangement is marvelous. But in the Pacific, most of South America and Africa, and the East Indies block ice is a rare bird except around a few commercial fishing operations. If you find the ice, you usually wouldn't want your food to touch it because of specks and doubtful water sources. As a practical matter for us, Margaret and I have found refrigerators and iceboxes entirely too much trouble.

So in port we let the shopkeepers pay for the refrigeration. Once away from land, or if we are coasting in an isolated area, we manage without refrigeration and we get along very well.

To the average person refrigeration is one of the necessities of life. When we mention that we have none on *Whisper*, the usual response is, "What on earth do you eat?" Our questioners imagine that we live on an endless diet of canned stew (ugh!) or corned beef hash (ugh!). Nothing is further from the truth.

In general, we take certain basic foods that keep well and use them as foundations for meals. We carefully add small cans of selected foods to the basics to broaden the variety and appeal.

Shore people store many things in refrigerators that don't need cooling at all.

Eggs (greased with Vaseline petroleum jelly), rice, spaghetti, potatoes, and onions will easily last four or five weeks—plenty of time, since most sea passages are under a month. Carrots and cabbage will keep ten days or more. Grapefruit, oranges, limes, and lemons—especially if carefully selected and wrapped in aluminum foil—will stay fresh for weeks and weeks. A piece of bacon, a Plumrose canned ham, smoked fish, and a large salami (if you like spicy things) will help the meat department. Cheeses covered with wax (Gouda, Tillamook, Edam, Bonbel, etc.) keep adequately.

Greasing fresh eggs with Vaseline petroleum jelly may seem like an old wives' tale, but the step will help them keep four or five weeks without refrigeration.

Even in the tropics bread will last ten days before you need to trim off the edges (crusty or double-baked bread is best). Then you can go to Scandinavian hardbread, water biscuits (my favorite) or bake bread. On *Whisper* we can make four small loaves at one time in the oven of our diesel stove. Of course we don't bake when sailing conditions are rough, but when we are becalmed or the going is light, someone is often busy sifting flour or kneading the gently rising dough. Then the yacht becomes filled with the delicious aroma of fresh bread.

We try all sorts of recipes—thick, crusty loaves of rough-textured whole wheat, lighter loaves of half white and half dark flour, and smooth, fine-grained white bread. We vary the results by putting in raisins or honey or even bananas (!). We make French bread which needs only four ingredients. Our recipe gives us six slim mouth-watering baguettes that generally vanish in a twinkling.

We have found that the traditional bread recipes which require two risings are best. The short-cut formulas (soda bread or miner's bread) taste dull and flat to us. We prefer the look of properly baked loaves to the ill-formed and unattractive products of quick recipes that are often prepared in frying pans or coffee cans.

We bake with dry yeast that comes in eight-ounce cans. We find that after a can is opened we use it up in three or four months. Unopened, a can will keep indefinitely. Three loaves of bread need seven cups or 1¾ pounds of flour and will last two people five or six days. At this rate, bread for a month requires about ten pounds of flour, which we stow in large jars with screw lids. We take along a few boxes of cake mix and birthday candles for special occasions.

Several years ago our friend Tee Jennings put us on to a Teflon-coated waffle iron from Norway, which has become a great asset for Sunday-morning breakfasts. The waffles are especially good with maple syrup, which we bought when we sailed in Canada and replenished recently when a friend from Vermont joined us for a few days. The waffles don't stick to the specially coated iron, which is easy to keep clean.

Fifty years ago, when the famous French pilot cutter *Jolie Brise* was making long sea passages, her English owner, Commander E. C. Martin, found that his greatest triumph was onion soup. We have made *Jolie Brise* onion soup many times on *Whisper* and think highly of it. The soup is quick and easy to prepare, uses ingredients common to most cruising yachts, and, best of all, is tasty and nourishing. (I have an urge to get up from my writing table and start making some now.)

Here is Commander Martin speaking from the pages of *Deepwater Cruising*, published two generations ago:

Get the largest and finest onions available. . . . Peel them, for choice sitting a few points to windward of them on deck; or peel under water, or one can see to do only about three. Allow about two for each man. Cut them into quarters and put them into a large saucepan with a cover. For five men I should cut up 12 onions. Pour in enough cold water to make plenty of soup for all hands; add two full tablespoonsful of Bovril; about one-quarter pound of butter; a dessert spoonful of Lea and Perrins Worcester sauce; black pepper, with caution; and if there is any, a small wine glass full of sherry, or rather more white wine, when the cooking is nearly finished. It seems best not to add any salt in the cooking. Allow the mixture to boil gently, and stir occasionally until the onions have all fallen to pieces and are perfectly soft. The soup is then made. I venture to recommend the recipe because we have found this soup to be one of the very best and most wholesome forms of food which one can have at sea. It is easy to make at any time when cooking is possible at all, and everyone seems to like it.

On *Whisper* we make a smaller amount (we are two instead of five) and substitute beef stock for Bovril, an English product that may not be available.

We carry various canned meats—corned beef, roast beef, chicken, turkey, ham, and bacon. One small can of meat is about right for two people for a main meal. We have found it best to buy the smallest-size cans (even if they cost more) and to purchase meats without gravies and sauces if possible. Stews, for example, taste better if the cook assembles her own chunks of meat, fresh potatoes, fresh onions, carrots, beef stock, and seasonings (including a dash of Angostura bitters). Warmed-up canned stew tastes exactly like warmed-up canned stew (mostly potatoes and very little meat). By all means make your own, which is cheaper and infinitely better.

The same reasoning applies with small cans of tuna, salmon, shrimp, or with fresh fish. Use the basic fish and make a cream sauce (melt two tablespoons of butter, put in an equal amount of flour, and add one cup of milk plus seasoning). You can vary the flavor with curry, tarragon, oregano, and many herbs. Fish dishes can be served on steamed rice, mashed potatoes, or toast. Margaret often adds unusual ingredients to pep up ordinary fare. She may put a small can of water chestnuts in a beef casserole, add canned bean sprouts to an omelet, or spicy pimentos to fish prepared in a cream sauce.

A typical recipe for corned beef is to cut off slices of the crumbly meat and to dip them in beaten egg. Then roll the moistened meat slices in toasted bread crumbs (or coarse whole-wheat flour) and fry them—together with onions—for several minutes in a pan with a little shortening. The corned beef can be served with noodles garnished with grated cheese.

One of my favorite foods at sea is curried lentils, which no doubt sounds like a ghastly health food of some kind. On the contrary, Margaret's recipe is tasty and nourishing.

1. Soak 1 cup of lentils overnight in fresh water.

2. Put the lentils in 2 cups of lightly salted water and cook 20 minutes in a pressure cooker.

3. In a frying pan sauté a large chopped onion in 2 tablespoons of butter or margarine and add 2 tablespoons of flour, 1 tablespoon of curry powder (watch it!), salt, and pepper.

4. While stirring, add 1½ cups of boiling water (or vegetable or meat stock) and simmer for 30 minutes.

5. Add the lentils to the sauce and serve with rice.

A one-pound can of butter will last a week or ten days. We also use margarine, which keeps several weeks, depending on the latitude. Canned butter is available in most countries, although it is sometimes hard to buy because of restrictive dairy laws. (In California—which exports lots of canned butter—I once had to promise a reluctant supplier that I would not open the cans until I was at sea!) In the tropics Margaret and I tend to eat less bread and consequently not so much butter or margarine. We fry food in Teflon-coated pans, which need little or no grease or butter. For frying onions or foods that we want to brown, we use a white vegetable shortening (Crisco), which seems to keep forever.

Leftovers are a problem in the tropics. If you are cruising on a budget, it is distressing to throw away food. Our solution is to keep the remains of last night's supper and to use the leftovers for a filling in omelets or mixed with scrambled eggs. For example, a cup of cooked rice and a few bits of spicy roast beef make a breakfast omelet tasty and filling. The ship's cat has the rest. The fish get what the cat doesn't eat, because we never keep doubtful food.

Milk is no longer a difficulty. I have always found the taste of evaporated milk in cans to be ghastly, but the excellent powdered milk (Marvel or Nestlé's in foreign waters) if always stored dry keeps for ages, goes into solution easily, and tastes rich and creamy. We use it for general cooking, breakfast cereals, puddings, and cocoa. Margaret and I are not big milk drinkers, but we have noticed that children seem to drink glasses of the Milkman-type products with gusto. You can also buy cans of Real Fresh Milk, a sterilized liquid product that tastes as fresh as if it came straight from a cow. The military services of the United States buy enormous amounts of Real Fresh Milk for use at isolated stations. Unopened cans keep for several years at least.

Among *Whisper*'s stores we also carry small cans of sour cream and Nestlé's cream (6 oz.) that we use with vegetables (spinach and green beans are improved), meat dishes, and fruit. Sour cream is especially good with meat. One idea is to sauté a few chopped onions, cook some roast beef with button mushrooms, and then put a little sour cream on top of the meat and heat the sour cream through. Delicious! Margaret does the whole deal in a single ordinary skillet to avoid washing extra pans.

One rule we have (after two disastrous scaldings) is for the cook to *always* wear an apron. It should be long and be of vinyl or some material that will deflect, not absorb, boiling liquids. Burns at sea are catastrophic.

We carry 78 gallons of water in two tanks plus another 10 gallons in plastic jugs. Our maximum water consumption at sea is one gallon a day for two people, which includes an occasional bird bath from a bowl and some sparse dish rinsing (after washing in hot, soapy salt water). We generally take water as it comes from a tap on shore; if the water looks suspect or we have been warned about contamination, we add a little domestic chlorine bleach (Clorox). We strain the water through a fine cloth as it goes into the tanks; it's surprising how many particles of mud are in supposedly clear water.

"When we're at sea in the tropics, I like to fix a lime drink," says Margaret. "The drink is simplicity itself—squeezed limes or lemons, sugar, and water plus maybe a preserved cherry if I'm feeling fancy. We find the drink refreshing, and I think it's good for you."

Fresh fish at sea are always welcome. The fish, however, tend to be of the tuna, wahoo, or dorado variety and are often three to five feet long. The trouble with catching large fish is that you can eat only so much. I generally make athwartfish cuts with a hacksaw to get steaks quickly and without fuss. In the tropics we feed leftovers to the sharks; in cooler Alaska we kept pieces of halibut for three or four days. When we were in Japan, we saw a lot of fish hanging up to dry, and we intend to try drying some ourselves.

Fishing gear needs to be heavy. We never had much luck catching fish until we tied up near *Fast Lady*, a Japanese yacht that we met in Western Samoa. The Japanese crew lived largely on fish that they caught, and the men couldn't understand how we could be so unsuccessful until they saw our small lures, puny hooks, and thin line.

"The fishing machinery of *Whisper* is for humor only," said the Japanese captain. "Fish of the open ocean are fierce fighters and all must be overstrong. We wish no disrespect, but your devices are for land stream fish only."

The captain of *Fast Lady* showed us his tackle, which was made up of colorful six-inch lures that sparkled with bits of glass and bristled with

The jaunty little Tancook Whaler Saro Jane was built by Bill Duffin, who is steering while a group of his friends relax in the cockpit. A fine-ended design derived from fishing vessels, this small yacht is suitable only for protected waters because of her large cockpit and low freeboard. Here on the smooth waters of San Francisco Bay with the hills of Sausalito in the background, Saro Jane is a real pleasure to sail with her simple, cheap, and attractive self-tending gaff schooner rig, which has plenty of area for good performance in light airs and is easy to shorten down. Except for less rake in her masts, Saro Jane's rig is similar to her larger and more famous sister, the America, which won and instituted the America's Cup a century ago. Note the absence of backstays.

feathers. Each hook was two inches long, evilly curved with a large barb, and four of the hooks were lashed together to make a fearsome trap for a fish. The line was ⅛-inch polypropylene with a breaking strength of 200 kilos. The machined swivels were the diameter of a pencil.

The crew of *Fast Lady* presented us with a selection of lures and line. Our fishing results improved at once, although generally we have had our best catches in the vicinity of land (occasionally we hook a tuna far at sea). We gave away a fancy rod and reel, and put the polypropylene line on a sheet winch and haul away when we hook a fish.

One reason the line and lure need to be so strong is because of the forward speed of the yacht. At 5 knots the pull from a twenty-pound fish is surprisingly hard. To keep the lure from tearing out of the fish's mouth when he strikes, we put a three- or four-foot piece of shock cord in the line.

We learned to drag the fishing line from the starboard quarter and the distance recording log line from the port quarter in order to keep the two lines separate. If the spinning log line gets around the fishing line, the snarls and knots are monumental.

"Good food and regular meals, as well served as possible, are, I think, the most important thing of all upon a long voyage," wrote a famous sailor a long time ago. "It is not often that several men can live at very close quarters and at times in considerable discomfort, without feeling the strain of it after a while, and I am sure that the best, and indeed the only way of having a happy ship, is to spare no pains in making the meals as wholesome, as varied, and as attractive as possible."[10]

When the weather is rough, Margaret and I (well wedged in somewhere) eat from bowls, perhaps having pilot biscuits, macaroni and cheese, and oranges. Usually, however, we eat from china plates with pretty decorative patterns. We like the feel and appearance of proper plates and silverware and pottery mugs; their use makes our mealtimes a little nicer. After all, the yacht is our home. Why not eat with a bit of style and elegance?

12

~~~~~~

Wrinkles

A century ago a famous English seaman named S. T. S. Lecky wrote a book on navigation called *Lecky's Wrinkles to Practical Navigation*. The book went through many editions, and *Lecky's Wrinkles*, as it was soon called, became a handbook of the sea because of its practical usefulness. I have borrowed the key word from Squire Lecky's title and present a few ideas that I have found helpful, not on navigation because the concern of this book is otherwise, but on general sailing.

1. When you are sailing in the trade wind zones, the easiest way to fill your fresh-water tanks is to use a water-catching awning. There is usually plenty of water around high islands and atolls in the tropics, but the problem is how to get it. Often you may be anchored a half mile out from shore in a shallow lagoon. This means you must row the jugs ashore and then carry them to a suitable place along a stream (above where the women are washing) or go to a cistern where you can draw water. This is generally beneath the roof of the church, the building with

One way to get drinking water is to hang a bucket on the main boom gooseneck and top up the boom a little. After a few minutes of heavy rain, the sail, boom, and bucket are washed clean and you can transfer bucket after bucket into the water tanks. This photograph was taken between the Galápagos Islands and Callao, Peru. I collected 40 or 50 gallons during a heavy downpour that lasted an hour or so.

the largest catchment roof on the island. To get 80 gallons of water may take most of a day. You row half a mile to shore and walk half a mile to the church while you try to balance water jugs that get surprisingly heavy.

A much simpler scheme is a water-catching awning. Not only is it easier, but the water is purer—you don't draw it from a cistern of doubtful purity or take it from a stream whose upcountry customers you may or may not like. A water-catching awning is handy not only in distant places but sometimes in the United States as well. Last year we sailed to Newport, Rhode Island, from Bermuda. Needing no fuel or supplies, I innocently tried to get water from the Texaco dock and was roundly insulted and turned away by the woman in charge. I retreated to an anchorage and unrolled the water-catching awning, which once again performed when dark clouds moved in.

A sun awning is generally adequate to catch water. On *Whisper* our awning measures 10 x 17 feet and rests on top of the main boom. The awning is supported by four athwartship battens. At the forward end the awning is secured to the lower shrouds and the mast; the after end is tied to the twin backstays; we tie light lines between the lifelines and the ends of each batten to keep the awning from flapping. We have a small triangular pocket at the forward starboard corner that takes a hose that leads to the water tanks. During a rainstorm we tilt the awning a little so the pocket area is low, which allows the water to collect and run down the hose into the tanks. If we put a clothespin on the hose, we can take a shower by standing underneath and releasing the clothespin after some water has collected. If the water stands for a while, the sun will heat it.

A problem with the big awning is that in strong rain squalls a good deal of wind often comes with the rain, which makes it necessary to roll up the awning. To get around this difficulty and to be able to catch water in places where we don't use the big awning (away from the tropics), we made a smaller awning especially to catch rain. This awning goes along one side deck and is 9 feet long and 2½ feet wide. It is cut to be lower at the forward end, which is over the deck opening for the tanks. A sewn-in plastic funnel and short hose lead directly into the filler pipe. To keep the awning from flapping in the wind, we weigh it down with the boat hook.

Another plan is to use the mainsail for water-catching. You can do it while either sailing or at anchor (you'll need both bow and stern anchors). You catch the water in a bucket at the forward end of the main boom. The first few buckets may be slightly salty but are good enough for washing.

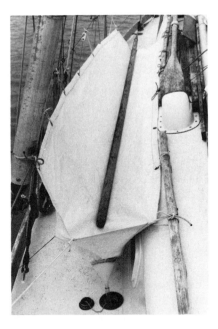

This water-catching awning fits along the starboard side deck and is cut lower forward so that the water runs into the funnel and into the tank. The boat hook keeps the awning from flapping in the wind that often accompanies rain squalls.

Does it rain in the tropics? I remember a rainstorm about halfway between Mexico and French Polynesia while we were sailing hard in the northeast trades. Did it rain? I'll say! In the darkness of night Margaret and I eased the main halyard a little and lifted the main boom slightly with the topping lift so the mainsail had a big belly in it. The wind was fair and the rain thundered into the sail and cascaded on deck near the mast. After the first few minutes the sail was washed clean, so we bucketed water into the fresh-water tanks, which were soon full. We filled the teakettle, the sink, the water jugs, the buckets, and took long drinks of the delightfully cool water. We washed our hair, wiped down the cabin sole, and, after plugging the cockpit drains, started doing the laundry. Even the cat got a bath. Did it rain? Two hours later it was still pouring. Talk about an un-nautical scene! Naked bodies, laughter, laundry flapping, a cat that looked like a rat—all while we footed along at five knots with a great silvery luminescent wake bubbling behind us. All we needed was a man playing the flute!

Still another way to catch water is to use the coach roof or a section of deck and to surround a flat, level area with low battens. Then, with a through-deck drain, a petcock underneath, and calm sailing, you can pipe the water to the tanks. Blondie Hasler used this idea on his famous *Jester*, and I saw a similar scheme on a ferro-cement yacht in Samoa. I suppose you might catch drinking water in an upright-stowed dinghy if it were cleaned out thoroughly. During his many high-latitude adventures, Bill Tilman often ferried water from freshwater streams to his Bristol Channel pilot cutter *Mischief* by means of a rubber dinghy that was washed out, filled to overflowing, and carefully towed out to the ship behind another dinghy.

2. Margaret and I go up and down the mast on metal steps or stairs that are fastened every twenty inches on alternate sides of the spar. Our eighteen steps extend to just below the masthead, where we have a fitting on each side—opposite one another—for convenience in working at the top or for looking out. In practice we find that we keep the rigging in better condition because inspections and work are easier. For big jobs aloft when you need many tools and a comfortable seat, it is still necessary to use a bosun's chair, which I hoist to the appropriate height and then climb up to on the steps. Or you can get into the chair on deck and someone can hoist it while you climb the steps.

I believe the steps are superior to ratlines on the lower shrouds, which move athwartships and which are dangerous to climb if the vessel is rolling. In addition, ratlines of thin line are impossible to climb barefoot. There is a problem of getting the halyards around the steps, but we have learned to keep the slack out of the halyards and to look aloft frequently when hoisting sails.

An important use of the steps is to go aloft at sea when there is a rigging problem. Mast steps are better than a bosun's chair or a rope ladder, although no scheme is safe on the moving ocean. Going aloft is an emergency situation and should be avoided if possible because of the danger of getting slammed against the mast or even of getting whipped off. In any sort of cross swell you may not be able to climb aloft at all.

I have gone up only once at sea, when we were sailing between Isla Española in the Galápagos and Callao, Peru. The yacht was close-hauled in a Force 6 wind and sea and I had lost a jib halyard because I had stupidly failed to close a snap shackle properly when changing a head-sail. The halyard end and shackle ran about three-quarters of the way up the mast, and the fitting and halyard wrapped around everything in sight. The bronze snap shackle then began to hammer away at the mast and made fearful destructive noises. On my first trip I got to the problem area but could do nothing because it took both arms and all my strength to hang on. We then dropped the jib, which had been hoisted on a second halyard, and ran off slowly downwind to ease the motion. On the

Mast steps are so practical that most cruising yachts now have them. Halyards and various lines do get around the steps, but you can learn to work around the problem. The steps are superior to ratlines for a small vessel and are ideal for checking the rigging, reeving halyards, or climbing aloft for visual pilotage.

second try I was able to get up and untangle the halyard and the new knots it had invented, although the experience took ninety minutes and rather flattened me for several days.

If you are planning to install mast steps, I suggest that you try climbing a mast with steps on someone else's yacht beforehand if possible. People vary quite a bit in their leg and thigh strength, and some otherwise athletic men are simply unable to climb mast steps. In addition, the spacing may be too little or too much for your leg and thigh length. When we put up the steps on *Whisper's* mast some years ago in California, there was a lot of curiosity about them. Many people tried climbing up, with surprising results.

There are so many things on a mast that I hate to clutter up the spar even more, but I feel the quick accessibility all the way to the top is worth it. The head-on windage is small; you can hardly see the steps from forward or aft from a distance. The steps make it easy for a lookout to climb to the spreaders for coral pilotage.

I had the steps fabricated of .085-inch marine grade stainless steel 1 inch wide except for the footstep, which is 1½ inches wide and rounded so that it is comfortable for bare feet. Each step weighs about seven ounces and is held to the mast with six stainless steel screws. The fittings have been put on both wooden and aluminum masts. The steps, now available commercially, were made by the Moonlite Marine Corporation. The workmanship and finish are superb.

3. At one time I kept my tools in fishing tackle boxes that were stowed in cockpit lockers. All sorts of gear got piled on top of the boxes, and not only was it hard to pull out the boxes but often you had to unload half a box before you found the tool you were after. It seemed stupid to lift out an entire box for one small tool. Also, it was quite easy to upset a box (generally at night when I was in a hurry). I never seemed to have enough room for all the tools, and after I half filled the boxes with salt water a couple of times I chucked out the blasted things.

I built permanent compartmented drawers and shelves behind the settee backs (hidden by the cushions), where I now keep the tools (separated into various sizes and grouped according to the frequency of use). In the same area I put all the fastenings and bits of hardware in two dozen or so labeled plastic containers with screw tops.

My theory of stowage is *compartmented areas for accessible stowage for frequently used items or classes of items* (daily use tools, first aid, sail repair, sewing, stationary, toilet articles, cameras and film, charts, signaling equipment, navigation books, etc.). Each stowage compartment has

To keep the masthead burgee from fouling its pole, I mounted the flag on a second short pole which is held to the main pole with two loose but snug scraps of PVC plumbing pipe. A screw eye in the short shaft and a retaining screw in the center of the main pole keep the second shaft in place. The long plastic bearing surfaces hardly wear at all, and the flag turns easily and silently with the wind.

its items and no others. Gradually we have switched drawers and compartments around so that the most used items are the most accessible. Instead of always fumbling for a pencil and dividers, I installed a little rack above the chart table. We fastened the sextant box where the navigator logically puts down his instrument. A vegetable box went into the galley. We grouped writing materials, the address book, and a dictionary where we normally do our letters. I mounted a cup rack for coffee mugs, and so on. We discovered that some things never got used and put them ashore— books that really didn't interest us, games that were never played, useless departure presents, impractical cooking implements, and so on. Vulnerable gear is stowed as far as possible from salt spray. We never put a camera near the main hatch, but the vegetable box is quite unharmed by a little shower now and then. In fact, the water may make something grow!

For long-term stowage Margaret lists everything in a notebook, which saves hours of frustration and hunting for things that may or may not be on board. For example:

> Item 37: Spare galley pumps. Under starboard
> forward forepeak. Quantity 2.

When I need a galley pump, I know exactly where it is and that spares exist. In some instances I have had good luck fitting spare parts and stowing away the originals to make certain the spare parts fitted. Metal items should be well oiled and wrapped in several plastic bags before being tucked away.

To deal with our food, Margaret keeps a notebook with two sections: *Total food stores* and *Food stores locations*. *Total food stores* lists (in cans or jars or packets or in bulk):

> meat
> fish
> soups
> vegetables
> fruit
> juices
> sauces
> bread—flour—noodles—cereals
> milk products and other fats
> sugar, jams, and preserved fruits
> tea, coffee, bouillon

When Maragaret buys a dozen cans of tuna, for example, she puts twelve checks after tuna under the heading of "fish." When she uses a can, she crosses off one check. This way she keeps a running total of food on board.

The second list, *Food stores locations*, tells in which of eight food-stowage areas on the yacht certain items or classes of items are kept. Margaret uses three stowage areas convenient to the galley for current requirements, but when she wants to go under the cockpit to a less used stowage area, for instance, she can look in her book and find that the boxes hold 49 cans of corned beef, 14 cans of roast beef, 10 cans of meat-balls (we bought heavily in Argentina), and 3 large cans of peaches.

Such a notebook is very little trouble if you keep it up to date and make an entry every time something pertinent is brought on board, moved, or consumed. We have found that Margaret's little red book saves hours of hunting and helps us to know where we stand. No inventory system is perfect, certainly, and because we're no paragons of orderliness, our scheme gets out of hand occasionally. Yet even approximations are help-ful (we have two 1½ inch copper elbows on board but no 1¼ inch, or is it the other way around?). A cruising yacht has thousands of things on board, and we must be able to find a one-inch, pan-head, sheet metal screw or a jar of chutney to go with the curry!

I bought this Aldis signaling lamp from Thomas Foulkes of London many years ago. The lamp uses 12-volt DC current and works on the principle of a high intensity silvered bulb whose light is thrown backwards into a silvered reflector. The lamp is aimed with a sighting tube at the top. The signal is quite powerful, and it is easy to send Morse code several miles or more. The bulb, however, is a special item, and you must carry spares.

4. For secure footing on the decks, cockpit floor, cockpit seats, bridge deck, and coach roof we add coarse coral sand to the deck paint. Some of our visitors think that our decks are too rough, but no one has slipped yet, a statement that can hardly be said for many fiberglass decks with supposedly skidproof patterns molded into them. (Once we had two toddlers from South Africa on board who talked about "the cobblestones" on the floor of the cockpit.)

We paint the decks with two-part epoxy paint and sprinkle the sand from a saltshaker. We paint a patch about three feet long, sprinkle the sand on it, let the paint dry a few minutes, and then lay on a second coat of paint—brushing lightly—before moving on. The two-part paint is extremely tough and combines with the sand to make a file-like surface that either bare feet or boating shoes can grip. We have found that a coarsely roughened surface is easier to clean than a lightly roughened surface.

5. Because we don't have the stowage space and we don't wish to buy special running sails with high cut clews for *Whisper*, we pole out our regular headsails in conjunction with the mainsail for downwind running (see page 63). For ease of handling and more room and safety on the foredeck, we stow our spinnaker poles up the mast with the mast ends of the poles permanently attached to the mast. With one end of a pole

Left: Whisper's *spinnaker poles are connected to the mast track with these large cast stainless steel sliders that allow side-to-side, up-and-down, and rotary motion. Each pole has a separate slider, which is hauled up and down by its lift and downhaul lines. Because our usual running rig is a single poled-out headsail, we generally keep only one pole and slider mounted up the mast to reduce weight aloft. We have the option, however, of using two poles and twin running headsails. You can make a point for having each slider and pole on a separate track and keeping one pole for port and the other for starboard. In practice, however, it is easy to raise the mast end of a single pole so the outer end can be dipped beneath the headstay(s). This hardware is first class and the system has worked well for many years.*

Right: To raise and lower the mast end of the spinnaker pole, we use a single line. One end is secured to the bottom of the pole slider as the downhaul. The other end is the lift and is reeved through a block above the spinnaker track and then down to the pole slider. This double horizontal Clamcleat mounted at shoulder level on the mast holds both lines perfectly, is simple and neat, and replaces two bulky cleats and an awkward arrangement.

firmly fastened to a substantial fitting, you can raise or lower or pivot the pole with safety; it's when the entire spar is loose and loaded with compression or tension from a sail or sheet that you get into trouble—especially at night or when you are jibing the rig by yourself.

It is not possible to wing out a sail with a clew three feet above deck level (or lower) with a spinnaker pole whose mast end pivots on a hinge point high on the mast. To get around this, we slide the mast end of the spinnaker pole down to clew height on a 12-foot track on the forward side of the mast. It would be easy to put both poles on one sliding fitting, but this would bring down both poles when generally we want only one (we employ both poles only when running with twin headsails). We have, therefore, mounted the mast end of each pole on a separate, independent cast stainless steel fitting (made by Spar Craft of Costa Mesa, California) that allows each pole to revolve, pivot up and down, and swing from the port lower shroud to the starboard lower shroud. Small-diameter lift and downhaul lines that go to a double Clamcleat control each slider. The outer end of each pole is raised by a standing topping lift that in our case runs from the outer end of the pole up to a forward lower mast tang fitting at the spreader base. (It is hard to visualize how well a standing topping lift works with a pole until you try it yourself.)

In the past we called the use of the spinnaker poles "foredeck combat." Now their employment is easy and safe because we have all movement under control. Stowage of the poles up the mast gives us more deck space and keeps the poles from damage.

6. Cockroaches are the plague of all human habitations in the tropics and nearby zones. Ships are especially prone to infestations because of warmth, dampness, darkness, food, lots of places for the pests to live free from harm, and the difficulty of fumigation. Seasoned voyagers to the tropics go to great lengths to avoid bringing cockroaches on board. Old hands prefer to anchor out, never bring cardboard boxes on the ship, and scrupulously inspect all foodstuffs coming by the dinghy (including dipping potatoes and bananas in seawater and in general scrubbing and rinsing all suspicious food).

What do you do if cockroaches are on board? Besides clobbering them with a tennis shoe whenever one appears, the best remedy is to spread boric acid around the edges of the galley and the perimeter of the cabin sole.

Insect powders come and go; boric acid, however, is effective and cheap. In exhaustive tests of various posions, powders, and repellents, scientists at the University of California confirmed that boric acid was "strikingly superior to other insecticides in long-term residual effectiveness." The tests included lethal chemical insecticides, which the cockroaches often learned to avoid. Entomologist Walter Ebeling said that it did no good to add chemical insecticides, sugar, or flour to boric acid. All the additives tended to repel the cockroaches and clearly weakened the effectiveness of the boric acid by itself.[11]

To pre-heat a Primus kerosene burner, we use this clip-on Tilley wick, which is kept in a bottle of alcohol. The wick holds enough fuel to pre-heat the burner, and the system is safe, simple, and quick.

7. We prime our Primus and Tilley kerosene stoves and lanterns with a Tilley wick. This is a little clip-on device that holds a small amount of alcohol, costs less than a dollar, and lasts for a year or so. We store the Tilley wick in a four-ounce jar of priming alcohol, which keeps the wick part (asbestos?) always saturated with alcohol and ready to use.

The advantage of this little device (and I apologize for writing about

My topping lift runs from the boom
end to the masthead and back down
along one of the standing backstays
to the transom. To help lift the boom
when the sail is full of wind, I have a
single purchase on the fall or hauling
part. To keep the block and line out
of mischief, I seized a nylon ring to
the line near the block. The nylon
ring runs up and down the backstay.
I lead the hauling part of the single
purchase to a small block at the back
of the transom deck and then to a
Clamcleat on the outside of the
cockpit coaming at a convenient
place (see description on page 186).

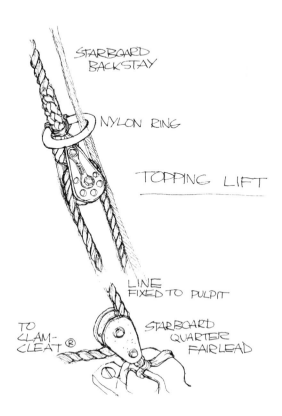

STARBOARD
BACKSTAY

NYLON RING

TOPPING LIFT

LINE
FIXED TO PULPIT

TO
CLAM-
CLEAT ®

STARBOARD
QUARTER
FAIRLEAD

Left: Veteran Caribbean delivery captain Cees de Graaff shows the simple safety harness he devised from a length of ⅝-inch diameter braid and a heavy-duty stainless steel snap hook. You put the line around your chest and tie a bowline with a long free end, which is then passed around your neck and back through the eye of the bowline. The harness is completed by tying a stopper knot or figure eight to keep the end from slipping through the eye of the bowline. The loops around your chest and neck should be somewhat loose, and it takes a little practice to get them the right size. With tension the line pulls against your neck harder than a strap (one reason for the stout line), but the design has worked out well, according to Captain de Graaff. "Except for the snap hook, the harness costs nothing at all," he told me, "because you can use a piece of line cut from an old sheet or anything handy. Line of ⅝ inch or 15 mm diameter is a good size and is plenty strong." It is remotely conceivable that you could get into a situation over the side where, with tension on the harness, it would be impossible to untie the bowline. You should therefore—like any good sailor—always have a knife handy in an outside pocket, particularly if you are wearing oilskins.

Right: My personal harness was made by Westerly Chandlers but is so simple that it can be easily put together with nylon webbing, two stainless steel rings, two snap hooks, and a piece of ⁷⁄₁₆-inch nylon line. The top and bottom straps are colored differently. This design is the easiest to put on of any that I have seen and is simple to roll up for stowage. The line in the photograph is ⅜ inch but should be increased to ⁷⁄₁₆ or ½ inch. Under some conditions a snap hook can trip itself open when clipped to an eyebolt or U-bolt. A new snap-hook design of M. S. Gibb is impossible to open accidentally.

Margaret prefers this harness made by Peter Haward, which is made in the form of a little vest and is easy to put on. Peter Haward is the originator of the formal safety harness, which he developed after a tragic accident in December 1949. Haward has tested many harnesses by "falling overboard" at speeds up to nine knots and feels that it should be possible to get out of a harness under tension. His products have a stainless steel clip that can be unhooked regardless of the pull on the safety line. (The addresses of the different companies are in the back of the book.)

such a small thing) is that when you light the wick you have only a measured amount of combustible fluid available. The fire cannot spread to anything else because there is no more fuel. Years ago we used a plastic detergent bottle with a rubber tube leading from the top to pour a little alcohol into the priming cup. One day the stove needed to be re-primed and the cook failed to notice that a little flame was still burning. When fresh alcohol was poured from the bottle, the fire shot up the tube and the detergent container exploded. Burning alcohol was thrown all over the galley and cook.

We determined to find a safe priming scheme and discovered the Tilley wick (available from Thomas Foulkes or Captain O. M. Watts chandleries in London). Now, after half a dozen years of daily use (and lots of gifts to sailing friends), we feel we have the perfect priming device for kerosene appliances.

8. I run the topping lift from the main boom up to a block at the back of the masthead and then down along one of the standing backstays to the transom area behind the cockpit. This gets the line away from the mast (one less line to slap), and it is handy to be able to adjust the topping lift from the cockpit. Because the lift is sometimes hard to haul on when the sail is full of wind when reefing, I have a single purchase in the fall of the topping lift. This purchase is merely a single block that rides up and down the backstay on a 2-inch nylon ring about ten or twelve feet above the deck. The fall of the topping lift is spliced to the eye of the block. The standing part of the purchase is tied to the stern pulpit. The hauling part leads down from the block and goes through a second small block at the transom and then to a side cockpit coaming, where it is held in a Clamcleat. To deal with the topping lift, you merely lean over the cockpit coaming and either haul on the line or ease it—simplicity itself. Once arranged, this setup works perfectly and seldom needs attention.

As Eric Hiscock suggested many years ago, we use ⅜-inch diameter nylon line for the entire topping lift. This line is ideal, having ample stretch and little chafing tendency on the leech of the mainsail. The line lasts for years and years. The topping lift block at the masthead needs to be of a type that cannot revolve; otherwise the two parts of the topping lift may twist together. In an emergency the topping lift can be used as a main halyard or for other purposes, so the masthead block should be extra strong and securely mounted. I always take up on the topping lift a little when the mainsail is being raised or lowered to prevent possible strains on the leech of the sail.

13

~~~~~~

What Does
World Cruising Cost?

The trouble with writing about the costs of long-distance sailing is that everyone has different standards of living. People's needs and wishes are as variable as the expressions on their faces. One man will drink local lager while another prefers imported bock. My neighbor next door may drive a Volkswagen while the man across the street demands an Aston Martin. Some of my friends wear suits of Italian silk; others are quite content with wash trousers and khaki shirts.

In terms of sailing, a two-speed stainless steel winch costs a hundred-fold more than a simple tackle. Yet both systems will haul in the head-sail sheets. We mustn't forget that many of the most significant trips to the far corners of the world have been made in very simple and small vessels that have little in common with modern racing yachts, whose yearly designs and annual new equipment purchases are as trendy and whimsical as women's high-fashion clothes. A hard chine gaff ketch that's forty years old can get from California to Tahiti just as well as the latest lofty-masted IOR creation. The older vessel may or may not take longer, but what difference does it make? If you're in a big hurry, take a jet airplane.

Coupled with the variability of people's individual demands and resources is the difficulty of defining cruising. There is a lot of talk about trips in small ships, but I have never seen anything written about the different *kinds* of cruising. One person will talk of an afternoon cruise to Green Island out in North Bay. We often hear about a two-week vacation cruise. Someone speaks of six months along the west coast of Mexico. There is the cruise to Bermuda or the Virgin Islands or the ultimate cruise around the world. All of these sorties under sail are certainly valid cruises, which I define simply as *distance sailing for pleasure without regard for a rigid schedule.*

Note that I mention *sailing*. There is a whole world of powerboat and motor sailer touring about which I know nothing. My interest is in small vessels propelled by the wind, and quite free from the noise and fumes of machinery.

The practical problems of long-distance sailing trips are a good deal different from cruises of one or two weeks. The farther the trip, the more important the planning and the more meaningful the cost figures. Obviously, if you go on the one-day trip to Green Island in North Bay and eat out at the restaurant when you get there, your costs are going to be identical with an evening out at any restaurant. As the trips get longer, however, and you go to more remote islands and distant coastlines, you become dependent on your own resources. Comparative expense records from other cruising experiences are helpful.

I equate the cost of a yacht suitable for ocean cruising with the price of a modest house. Like the house, the yacht can be large or small, new or old, run down or shipshape and Bristol fashion. In 1965, I contracted for thirty-five-foot *Whisper*, which cost about $20,000 including sails and a 15-horsepower diesel engine. In 1977 I estimate her new cost would be about double because of inflation.

Regrettably, the initial cost is only the first of many bills. To equip a new cruising vessel costs an additional 25 percent of her purchase price—more than $5,000 in my case (or $10,000 in 1977). This is one reason why it is prudent to consider purchasing a used cruising yacht. You often get a substantial inventory at little cost. Ocean voyaging is a lot different from day sailing or racing around the buoys. When you go to sea for long periods, you need all kinds of things—dinghies, warps, anchors, medical supplies, mountains of food, sextants, stoves, a steering vane, light- and heavy-weather sails, an awning, spare rigging wire, lots of tools, Pilot books, and so on *ad infinitum*. Some of the costs are hard to escape. All chart prices have risen in recent years, and will probably increase further. You may easily need a hundred charts or so for any extensive cruise.

Here Stornoway thunders along with full sail while on a broad reach. Gaff-rigged yachts are marvelous across or off the wind. Their masts are short, massive, and heavily stayed. The sail area is low, and the vessels can generally stand a lot of wind before reefing. Like long dresses or mini-skirts, the popularity of double-enders comes and goes. Colin Archer's name is revered by some and scorned by others. But yachts based on his designs continue to sail the oceans in substantial numbers.

I'm sure everyone knows the old story of the sailor and the marine catalogue. The man went through the book and made three lists. List 1 was of the things *he wanted.* List 2 was of the things *he needed.* List 3 was of the things *he could afford.*

If you are clever with your hands or good at finding sales bargains, you can reduce your expenditures in dollars but your time investment will be heavy. In any case, getting a new vessel ready for sea and working out all her gear not only takes a lot of hard work over a period of time but requires a fair investment. If you have x dollars set aside for a new cruising yacht, I suggest that you spend only ¾x for the yacht and reserve the rest for outfitting, which will cost more than you think.

When you own a vessel that is used a great deal, there is not only the general upkeep but there is an area of work that I call capital improvements. As the sailing years go by, you find various major installations that do not work out for one reason or another. Generally the cost of the change—the labor—about equals the cost of the item itself. For example, *Whisper's* mast developed an alarming S curve after several years of sailing. Our friend Bill Duffin of Sausalito made a magnificent new spruce spar which Margaret and I undertook to finish and rig. But the job took almost a month of half-time work.

One's tastes and desires change, improved gear becomes available, and equipment wears out. You must budget something for new sails, new cushions, new rigging, and so on. The standard of maintenance on world cruising yachts is surprisingly high, because it is important for everything to work and to be in first-class order. To keep a forty-foot vessel in top condition can easily take the full-time efforts of one man.

Finally, however, sailing day comes and we head for the Great Beyond. The check writing has ended at last, because the temptations of the fleshpots and the marine catalogues are no longer available. In many of the best cruising grounds it is hard to· spend any money at all. Or you may only need to purchase a little food now and then. In some of the tropical islands of the South Pacific we found that by doing a few favors for the local people—taking them for a sail or repairing an outboard motor—we got all the food we wanted. Sometimes I was asked for an old pair of trousers, which was always worth two fish and half a dozen drinking nuts. In Alaska we entertained fishermen now and then and were given plenty of salmon and halibut. In the Cyclades and Dodecanese Islands in the Aegean Sea we spent a few drachmas for food, but not many, for there simply wasn't much to eat on some of the small islands. In the Chilean channels we had unlimited supplies of large mussels; in Maine the clams were easy to dig.

One cruising truth emerges: when you are on a sailing passage or visiting obscure islands and little-known coastlines, your financial requirements are low. Many of your meals will be from stores on board, and in effect you will be eating from a food bank. I recall periods of up to two months of not spending a single dollar. When we sailed around Vancouver Island in 1971, our main expense was for an armload of oiled wool for two sweaters Margaret was knitting.

One fast outlet for money is in the big ports, when you produce a two-page shopping list and are tempted to eat out in restaurants. In some places it is easy to get involved in a complex social game with high entertainment costs. I think that sailors on a shoestring budget should avoid big cities and yachting centers.

A few years ago I discussed this problem with Guy Cappeliez, a Belgian doctor, when our yachts were anchored near one another in the Marquesas Islands.

"We like to eat well, but our cruising fund is not too big," said Guy, who was sailing around the world on his blue double-ender *Procax*. "Viviane and I always buy first-class foodstuffs, which we prepare on board the ship. We feel that our meals are infinitely better than restaurant fare, and of course our costs are infinitely less."

Sightseeing in foreign places is part of the fun of cruising. Often you can take the local buses or rent bicycles or a motorcycle. Or you can walk! Sometimes we have entertained people who were so proud of their local area that we got a grand tour the next day. In Ketchikan, Alaska, I recall that Virginia Head, the wife of a logging camp operator, not only urged us to climb the local mountain—"You must see the view from Deer Mountain"—but she accompanied us to the top. Often the sightseeing is easy and close, because you can sail to the very heart of the best places in your vessel.

The increasing number of cruising yachts means that they are not such a curiosity. There is less interest and perhaps less help is offered than in the past. Fifteen or twenty years ago the arrival of a small ship after an ocean crossing meant a newspaper story. Today city editors are bored with yachts unless they get into trouble.

Cruising vessels tend to follow well-worn trails. Numerous yacht clubs, marinas, and cities in the path of these yachts have begun to deal with their nautical visitors on a business basis, rather than as distinguished guests. If you pull into many marinas or yacht clubs these days, a cost-oriented manager may be waiting on the dock with a contract for you to sign in which you agree to pay 40 cents a foot (or whatever) per day starting now.

Lots of singlehanders, cruising couples, and vessels with a crew of three or four do their own maintenance, the exception being an infrequently hired specialist (a sign painter to do the name on the transom, a welder, or a sailmaker). We carry bottom paint, brushes, and many spares bought in bulk to maximize savings.

Charts are a problem because they're necessary and costly. I never skimp, perhaps making a fetish of having lots of them. Cruising people often lend them to one another. The danger, of course, is that an outdated chart will fail to show an important change. If you use old charts, you should certainly have new light lists and Pilot book supplements. It is not difficult to update charts from Notices to Mariners.

Unfortunately, for a sailing vessel even the wind is not free. If you buy $1,000 worth of sails which last for 25,000 miles, the cost works out to be four cents a mile.

Harbor dues have seldom been a factor, although with the astonishing increase in yachting I think we may have to pay harbor charges as is done in many places in Europe.

Most cruising vessels that Margaret and I have met do not have insurance because it is too costly. Years ago we carried hull insurance, but for one trip our premium was raised to 15 percent. When we objected, the underwriter smugly suggested that we cancel, which we did. (The broker is now out of business; we are still sailing.)

I note that the safety record of offshore yachts is reasonably good. I think they should be treated separately as a class and not grouped with novice, marina-hovering boatowners who frequently get into trouble and pester insurance brokers with small claims. An attitude of many companies is that if you are twenty-five miles from land and at sea you are in mortal danger, when the opposite is, of course, true. Big and little ships get into trouble around land; seldom do they founder at sea, and then only to the great drums of publicity. No one ever makes a sound when you pay insurance premiums for ten years and file no claims. I believe that cruising yacht owners are not concerned with small claims but with insurance for catastrophes and would prefer to buy coverage with a high deductible clause, say $500 or $1,000.

Fuel costs for the engine are insignificant. We use about four gallons of oil a week in the Dickinson stove during a cold winter. When we cook with kerosene in warm weather, we use three gallons a month ($1.50), although some of the fuel gets burned in the cabin lights. Personal expenses have torpedoed many a voyage, for even at sea any mortgage charges and loan payments go on and on. Fortunately, I do not own a car, house, or credit cards. I do not subscribe to insurance, a telephone, or use installment payment programs. Medical care is a problem. I like hospitalization in case of a major accident or illness, but insurance now costs $50 a month for two (up from $30 in 1972) and I am uncertain how good the coverage is when you are in a distant country.

In 1973 I wrote:

We believe that we can cruise for $175 a month and have a wonderful time.

The Blue Water Medal is generally awarded annually by the Cruising Club of America for "the year's most meritorious example of seamanship." Since its inception in 1923 the medal has been presented 47 times and has been given to small ship sailors from Argentina, Belgium, Canada, Denmark, France, Great Britain, Sweden, and the United States. Many of the awardees' names are well known in the field of yacht voyaging and include such men as Marcel Bardiaux, Francis Chichester, Vito Dumas, Alain Gerbault, John Guzzwell, Eric Hiscock, Bernard Moitessier, Harry Pidgeon, William A. Robinson, Miles Smeeton, Roderick Stephens, Jr., Eric Tabarly, and H. W. Tilman.

This assumes that the vessel is well prepared beforehand, has no complex machinery or electrical gadgetry to maintain, and that we both watch our expenses, do our own maintenance, and have no shore-based payments. This figure works out to about $1,050 a year per person.

Charles and Liev Kennedy and their son Curtis sailed 36,000 miles on *Kelea* during four years and reckoned their expenses as $1,000 per year per person. Al and Beth Liggett circumnavigated the world on *Bacchus* and figured their costs at $7 a day for two people or $1,275 a year per person. On *Strider* the Heacocks, another cruising couple, reported costs of $3,000 a year or $1,500 each. Bob and Jane Van Blaricom calculated a leisurely England-to-San Francisco trip at $1,350 per person per year.

The average of these five cruising couples was $1,235 per person per year, or about $100 a month. But these trips were made years ago when prices were reasonably stable; in 1977 the costs have doubled because of inflation.

These sums are reckoned on a long cruise with minimal yacht expenses. Afterwards, however, there are usually heavy charges for a major refit and the renewal of spent or broken items. With excellent preparation you can make extensive passages without much cost. Many people have sailed around the world with only two haulouts and little other than the replacement of a sail or two. But continued cruising necessitates substantial expenses for putting the yacht back into first-class condition. From time to time you must buy oilskins and replace worn halyards and sheets. You may lose an anchor, or a winch may pack up. Oars may be lost; the dinghy may vanish. You may need a new propeller shaft bearing or injectors or rings for the engine. Zincs need replacing. A battery may no longer hold a charge. Deck gear and robes are stolen. The anchors and chain may require galvanizing. Woodwork may be broken and necessitate an expert joiner, who will use costly hardwoods and fastenings. The price of haulouts has increased, and the cost of anti-fouling paint has at least doubled, as have the wages of machinists and sheet metal men. All these items are based on the status quo. If you want to replace your winches with a larger size, if you decide on new light-weather sails, or if you allow yourself to have the topsides spray-painted by an expert, your yearly charges will increase by several thousand dollars. Major alterations and the repair of accidental damage are additional categories that must not be forgotten.

A cost analysis of long-time yacht cruising soon shows that the big item is the upkeep of the vessel. Food and miscellaneous personal costs are not high. On *Whisper* in 1976 the expenses for Margaret and me were as follows:

(1) Food	$100 a month or $1,200 a year
(2) Medical (health plan, doctor, dentist)	$70 a month or $840 a year
(3) Personal (clothes, mail, local transport, toilet articles, stationery, books, magazines, gifts, souvenirs, laundry)	$100 a month or $1,200 a year
(4) Maintenance and upkeep of the yacht to a high standard (includes fuel, charts, clearances, and moorings)	$250 a month or $3,000 a year
	$520 a month or $6,240 a year

These costs compare closely with the expenses reported by our friends Michael and Jane DeRidder of *Magic Dragon*, who have sailed widely and far for many years. Elsewhere I have noted that maintenance costs escalate rapidly with increasing over-all length. A mitigating expense consideration, however, is that three or four people (or a couple with two children) can sail on a yacht and the vessel's expenses remain about the same. The food, personal, and medical costs increase, but the yacht's running expenses are no more.

I want to make it clear that this chapter is about traveling and upkeep costs of voyaging yachts that pay their way as legitimate enterprises. I suppose it is possible to bum your way around the world, scrounging meals, hospitality, parts, and services. This is not the way I travel, however. I am not a seagoing hobo, because I don't believe it is ethical. I pay for what I need or trade something I have for an exchange or favor from another person.

Practically all the long voyages have been made by modest, ordinary people with more adventure in their veins than dollars in their pockets. As long as your vessel is sound and well stocked, you have something set aside for emergencies, and there is a little to live on, you can get by. If a person is diligent and willing to work, he can always get a job, even if it's teaching English, painting houses, or typing bills of lading. It's not the work that's important but the cash to continue while the faraway light is still bright in your eye.

Remember that my whole case is based on sailing and going somewhere, not sitting in a marina and talking. Marina disease is a terrible plague! And expensive!

Another scene of happiness and joy. The engine is out for the correction of a few problems while we swing on a mooring in Aburatsubo, Japan. We have lifted the 485-pound engine with the main halyard. Another time, when at anchor in Callao, Peru, we removed the engine and somehow manhandled it (with four men) over the side into a launch. It's remarkable what you can do with patience and the equipment on board. Generally by the time the engine is back in and running, you are so fed up that you feel like reading the burial service and committing the engine to the deep.

14

~~~~~~

The Cruising Engine: Necessity or Monster?

Ever since auxiliary engines were first installed in pleasure sailing vessels, men have compiled long lists of reasons both for having and for not having engines. At one extreme is the purist, who disclaims any alliance with mechanical propulsion. "The natural wind is enough for me," he says loftily—until the wind dies and he wants to get somewhere. At the other extreme is the proponent of the motor sailer, whose life and often existence seem to revolve around large engines and masses of complex machinery.

Without detailing the arguments on both sides, I believe that if you take a vessel with reasonable sail area from an anchor or a mooring in a region where the winds are generally predictable, you can manage without an engine. Long ocean passages usually don't require an engine; it's the ports and headlands at each end that may demand some expert sailing. More rarely an ocean journey may include a portion of the doldrums, where a few hundred miles of powering can take the place of a week of sail slatting and terrible rolling.

In areas where winds are fickle, in regions where tidal streams run like flooded rivers, and for ports with difficult entrances and complex docks and jetties, a small engine can be very helpful. You may lose the wind outside a port with bad weather coming up; you may wish to transit a canal or a narrow strait. You may need to shift your berth at night with an ill wind blowing. It seems to me that all these situations are legitimate uses for a small auxiliary.

The captain of a cruising yacht should be able to deal with these problems under sail alone. Or at least to make a courageous attempt. With patience, light-weather sails, a bit of anchoring now and then, the use of one or two oars, and a few lines to warp the vessel around, you can do astonishing things. Instead of a panic call to the Coast Guard when the wind dies and the engine won't start, you might drop a light anchor and wait for the wind like our forefathers.

Ship handling in narrow or crowded waters is fully as important as navigation or anchoring. Personally, I find that the tactics of maneuvering in difficult circumstances are a challenge, a lot of fun, and eminently satisfying. One of my greatest pleasures is to enter and leave ports under sail. Sooner or later the engine will be out of order anyway, and you will have to sail under marginal conditions. Then the practice will pay off. Competent maneuvering under sail may save your vessel and even your life.

I mentioned oars. On *Whisper* we carry a 13-foot oar, which I lash to the transom. I find that I can scull the yacht at one knot if the water is smooth and there is no current or tidal flow. I suppose some readers will snicker at my mention of oars, but I can assure you that they are a most seamanlike accessory that I have seen employed with skill and results all over the world—not only by local boatmen but by competent yachtsmen as well.

Some of my most pleasant sailing is in very light winds. With ghosting sails on *Whisper* we can glide along at a knot or two, often over water that scarcely shows a ripple. At such times I feel very close to the sea and her moods. You can see fish and sea creatures beneath the surface of the unbroken water. Sounds travel for miles. Sometimes birds circle you curiously. The feeling is one of calmness and tranquillity. It is all spoiled when you turn on the noise and fume machine.

Today there are thousands of cruising yachts tied up at marinas and docks. More are being built and launched every day. The proud owners of these vessels are often anxious to make extensive trips, but as we have seen in these chapters, it is a complex business to prepare a small ship for ocean passages. And an even longer process—five years? ten years? twenty years?—to turn a boatowner into a seaman. The more you learn, the more you realize that you will never know enough.

You can make a distinction between (1) a pure sailing ship, (2) a sailing vessel with a small auxiliary engine, and (3) a motor vessel with auxiliary sails that are used when the wind is favorable, *a sail-assisted vessel*. Most accidents happen to category (3), because many owners of so-called "full-power auxiliaries" are more motormen than sailors and don't know how to maneuver and control their ships under sail. These yacht owners often have no concept of storm management, how to sail an anchor out, how to heave to, and so on. Instead of knowledge and practice, they rely on engines that may work or may not. These expensive vessels are often heavy, with emphasis on accommodations and machinery, and typically have a cut-down ketch rig for easy handling in heavy weather. Unfortunately, such a rig—in combination with the drag of a large three-bladed propeller—gives no light-weather performance at all. I think this design trend is deplorable for long-distance voyaging. People who have sailed long distances know that light-weather performance is most important and that cut-down rigs are ill-advised. I think it is worth repeating that 40 or 50 percent of all winds at sea are 15 knots or less.

An engine will not substitute for seamanship under sail. The confidence that an engine gives to a new boatowner is based on the spurious logic: "I'll be twice as safe with a 60-horsepower engine as with a 30-horsepower." If you own a cruising vessel and don't know how to sail it, you should either hire an experienced man to teach you or attend sailing classes and learn to sail a dinghy. One must serve a bit of an apprenticeship.

In my judgment the only practical engine for a cruising yacht is a diesel. Gasoline is out of the question for three reasons:

1. Acute fire danger from the fuel.
2. High fuel consumption.
3. The difficulty of keeping an ignition system operating in an environment of salt water.

While diesel oil will burn, it is very much less flammable than gasoline, whose vapors are extremely explosive. Yachts with gasoline engines burn up regularly every year. I know, because a former yacht that I owned was destroyed by a gasoline fire, even though I believed I was conscientious about dealing with the fuel. Another time Margaret and I watched in horror when a gasoline-powered ex–Coast Guard vessel blew up with a tremendous 100-foot-high explosion in Sausalito and killed the owner. We saw it happen.

Diesel fuel consumption is about two-thirds that of gasoline; diesel fuel is also cheaper, so the hourly cost is about half that of a gasoline engine.

At cruising revolutions a marine diesel of 10 to 30 horsepower will use only a quart or two of fuel. A diesel requires no ignition system at all. The original investment is more than for a gasoline engine, but the advantages soon compensate for the higher initial price (which is falling each year). Very little carbon monoxide is produced by an oil engine.

A marine diesel is strongly made, with a massive crankshaft, heavy cylinders, and sturdy bearings. Reduction gears are usually fitted to enable an efficient, large-diameter, high-pitch propeller to be driven smoothly and easily hour after hour. A big fixed propeller, however, produces substantial drag when the engine is shut off and the yacht is sailing. The excellent Sabb engines and some models of the Volvo-Penta get around this problem by fitting a feathering propeller actuated by a mechanism within the propeller shaft.

A diesel engine weighs perhaps 25 percent more than a gasoline engine of equivalent horsepower and requires sturdy mounts to withstand its greater vibration. A small diesel can easily drive a 30- or 40-ampere alternator to generate electricity for lighting and accessories such as a powerful belt-driven bilge pump or a refrigeration compressor.

The engines we use are four-cycle models in which the first downstroke of the piston draws in air, which is compressed on the upstroke to about 600 pounds per square inch. At the top of the stroke a small charge of oil is sprayed into the cylinder through an injector. The heat of the compression ignites the oil and the rapid expansion of the gases created by the explosion drives the piston downward. The next upstroke forces the waste gases out the exhaust port and the cycle is complete.

The sole demand of a diesel engine is clean fuel and plenty of air (if it has a protected air intake, the engine will run submerged). You must be scrupulous about running the fuel through a series of filters to remove water and foreign matter. The slightest bit of blockage will clog an

Whisper from aloft while reaching along with a good sailing breeze. With moderate tension on her headstay, the genoa luff sags off to leeward a little but the luff has been slightly hollowed by the sailmaker. Because we were doing a lot of tacking when the photograph was taken, the inner forestay was disconnected and held out of the way on a thumb cleat on the forward side of the starboard spreader. Four lashings keep the dinghy in place, and we have a cover over the anchor windlass to protect it from salt water. Spinnaker poles stowed up the mast help keep the decks clear and uncluttered.

injector and stop the engine. One filter is not enough; generally three are employed. Sometimes a partially blocked injector will pump raw fuel into a cylinder. The engine will run roughly while the raw fuel washes the lubricating oil from the piston and cylinder walls. Suddenly a horrible squealing will announce that the piston has frozen in the cylinder (I spent hundreds of dollars to learn this lesson).

You can guarantee clean fuel if you pay attention to the fuel that goes into the tank and change the fuel filters regularly. If you install an hour meter on the engine, you can put in new filters every so many hundred hours. Or if you don't log a lot of engine hours, it may be prudent to change the filters every so many months. The cost of the filters is trifling compared to their importance.

Ever since a well-meaning but naïve oil delivery man in Western Samoa pumped 20 gallons of sludge into *Whisper*'s fuel tank, I have filtered all the fuel coming aboard. Even in industrial countries it's worth slipping a piece of old nylon stocking over the pump nozzle; it's often astonishing what you find. Every month or two I pump several quarts of fuel from the bottom of the main bilge tank with a small hand pump. As I pump I move the intake pipe of the little pump around the bottom of the tank. I am always amazed at the water and particles of sludge that my midget vacuum cleaner picks up. From the tank my fuel goes to a high-quality cylindrical filter (4 inches in diameter and 8 inches high) with a water drain at the bottom, then to a second filter on the engine which has a superfine screen, and finally to a third filter with a complex paper element.

It is a good idea to have a slight positive fuel pressure in the line between the tank and the injector pump. I have installed a black neoprene squeeze bulb hand pump from an outboard engine in my diesel fuel line. A few squeezes on the bulb give enough pressure to draw fuel from the tank, to fill the filters, and to show up any leaks in the various lines and connections after the system is bled of air.

What size engines do twenty-five- to fifty-five-foot cruising yachts require? You will need a smaller horsepower rating for a diesel than for a gasoline engine because gasoline horsepower is based on *intermittent* usage. Diesel horsepower is based on *continuous* duty. This means that the power of a 15-horsepower Lister diesel, for example, will roughly equal an Atomic Four gasoline engine rated at 25 horsepower.

I believe one to two *continuous* rated horsepower per ton of displacement is sufficient. My friend Tom Colvin has a 10-horsepower Sabb in his forty-two-foot *Gazelle* and reports a steady 4 to 5 knots in calm water.

A 10- or 15-horsepower engine is ample for *Whisper's* eight tons. An engine of this size pushes us along at about two-thirds to three-quarters of hull speed at cruising revolutions, depending on the condition of the bottom of the vessel. An engine of this size has reasonable power for maneuvering and is very easy on fuel, its consumption being measured in quarts instead of gallons, as I mentioned earlier. Best of all, I can hand-crank my engine, a feature of primary importance to me.

There are excellent engines available with hand-cranking capability (Lister, Farymann, the Norwegian Sabb, Volvo-Penta, Kelvin, Yanmar, etc.). These range in size from 8 to 35 horsepower and are quite reliable and adequate for vessels of moderate displacement up to fifty-five feet long. Perkins, Westerbeke, and Mercedes-Benz diesels are superb machines, but they lack hand-cranking capability and are dead fish without electric starters.*

Raw seawater cooling seems quite adequate for these small engines and is cheaper and simpler than fresh-water cooling, which requires an extra pump, tank, plumbing, and generally an oil cooler because of higher operating temperatures.

A second criterion for engine choice is the availability of parts. This is a real problem for long-distance voyagers. In spite of endless claims to the contrary, it is hard to get engine parts when you are in remote places. The big companies are the greatest sinners in this respect, because they have "worldwide networks of dealers" who don't stock the part you want, generally don't give a damn about your small order, and often need to be pressured into ordering your valves or big end bearings or whatever. In my experience, you simply cannot take the word of the factory advertising men that parts will be available when you need them. The truth, I believe, is that the sales volume of small diesels is modest, and it is simply not a paying proposition for dealers in Tahiti and Nassau and Seattle and Guayaquil to stock parts that may never be sold. On *Whisper* I have a two-cylinder Volvo-Penta, and I have repeatedly been unable to purchase rings, valves, thermostats, bearings, and so on—parts that should be available. The answer of the regional dealers is that they will order the parts. But to ease the shipping and customs charges, the dealers often wait until they collect a sizable order. Meanwhile you wait— week after week. In Newport Beach, California, I once marked time for seven weeks to get a tiny thermostat that could have been airmailed from

---

* I have seen these engines started by winding a line around the flywheel and leading it to the main boom, whose end is suddenly heaved on with the topping lift. This is a heroic operation and generally takes three people and some clever work.

In this photograph we are looking vertically downward into the bilge of the
43-foot wooden yawl Cimarron. At the left (toward the bow) we see the
after end of a Perkins 4–107 diesel engine. At the right (toward the stern) is
the exhaust system and muffler, which is based on a homemade waterlift box
constructed of fiberglass. The box is roughly the size of a two-gallon tank, but
the size and shape are not critical. Both the inlet and outlet pipes (1¾ inches
outside diameter in this case) are also made of fiberglass. The inlet (at the
left) stops two inches below the top of the waterlift box. The outlet (at the
right) projects downward to within two inches of the bottom. There is a bronze
drain plug in the bottom of the tank for occasional cleaning or draining
in case of winter layup. Otherwise the waterlift box and pipes are made
entirely of fiberglass, with a number of layers of mat and roving for
strength and resistance to the hot and corrosive exhaust fumes.

In operation the engine cooling water is mixed with the exhaust gases at
the elbow (shown in the small photograph at the left on page 208). The water
and gases flow into the waterlift box until the water reaches the level of the
outlet pipe. The pressure of the exhaust gases forces the water out of the
waterlift box and overboard through flexible hose.

With the engine mounted below the waterline, cooling water will continue
to flow when the engine is shut off because a siphon has been established.

The water will fill the waterlift muffler and then back up into the engine. To prevent this, it is necessary to fit a siphon breaker or a bleed line to the atmosphere to stop the siphon. In the system illustrated, a ¾-inch inside diameter bronze Onan anti-siphon vacuum breaker (shown at the right on page 208) is installed 12 inches above the waterline. The siphon breaker is mounted at the top of an inverted U-shaped line (made of collapse-proof hose) between the water-injected exhaust elbow and the engine cooling water outlet. In other installations the siphon break valve or bleed line outflow is led overboard, sometimes being piped to an elbow at the exhaust line transom fitting. (If this is done, put a high loop in the line to prevent outside water from entering.)

The waterlift box must be mounted below the level of the engine exhaust manifold, but the maximum lift of the water and exhaust gases should not exceed four feet. The box should be located as close to the centerline of the yacht as possible and should be large enough to hold all the water in the pipes that drain into it. The exhaust overboard line needs the usual high loop under the transom (or elsewhere) to prevent water from entering when running hard in big seas.

This system is relatively foolproof, reliable, and easy to install. The fiberglass waterlift box should last indefinitely. There is no costly metal tank to corrode or rust or fall apart from galvanic action (especially at the welds). Additionally, there are no awkward water-jacketed pipes, no flexible metal lines (belly-wrinkle), and there is no need to wind yards of asbestos around hot pipes leading from the manifold. The rubber piping is ordinary flexible marine exhaust hose, which is simple to install. You can make the waterlift box yourself. The whole system should cost no more than $100.

According to long-time sailor Juan Casasco, who made the exhaust system shown in these photographs, the scheme has worked perfectly. "It makes life easier for the serious yachtsman who needs a trouble-free marine exhaust installation," he writes. "I urge all naval architects, boatbuilders, and the yachting industry to adopt this system."

For the last several years the waterlift-box arrangement has been used in Onan marine generators in the United States and by various companies in Europe. The Volvo-Penta Company, for instance, recommends it for all of its small diesel engines. The Volvo scheme, however, uses a waterlift box made of heavy-gauge steel, which will corrode and rust out in time. The Volvo people also insist on a vacuum valve when the distance between the exhaust pipe flange and the waterline is less than 8 inches. The company recommends that the valve be fitted about 20 inches above the waterline.

Left: Ordinary galvanized iron plumbing lasts quite a long time and is simple and inexpensive to replace. Here a reducing T (so called even though it is an elbow) is used to mix cooling water (small pipe) with the exhaust gases (larger pipe). A bit of asbestos—held in place with soft iron wire—has been wrapped around the uncooled part of the pipe.

Right: This Onan anti-siphon vacuum breaker prevents water from backing up into the engine via the waterlift box.

Sweden in three days. The irony of it is that in the days before the dealer network I could purchase directly from the factory and get both immediate airmail service and far lower factory prices. Now I get neither.

The only hope for a far-ranging cruising yacht is to order a comprehensive set of spares months in advance. Buy plenty of gaskets, fuel pump parts, O rings, pump impellers, valve springs, and so on, and don't be afraid to acquire a few complete assemblies—fuel pumps, injectors, alternators, and the like. Probably the most important spare part is a rabbit's foot for frequent stroking!

If the engine parts catalogue shows any special tools, I would buy all the small tools and carefully look over the larger items. I feel it's better to spend fifty dollars now than to be stuck for a special tool in some remote place and have to make the needed puller or wrench or whatever. I once had to remove the flywheel of a Volvo-Penta to replace a front oil seal, and without the special flywheel puller I wasted days and days and in the end spent about three times the cost of the factory-made puller.

You can make a strong case for an air-cooled engine in a yacht, the English Lister being an excellent example. A fundamental fault with a water-cooled engine is that you introduce a hostile, alien substance into the vitals of the engine, certainly the last place you want a fluid that can easily destroy the bearings and delicate machined parts. It is quite logical to keep water as far from a marine engine as possible. Few marine engines wear out; they are destroyed by corrosion from water that gets inside—from a faulty head gasket, bad seals on a salt-water pump shaft, or from water backing up into the exhaust system. A dry exhaust and ducting for an air-cooled engine can be worked out. Certainly in the horsepower range we are discussing, these problems are not insuperable. The advantages of keeping all water away from the engine are considerable. (Incidentally, the lubricating oil in a diesel is usually a rich, thick, lustrous black; if it appears grayish and thin, look for an internal water leak.)

Water-cooled models of Farymann diesels attempt to get the best of both worlds by surrounding the engine cylinders with water-filled plastic jackets (through which seawater is pumped) that are in contact with the cylinders for cooling but whose plumbing is separate from the engine. If you should get a leak from a cooling jacket, the water simply runs into the bilge instead of inside the engine.

The exhaust system of a sailing vessel should have a large gate valve near the engine. When you are sailing, the valve should be closed to keep out seawater. I know that exhaust systems usually have a high upward bend in the exhaust hose to hold seawater at bay, but an accessible, easily closed valve is a positive door *that can be closed for certain.*

And speaking of accessibility, the best mechanic in the world cannot service an engine if it is enclosed on four of its six sides and shoehorned underneath a galley sink or jammed beneath a cockpit with its vitals reachable only by midgets under hypnosis. I just wish that some of the architects had to service the engine installations they design. I am forever being asked: "How many people does your yacht sleep?" I am never asked: "Is the engine accessible for reasonable service?" Certainly the prospective purchaser of a yacht should take a hard look at the engine installation. How much trouble is it to replace or service units at the back and sides? For example, how difficult is it to change the oil filter? Can you remove and replace the salt-water pump at the back of the engine? If you drop tools, where do they fall?

I wrote much of this chapter at Isla Fernandina in the Galápagos Islands, when Margaret and I were anchored next to a handsome forty-three-foot motor sailer named *Vagabond*, which was built in Holland and is owned by a Swedish couple who are sailing around the world. The sturdy blue and white steel yacht was filled with machinery—generating plants, ham radios, electric stoves, pressure water systems, a complex heating system, and so forth.

"Everything works," said owner Lennart Martinson to me one day, "but the price of all this is that I am always fixing something. It's all too much and is seriously interfering with the enjoyment of my world cruise. If I were to do it again, most of these things would remain on the dealers' shelves.

"It's only gradually that I have begun to realize that one's enjoyment is inversely proportional to the time you waste on mechanical annoyances. When maintenance and frustration turn a pleasure trip into drudgery, it is time to re-evaluate one's equipment and vessel."

15

~~~~~~

The Dinghy Problem

The main functions of a dinghy on a yacht are twofold:

1. To get the crew and supplies to and from the shore.
2. To lay out a stout anchor and cable in case of a storm, grounding, or the yacht going ashore.

Even if you habitually sail from a marina dock or a mooring, you should always have a dinghy along adequate enough to put out a suitable anchor in case you go aground. Sooner or later all yachts are stranded; with prompt anchor work you can generally get the vessel off. A delay of even a few minutes, however, can be disastrous. A rigid, proper tender is easy to row and is the only real way to lay out a second anchor against a strong wind, to put out a kedge when accidentally aground, or to take a line ashore or to another vessel.

A further use for a tender is for sightseeing, socializing, and exploring. I carry an excellent rigid dinghy which rows superbly and is a real pleasure to take on a tour of a harbor, especially with one person aboard, when you can get up good boat speed. In the dinghy we generally have a bailer (half a coconut shell is good), a life jacket, a sponge and a 5-pound grapnel with 50 feet of ¼-inch diameter line. I have had hours of silent pleasure rowing about new anchorages on quiet mornings, watching birds wading along grassy shorelines, and skimming along to a local settlement to mail a few letters and to do a little shopping. With two people aboard (one rowing and one in the stern) the dinghy rows less well. With three

adults (one rowing and one each in the stern and bow) the performance
is better because of improved balance and more weight.

When Margaret and I first sailed to foreign ports, we were surprised
at how much we used a dinghy. In most parts of the world, vessels without
important dock business anchor out (if indeed there *is* a dock). For
yachtsmen this is better in many ways. People trouble you less when
you're at anchor. Generally the view is better and your life is quieter.
In the tropics there is more breeze at anchor and the ship can swing head
to wind so that you can use a windsail to funnel air down the front hatch.
You don't scratch and gouge the topsides of the yacht by banging against
rough docks. Insect visitations may be less, and you avoid rodents completely. If there is a wind change, you won't be pinned against a wharf.
Finally, it is easier to get under way from at anchor.

Many river and bay and lagoon anchorages are quite shallow, or there
may be a substantial tidal range, which can mean that some docks dry
out. In the lagoon of Abemama in the Gilbert Islands in the western
Pacific we lay three-quarters of a mile from the main village because the
water shoaled to less than a fathom far from land. Again, at the mouth
of the Tawenjokola River in Ponape in the Caroline Islands we
anchored half a mile from the wharves of the main settlement because
of silting problems. During a summer's sailing in Maine and New Bruns-
wick we stopped at more than fifty anchorages and used a dinghy in all
but a handful.

Anchoring when cruising is usual and preferred. Tying up at a dock is
exceptional.

A good many new boatowners naïvely think that there are fancy
marinas with running water and electricity all over the world. No belief
is more mistaken. We're well used to ferrying water or catching rainfall
in an awning. Except for a few boatyard jobs, we haven't had shore
power aboard for a decade. In most ports visitors anchor out or tie up
with fishing boats. In the Mediterranean or Japan small vessels usually
drop a bower anchor and run a stern line to a wharf. We have used
moorings in Bermuda, Rio de Janeiro, Western Samoa, Valparaiso,
Nantucket, and Newport, to list only a few places. In all these ports
and many more we were pleased to have a good rowing dinghy. Indeed,
the dinghy was the only way to get to and from the shore.

But however good a tender is for transport and for other vital purposes,
it is a bother to deal with on the yacht. The problem is like that of
parking an automobile in a downtown section of a crowded city; it
would be ideal if you could rub a magic lamp and have a genie whisk

the dinghy away, only to have it magically reappear when you clap your hands.

The principal dinghy problem is stowage. On *Whisper* we store our 8-foot fiberglass dinghy upside down on the coach roof immediately abaft the mast. We lash the tender in place with a line passed back and forth over the dinghy from the handrails along each side of the coach roof. We could store the dinghy right side up, but it would require more vertical space, special chocks, and a cover to keep out water. Besides cutting down forward visibility even more, an upright dinghy becomes a general repository for scrap lumber, empty bottles, half-full paint cans, and odds and ends of junk better stowed elsewhere or tossed out. If the dinghy is stowed upside down, it will often cover a coach-roof skylight, which sometimes can be left open at sea to help ventilation. On some yachts the tender can be lashed upside down over the front hatch forward of the mast.

We have a painter spliced to an eye at each end of the dinghy, and to launch it Margaret and I each pick up one end, hold the painters with a little slack, and flip the dinghy over the side into the water, turning over the tender as we let go. This takes only a few seconds. One person can launch the dinghy, but it is easier with two people.

One crewman can recover the boat by bending the bow dinghy painter to the main halyard and winching up the tender vertically until it almost clears the lifelines (this is a good position to throw in a couple of buckets of seawater to wash out beach sand, pebbles, and land dirt). I hoist the dinghy over the lifelines and turn it so that its bottom faces aft, which is easy with the halyard holding the weight. I then pull the stern of the dinghy aft toward the cockpit and lash the stern lightly to the boom gallows (or anything handy), which angles the dinghy at about 45 degrees. If I then lower away on the main halyard, the dinghy drops inverted on the coach roof. (This reads harder than the job is.)

Usually, however, two of us get the boat back on board by simply hauling up on a painter at each end of the dinghy.

I find that one-piece spruce oars are quite good and last a long time. I prefer one-piece oars, because the glues in laminated oars do not stand up to continual wetting and drying out. I used to paint or varnish oars, but—as with a boat hook—the life of oars is a continual series of knocks. It is more practical to leave oars unpainted except for a coat of polyester resin.

Rowlocks (some people call them oarlocks) and rowlock or oarlock sockets are troublesome accessories. In order not to lose them, I slide

This Whisper rowlock socket will never come adrift, because it is through-bolted with four stainless steel fastenings. The large plate distributes the load over an area of 2 x 3½ inches. The socket itself has a bearing depth of 2 inches, and the rowlock is a precision fit. All stainless. Not available commercially.

circular, not horned, rowlocks over plastic oar collars, which I tack to the oars with a few short brass brads. To keep the rowlocks from sliding off the other end, I then either put a hose clamp or tie a Turk's head at the opposite end of the oar collar (see photograph). This way the rowlock cannot get off the oar to fall over the side or to be misplaced. A dropped oar will aways float. My spare oars have spare rowlocks in place.

Most rowlock sockets are made of soft brass, whose rowlock holes soon wear oval-shaped. If the rowlock sockets are galvanized iron, the wear of the rowlocks soon goes through the zinc coating and the bearing surfaces become a rusty mess. But the greatest fault is that rowlock sockets are almost always secured with small, short, easy-to-pull-out wood screws that are totally inadequate. If a rowlock socket comes adrift when you are rowing out to the yacht during a spring ebb or at other crucial times, you can be swept out to sea. To get around this difficulty, I finally had special rowlock sockets made up of small stainless steel plates ⅛ x 2 x 3½ inches with 2-inch stainless piping welded to the plates to take the rowlocks. I bolt the plates on with four 10–24 bolts. This way I have large bearing surfaces on the hull to resist the pressures of rowing, and rowlock sockets that are extremely secure and long wearing (with a touch of grease). If you use commercially made rowlock sockets (the best are Wilcox-Crittenden), I suggest that you bolt, not screw, them in place.

I recommend an extra pair of oars with fitted rowlocks. Also put extra rowlock sockets on board. In a pinch a useful idea to remember is that you can make a vertical tholepin of any small stick (even a ball-point pen). If you cut two small holes through the hull just below the gunwale with a knife, you can lash the tholepin to the boat with a shoelace or a strand cut from the painter. If, in turn, the oar is lightly lashed to the tholepin, you will find that it will do very well for an emergency rowlock and rowlock socket.

Of course, it is handy to be able to scull, a technique I am trying to teach myself. A transom sculling notch is also useful to lead a warp through when running out a line or heaving up on an anchor.

I am not a fan of having a tender in davits for ocean passages. I object to the aesthetics, and the windage aft may interfere with steering in strong winds. I would hate to have a boarding sea strike a dinghy in davits behind the helmsman, although I have spoken with sailors who have had no problems at all. The difficulties of both mounting a wind-vane steering gear and having a dinghy in davits may be insuperable.

We never tow a dinghy, for I consider this to be an unseamanlike procedure which is liable to result in loss of the tender, a line around the rudder or propeller, or more serious problems from inattention because of fumbling with the dinghy in worsening weather. We find that it only takes about ten minutes to get a dinghy on board and to lash it down.

Excellent rigid dinghies are built of many materials—aluminum (generally riveted), fiberglass, and all forms of wood. Prams are often made of thin plywood with a layer of fiberglass cloth and polyester resin on the outside. Many dinghies are constructed of thin—say $\frac{1}{8}$-inch—fiberglass moldings which have little strength in unsupported panels. However, with the addition of a few stringers, molded-in buoyancy tanks, seat supports, knees, transom braces, mast steps, wooden gunwales, and so on, the strength increases rapidly. My favorite is cold-molded construction—two or three layers of 4- or 5-inch wide strips of $\frac{1}{8}$-inch hardwood laid up and glued over a male mold to make form-following plywood that is quite strong, light, and easy to fasten to. My friend Raith Sykes used a fiberglass dinghy for a male mold and constructed a splendid nine-foot cold-molded tender which, when varnished, was both handsome and lightweight.

A dinghy needs a heavy brass or stainless steel (no iron, please) rubbing strip on the bottom of its keel to protect it from rocks, coral, and gravel when the boat is dragged across beaches. On my tender I have a 9-foot length of $\frac{3}{4}$-inch stainless steel half round that curves down from the bow and runs all the way to the transom. A bronze lifting eye goes through the strip to hold it at one end. The metal is through-fastened along its length with 10–24 bolts or 1¼-inch No. 12 stainless steel screws to make a really tough bottom bumper that will never tear off and greatly increases the strength and utility of the dinghy.

A tender should also have an encircling bumper strip of soft rubber, old fire hose, 2-inch diameter manila line, or split vinyl hose fastened entirely around the gunwale and stern to minimize knocks, chafe, and noise between the tender and the things it touches. If the bumper strip is screwed or nailed to the upper outer corner of the gunwale, impacts will in time tear off the encircling bumper. A better scheme is to fasten the strip an inch or so below the outside of the gunwale so that any impacts will merely compress the bumper strip.

All dinghies need built-in buoyancy to make them and their occupants unsinkable. The buoyancy can be flotation bags, large pieces of closed-cell foam, metal tanks, or closed flotation areas built into the hull.

There are four main types of dinghies suitable for use as tenders for yachts. None of these small boats are lifeboats or life rafts, which are something entirely different. The main requirements for a yacht tender are good rowing and load-carrying ability combined with safety, reasonable weight, and ruggedness. A small high-performance sailing dinghy with oars added afterwards is the wrong approach. In reality a 7- or 8-foot boat is only a tolerable dinghy at best; a 9- or 10-foot tender is much more satisfactory, because it is safer, easier to row, faster, has a larger carrying capacity, and is better suited to a small sailing rig, perhaps with one sail and a leeboard. If you have room, by all means take the largest small boat you can.

The first type of dinghy has a pointed or rounded bow, a transom stern, a flattish floor, and a long skeg. Generally these dinghies—with attractive curved lines—are the best boats for rowing, but they are heavier and more costly because of their curved construction.

The late Hamish Davidson of Vancouver, who built *Whisper's* dinghy *Wisp* along with 8,000 others during a career that dated back to World War II, felt that a good rowing dinghy needs a modest keel carried back to the transom in the form of a straight skeg to keep the dinghy on course. "In addition, I favor a reasonably pointed bow to help the craft slice through small seas," Davidson once told me in his West Georgia Street shop. Davidson also argued for ample sideways and fore-and-aft curvature of the hull lines at the stern to allow water to flow away easily. "Plenty of beam and freeboard help the load-carrying ability without hampering performance as long as there is adequate hull curve," he said.

The second variety of yacht tender is a pram, with a flat transom at each end and hard chine construction, with a slightly veed and cambered bottom. Around 8 feet long, they are easy to make from kits or plywood sheets, row reasonably well, and can be sailed. An adequate second choice.

Flat-bottomed dinghies make up the third class and are simply water-going bathtubs with flat bottoms, a kind of giant soap dish made of inexpensive plastic. A flat-bottomed boat or barge has high initial stability but, once it is inclined to a certain point, will flip over with no advance warning. An example is the Sportyak. These tenders stow easily, are unsinkable, and can transport a lot of weight. They row poorly, however, and with their low freeboard are easily swamped. Not recommended.

The fourth class of yacht tenders comprise folding, take-apart, and inflatable boats. In many sailing yachts under thirty feet, such dinghies are the only possible ones. This class of dinghy will always be popular, because it is an attempt through clever (though often cumbersome) design to get a larger dinghy that collapses for convenient stowage on board.

Prout Marine on Canvey Island in Essex, England, used to make a small folding dinghy with wooden sides, a canvas bottom, and canvas ends, whose fabric portions folded together athwartships so that you got an almost two-dimensional parcel about the size of a seven-foot surfboard that was easy to tuck away. The Prout dinghy seemed a ramshackle affair, but many a yachtsman swore by his. I have always hoped that a clever manufacturer would update the design with modern materials and make a larger model. The design is simplicity itself, and a $100 Prout could be sold by the hundreds—perhaps thousands.

I once had a two-piece take-apart dinghy called a cup and saucer. The two halves of the tender were joined at the center with alignment pins and clamps. Each half was about four feet long, and one section nested inside the other to make an easily stowed box. The concept of the dinghy was excellent, but the structure needed a few improvements. Ed Boden of *Kittiwake* fame has recently designed a 12-foot dinghy made of three 4-foot sections that nest. A Dutch builder (Jachtwerf Zuiderzee B.V., Julianaweg 145, Volendam, Holland) offers a 14-foot 5-inch roomy plywood dinghy that knocks down into nesting halves. This Dutch tender is quite a proper rowing and sailing dinghy with two sails that total 86 square feet. Under light-weather conditions it might be used as a lifeboat.

At least you would have a chance of helping yourself. The beam is 4 feet 11 inches.

The inflatables are well known (Zodiac, Pirelli, Callegari, Avon, etc.) and have the advantage of requiring little stowage space, although inflating and deflating each takes ten or fifteen minutes (why not use a pump to extract the air?). These tenders have excellent load-carrying ability and are almost impossible to capsize. They are perfect for visitors not used to tippy dinghies, for landing on surf-washed beaches, or among rock-strewn shorelines. Their fabric is surprisingly tough and durable. The smaller models are quite easy to haul up on land or a dock and to store with a friendly shopkeeper or harbor master. In my opinion, however, the inflatables have two major disadvantages.

They are very expensive. Even the cheapest model costs three times or more as much as a rigid dinghy. Many necessary items—oars, engine mount, floorboards, etc.—are extra. Not only do thieves like them, but sometimes it is quite hard to leave an inflatable at a dock because children find them fascinating.

The rowing performance of inflatable dinghies is abysmal. In strong wind and sea conditions it may be impossible to lay out an anchor, which, as we have seen, is a vital and important business for the tender of a cruising yacht. The glib-tongued sellers of inflatables (most of which are sold to fair-weather boatowners) try to gloss over this basic fault. I note that the advertising photographs with oars are always taken in smooth water with crews of smiling, bikinied girls, not of a cold and wet sailor trying to manhandle a fifty-pound anchor on a horrible and nasty night.

The performance of an 8- or 9-foot Avon dinghy with oars or a 2- or 3-horsepower engine is truly pathetic when heading into even a light chop. With three adults aboard, the performance reminds me of a centipede crawling over a bundle of broomsticks.

I refuse to have an outboard engine on board because of the noise and fire danger of gasoline, but if you can tolerate an outboard, I think you are much better off with a slightly larger Zodiac or Avon (or other make) sport type, with inflatable side and bow buoyancy tubes, inflatable keels, and a plywood floor and transom. Depending on the model, such craft take an outboard of 8 to 20 horsepower. If the engine has a forward, neutral, and reverse shift, you can with practice maneuver the dinghy astern and in close quarters and use it to lay out an anchor. Such a craft has better speed and is quite good for traveling long distances around harbors and islands. But a large inflatable and outboard can cost a surprising amount and is highly attractive to thieves. Some owners make it a policy to put the dinghy aboard at night and to chain the engine and dinghy to a pier or float while ashore (watch out for a rising tide).

You can make a good argument for carrying two tenders on board a cruising vessel—a rowing dinghy for the principal tender and an inflatable for a spare or second. If you are at anchor with two or more people on board and one person goes ashore for any reason, the other person(s) is marooned until the first person returns. Also, a second dinghy gives you an alternate for different conditions. You have a second choice if one boat is damaged, lost, or stolen, a real consideration in remote places.

To keep the dinghy quiet while *Whisper* is at anchor, I usually drop a fender between the yacht and the tender and tie it up alongside with short fore and aft lines. Or we stream it aft if there is any wind or tidal stream. If the dinghy persists in being unruly, you can put out a spinnaker pole and haul the boat away from the yacht a foot or two with an endless line rove through a block at the end of the spinnaker pole and tied to one end of the dinghy. Or the same with a stern anchor line.

16

~~~~~~

Questions and Answers

Q. *"What sails should I buy for my new cruising sloop? I'm short of money."*

A. For a bermudian sloop I would buy five sails. A mainsail, a storm trysail, a medium-size genoa, a working jib, and a storm jib. This basic inventory favors the heavy-weather end of sailing, but you must have storm sails in case of strong winds. You can add a light-weather drifter and a large genoa at a later date.

I do not recommend a spinnaker for a short-handed cruising yacht. A spinnaker can be a marvelous sail—easy to put up and with the pulling power of a mule. Getting the sail down is sometimes difficult, however, and if the spinnaker becomes wrapped around the headstay at night, you

Naval architect John Atkin designed this 7.3 metric ton brigantine for Dr. John Osborn, an enthusiastic fan of square-riggers. Perhaps a bit impractical in an over-all length of only 32 feet, and complicated with a maze of masts, booms, spreaders, yards, stays, and shrouds, plus a spiderweb of special lines to control the three square sails, Anna Maria was nevertheless taken to Mexico by her California owner's son, who had a marvelous cruise and returned home full of praise for the vessel. Anna Maria has 70 different running lines, 40 blocks, and some 2,000 feet of running rigging. It is interesting to compare this rig with Jester's sail plan in the photograph on page 298.

have a real problem, particularly if you must change course and go to windward. Even if the sail blows out after it has wrapped around the headstay, the remnants may prevent the hoisting of a headsail.

You should share your cruising plans with your sailmaker and let him know that your life may depend on his good work. No trial balloons or experiments, please.

I recall that a few years ago the *Spray*, the publication of the Slocum Society, had a horror story about a sailmaker who was trying out a new sewing machine with a novel thread-tensioning device. His unfortunate customer went offshore and the stitching simply ripped away from *brand new sails*. The poor sailor had no choice but to sew and sew and sew. He used up all his thread and was obliged to finished up with dental floss. When he finally made port and his hands had healed, he telephoned the sailmaker.

"Bring in the sails sometime and I'll try again," said the sailmaker. The sailor was last seen sewing a noose.

Fortunately this story is the only one I've ever heard about an irresponsible sailmaker; all I've known are as honest as Maine fishermen.

If possible, get the sailmaker to measure your vessel before he cuts the sails. It's surprising how many masts and booms have lengths that are different from those specified on the architect's plans. When the sails are delivered, arrange for the sailmaker to go out with you so you can try the sails together. Be sure to set every sail and to work out the sheeting arrangements. Practice tying in all the reefs or using the roller reefing gear in the same manner that you will be when you are cruising. If there are any problems, the sailmaker can then deal with them. You can get extra battens, hanks, chafing patches, and repair materials at this time. Sailmakers are very knowledgeable people, and I always learn a lot when I go out with these specialists.

I want to emphasize the advantages of getting a sailmaker to measure your spars and to go sailing with you. While the workmanship of the Lee Lung loft in Macao may be impeccable, what do you do if there has been a misunderstanding or error? How do you rectify a mainsail cut eight feet too short on the hoist when the sailmaker is ten thousand miles away and you have just fought the shipment through customs after a long wait? If you decide to order sails at long distance, measure everything carefully and type out the order. Then have a friend re-measure and write out the specifications independently. Finally, compare the measurements. Send Polaroid close-up photographs and dimensioned sketches of the outhaul and gooseneck fittings, and be sure to tell the sailmaker the type and size of slides on both the mast and boom tracks. Better yet, send samples of the slides. The sailmaker will need to know the halyard and tack arrangements and the sizes of any special snap shackles or fittings so he can make the eyes and splices at the tack and head to fit your hardware.

I specify the best quality Dacron material and order triple stitching for every seam. I ask for $\frac{1}{16}$-inch thick leather to be sewn under each hank along the luff of the headsails to keep the hanks from chafing the fabric around the luff rope or wire. I have a row of 1-inch grommets (sewn-in metal rings covered with circular brass thimbles) spaced along the luff of the trysail so the sail can be laced to the mast in case of problems with the track. The circular brass thimbles should be smooth and rounded, not lumpy and wavy. Ideally, all such thimbles should be heavy stainless steel, but these require a powerful hydraulic press that is often not available. I ask for three closely spaced slides to be put at the head of the trysail. The words "tack," "head," and "clew" should be stenciled on the appropriate corner of every sail. The letters should be large, be put on both sides of the sail, and be horizontal (not parallel to the nearest edge). Such lettering is of great help when changing sails. Each sail bag should be a different color, be labeled, and have a handling strap at the bottom.

We carry the tacks of headsails about 24 inches above the deck to keep water out of the sails and to prevent the foot of the sails from chafing on the lifelines. I like to have the clews cut as high as possible, which both helps visibility and makes it easier to wing out the sails for running because the pole is at a more convenient height.

If you need battens to support the roach of your mainsail, you might consider thin plastic battens, which can be carried in drop-in-type pockets made of *two* thicknesses of material. After the battens—with smoothly rounded ends—are slipped into the pockets, you can put a few quick hand stitches across the openings to prevent the battens from escaping. Batten pockets should not fall on panel seams, because if you need to repair the seam, you must first remove the batten pocket, which is a good deal of trouble. With roller reefing, the lower battens should be parallel with the main boom, not at right angles to the leech.

If you want a mainsail without battens, the leech of the sail will have to be cut with a hollow in it. This makes the headboard superfluous, and the battenless mainsail will then be very much like a genoa. I think you will find that the slightly reduced area is of little consequence and that freedom from the expense and trouble of battens and batten pockets

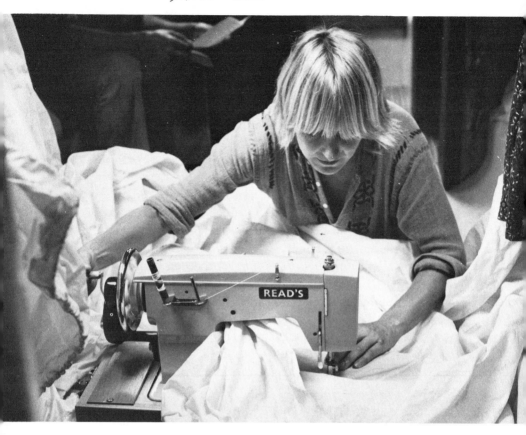

Lisa Pittoors repairs a torn sail with a zigzag stitch on her English-made Read's sewing machine. This rugged machine works very well either by hand or with an electric motor (various voltages are available). The machine can easily handle many thicknesses of heavy sail fabric. Sometimes (as in the photograph) it is troublesome to pull the heavy bunched material of a large sail through under the arm of the machine when a seam is sewed. The job is often easier with two people—one to guide the material while the second sews. The machine can make many kinds of different stitches, and with practice a clever person can sew awnings, sail covers, and clothes as well as sails. The machine is heavy, however, and is one more thing to buy and stow and to protect from salt water. For a yacht under 40 feet it may be more expedient to sew by hand.

is a big gain. Also, it is easier to hoist a mainsail without battens, which may jam behind a lower after shroud if it is inconvenient or impossible to head into the wind.

Sailmakers agree that battens and batten pockets are their biggest repair items. Battens exist only as rule-cheating devices to gain un-measured area for racing anyway, or, more rarely, for use in high aspect ratio staysails or narrow jibs with nervous leeches.

Earlier in the book I discussed the use of all-Dacron halyards. I prefer all-Dacron luff ropes for the same reason—much simpler furling and stowage of the sails. Flexible wire of 7 x 19 construction of ⁹⁄₁₆-inch diameter has a strength of 3,900 pounds; for ¼-inch, 6,600 pounds. Half-inch braided Dacron line has a strength of 6,200–6,800 pounds. The sail with a Dacron boltrope is infinitely easier to pull down and to stuff into a sail bag.

At one time I shopped around for sails at the lowest price. I now realize that price quibbling is ridiculous. The sails are the primary es-sential for propulsion, and for offshore work you want the best material, the most expert cutting, and the finest workmanship. We all know that for a sail to give good performance it must have a smooth airfoil shape when filled with wind. To produce the proper parabolic curves, the cloths of adjacent panels are carefully overlapped when the material is positioned and cut; the foot and luff of the sail are curved and designed for certain tensions. It takes a sailmaker years to learn these technical skills. Plus all the problems of sewing the slippery Dacron together and completing the intricate finishing details. A good sail has to be expensive.

While we all owe a lot to the wisdom and developmental skill of sailmakers who cut racing sails, we are not really concerned with Cunningham holes, Barber hauling, booms that bend, hydraulically controlled stays, foot zippers, and super-light materials. A cruising vessel needs well-made basic sails; we don't require the racing extras. I don't mean to suggest that cruising sails need to be super-heavy and cut like barge awnings. We want strong, light, easy-to-furl, and well-setting sails without frills.

Q. *"What do you do at night when you're at sea?"*
A. This is a common question. Some people think we take down the sails and go to sleep. Others believe that we anchor every night with five miles of chain in a depth of 1,000 fathoms. On *Whisper*—as with most vessels at sea—we carry on around the clock. If we stopped at dark, our progress would be halved and we would never get anywhere.

We can generally get the vessel to steer herself, which means that someone doesn't have to hold the tiller every minute. If the weather is settled and the yacht is going well, we don't touch a thing when the sun goes down. If some nasty-looking clouds are around, however, and we have been on the verge of a sail change, we may swap headsails and pull down a reef in the mainsail while it is still light. We keep a careful lookout at night, especially in shipping lanes and in fishing areas, much more than during the day, when other vessels can see our sails. Staying up half the night means that you must sleep during the day.

Margaret and I know *Whisper* well, and we can easily hand a sail in the dark in case of a squall. As mentioned in Chapter 4, we find it simpler and quicker (and easier on the hands) to use halyards of all-Dacron line. We have two lights on the mast if we need to sort out something. If the vane is steering, we try to wear safety harnesses.

When conditions require us to steer, Margaret and I take turns three to four hours at a time. If the navigation is attention-demanding and your watch is occupied with lights and buoys and shipping, the time passes quickly.

To improve night vision, we use red-coated bulbs in the compass and over the chart table, and I try to banish white lights. In addition to an Aldis signaling lamp, we keep a flare gun loaded with a white flare in case an approaching ship doesn't see us.

In practice the steering vane usually guides the yacht while one of us spends a lot of time standing in the companionway with his arms resting on the hatch runners. We check the compass course, look around, perhaps watch the disappearing lights of a ship, and see how many stars and planets we can identify. In many ways the quietness of night is the best part of the twenty-four hours.

Q. "How do you handle laundry on board a yacht in out-of-the-way places?"

A. Laundry is a constant problem, because in many areas of the world there are no washing machines and no commercial laundry facilities. In addition, fresh water is usually limited on board.

In some places you can take a bag of laundry ashore, find a sparkling stream—often in beautiful surroundings—and then carry on in the time-honored way by using a bar of soap, scrubbing on a smooth rock, rinsing well, and then spreading the clothes on bushes to dry. An old-fashioned washboard is easier on the clothes than a rock, which takes a heavy toll of buttons. Another scheme is the two-bucket system, either on the foredeck or at the village pump. If you do the washing on deck, it helps to soak the clothes overnight in soapy water to loosen the dirt. Put additional detergent on extra-soiled places and use bleach in the soaking water, because clothes washed in cold water tend to get gray after a while. The problem with the bucket system on deck is not the washing but the rinsing, because it takes a lot of water. Salt water can be used for washing and the first and second rinses (to get out the soap), but the salt water *must* be followed by a thorough rinsing in fresh water; otherwise the clothes will never dry. Bernard Moitessier claims that if you let clothes or towels flap vigorously in a breeze, the salt crystals will fly out. I have my doubts about this and have lost too many clothes over the side to allow my washing to do much violent flapping. Besides, I can't stand the noise.

For heavily soiled laundry you can put a galvanized iron bucket of soapy water and clothes on the stove and boil the water for a few minutes. But you must be careful that a large bucket of clothes doesn't overbalance a gimbaled stove and upset.

During passages with strong tropical rain we sometimes do a bit of laundry by plugging up the cockpit drains and using the cockpit as a tub. We wash only small items, however, because drying sheets at sea is impossible. At anchor in the tropics it is easy to dry clothes in the sun, which bleaches the cottons and makes them smell fresh and nice. In the tropics the laundry is mostly sheets and towels—not many personal clothes—and if you do a few things every day or two, you can stay ahead of the job. Be sure to use lots of clothespins when you hang things up *even if it is dead calm,* because as soon as you turn your back, a gust of wind will whisk the clothes away. Take plenty of clothespins, for they are forever falling over the side. In the high latitudes, drying clothes is more difficult; sometimes our diesel stove is festooned with socks and underwear.

Of course, you always hope there will be an inexpensive laundry in the next port.

Margaret has a kerosene iron which she uses to touch up our shoregoing clothes from time to time. Not many people have seen kerosene irons, and the few times visitors have been on *Whisper* when Margaret was ironing they were amazed at her nifty little red Tilley iron and a neat pile of beautifully ironed laundry. The technique may seem stone age, but the results are perfect.

Q. *"How practical is it to ship a yacht a long distance?"*
A. There is a good deal more of shipping yachts by sea or truck or road trailer than you might realize. In the United States there are several trucking firms that have substantial traffic between Florida and California. Europe is crisscrossed with specialized shippers. It pays to shop widely, for the rates vary by astonishing amounts. If you are considering shipping by sea, you might do well to inquire personally among ship's

captains who are going your way. There is such a thing as captain's option (variously titled). Discuss any shoring or cradle arrangements, and be sure the deal includes both on- and off-loading, because the stevedoring charges in some ports are scandalous. I have heard of a rate of $4,000 for a 33-foot sloop between Athens and Lima, and I have knowledge of a $750 charge for a 36-foot vessel between Amsterdam and San Francisco (done by means of captain's option).

Hauling thirty-foot yachts on trailers is common. A few years ago John and Pati Letcher had their twenty-five-foot cutter *Aleutka* trucked from the west to the east coast of Mexico. Recently several yachts have been taken overland from the Red Sea to the Mediterranean via Israel to bypass the Suez Canal.

If you want to make sailing trips in distant places but dislike ocean crossings because of the time involved or for other reasons, you might consider a yacht design that is particularly easy to ship. For example, Mr. S. A. Simpson and his wife shipped their thirty-foot yacht *Iota* from Sydney to Taiohae Bay in the Marquesas Islands on the merchant ship *Caledonien* and then sailed with mostly fair winds through the various island groups of French Polynesia. Simpson had limited vacation time and wanted to sail in selected places, so he chose a design that was easy to load and didn't require a complicated cradle for shipment. His thirty-foot Waterwich ketch is a barge-type yacht with an almost flat bottom, leeboards, a simple lifting sling, and masts in tabernacles so the little vessel "can be carried as deck cargo cheaply and without fuss." With lifting slings that attach to keel bolts, masts that collapse for stowage, and a small shoal-draft hull that requires no cradle at all, shipping is a cinch. Another point in favor of Simpson's choice is that shipping companies like cargo that is easy to load and may quote more favorable rates.[12]

A built-in lifting sling makes hauling for bottom painting or shipping quite simple and trouble-free. The sling (made up and kept on board) can be fastened to keel bolts (by way of overhead ventilators or access ports through the coach roof) or shackled to large eyebolts on the deck, in the case of a steel yacht. If a lifting sling is considered at the design stage, it can be made for little cost.

Q. *"What do you do about bumboats?"*
A. I hope they'll go away.

Sometimes the little boats that come out to see you when you anchor in a new place are simply curious. It takes a bit of enterprise to paddle

Why not a bit of pattern and color on sails? This vestigial U.S. flag on the mainsail of a small Herreshoff design is great fun. Psychedelic colors may not wear well, but an occasional bit of design and a color other than blank white can be distinctive and personal.

or row or motor out to you, and the person in the bumboat wants something—a look at the yacht, cigarettes or mayonnaise, employment, a passage to the next port, or to sell local guide service, ice, laundry service, girls. . . . In the West Indies we once had a delightful evening by hiring a steel band that operated entirely from a small pulling boat. In Kos in the Dodecanese Islands a charming chap named George—who turned out to be an ex–Spitfire pilot—took us around town and showed us where to shop and saved us his modest fee ten times over. At Atka village in the Aleutians a bumboat full of teen-agers suggested a better anchorage, helped us move, and carried out a second anchor.

Margaret and I show *Whisper* to anyone who asks to see her. Believe me, we have shown her to thousands of people. This is sometimes a bore, but we oblige and try to answer reasonable questions. We also ask a few questions ourselves (Village stores and shops? How is the harbor in case of storm? Thieves? Where can we buy vegetables, fish, bread, fruit? Drinking water? Local buses? Attractions?).

If the bumboat is difficult and becomes a bother, I tell the owner that I'm tired and want to sleep and ask him to come another time. Or I begin doing a job on deck and ignore him; generally the bumboat will go away. Don't be too short with bumboats. You never know who might be on board.

Somewhere in the Portuguese Atlantic islands a newly arrived yacht was visited by a bumboat sculled by a man dressed in an ancient business suit and a particularly tattered shirt and tie. The man took off his hat and began to speak and tried to give the captain something, but he was waved away by the impatient owner of the yacht. The owner's wife came on deck and listened to the man, who turned out to be a steward bearing an honorary membership card from the local yacht club.

Q. "My husband is very strong. Unfortunately I am not. How can a 100-pound woman sail a 43-foot ketch with heavy gear?"

A. If the gear is too heavy, you need mechanical assistance—winches for the sheets and halyards and a windlass to recover the anchors and chain. On Whisper we have seven mechanical aids: two powerful two-speed sheet winches, three small halyard winches, one reefing winch, and a two-speed hand-operated anchor windlass with a pulling power of 900 pounds. I consider these devices indispensable. On your ketch you might want additional winches for the mainsheet and perhaps the mizzen halyard.

The nastiest job on a yacht is to lift the anchor (often dripping with horrible black mud) on deck after the anchor has been raised to the stem-head by the windlass. If you do this by hand, you have to lift at a bad angle while leaning out over the pulpit, and you are liable to strain your back. It's not hard to design a bow roller scheme so that you can employ the power of the windlass to pull the anchor on deck or on top of a roller on the bowsprit (such a system also makes it easier to let the anchor go).

We routinely hoist our rigid dinghy on board with the main halyard to get away from another awkward lifting job. Our halyard winches make it easy to haul a person aloft in a bosun's chair.

I would plan for adequate sheet and halyard winches and a powerful anchor windlass right from the start. If you budget the cost over several years, the shock is not too great. I hold no brief for overloaded, inadequate winches that are liable to fail and are so much work to use that you gain little. Marginal winches ruin sailing pleasure by making tacking an event for supermen and gorillas. If your husband won't budge, give him a set of Barient or Barlow or Lewmar winches for Christmas. He'll be so pleased with the polished stainless steel and the clicking ratchets that he'll never notice the bill on January 15. You can halve the cost of a pair of sheet winches by mounting a single winch in the center of the cockpit or elsewhere and leading the sheets to it in turn.

You might learn to use a handy billy, a portable multiple tackle run between a strong point and a line that will increase your hauling power by four. Tackles are more cumbersome and slower than winches, but the lines and blocks are usually on board. You can read all about tackles and complex purchases in *Rigging,* by Harold Calahan (Macmillan, 1940).

If all else fails, you had better recruit a couple of strong boys about sixteen. But then you'll spend all your time cooking for them.

Q. *"How do you handle money and mail when you go off on long trips?"*

A. I believe the best way to carry personal funds for world voyaging is in small denomination ($10 and $20) American Express traveler's checks. The reason I select American Express is that the company is by far the best known; the checks look familiar and are accepted. These words no doubt make you think that I am a hireling of American Express, but I have seen checks of Thomas Cook, National City Bank, Bank of America, and others refused many times simply because the checks were unfamiliar. My wife and I each take half of whatever funds we have so that either of us can deal with money matters if the other person is absent or ill.

Letters of credit are not satisfactory. The sums are too small, the correspondent banks are often found only in distant metropolitan centers, and the whole apparatus is time-consuming and cumbersome. I once had funds sent to Japan, but the receiving bank did not have my sending bank's authorized signature on file and would not honor my order. The bank officers were very sorry but unmoving. They sent off a cable at once; nevertheless I was stuck in a strange city without funds after a long train ride from a coastal port. If you have money mailed to you directly, be sure to specify a formal bank check; some savings-and-loan associations issue glorified personal checks that are quite non-negotiable in foreign places.

We also tuck away a few new one-dollar, five-dollar, and ten-dollar U.S. bills, which are often useful. We take half a dozen cartons of cigarettes, which are even more negotiable. In remote areas credit cards are worthless. In many Pacific island groups there are no banking facilities at all; the governor or his staff or the post office takes care of money affairs, changing a check or forwarding a payment. Another useful dodge is to buy a little currency of the next country on your itinerary ahead of time, particularly if you plan to stop at outlying islands before you reach the main business areas. The storekeeper in a small village may not accept your national currency, but if you had the foresight to buy some of his local currency you can deal with him.

Of course, one blessing of remote places is that you can't spend much money. You are obliged to be frugal whether you want to or not.

Credit cards are more helpful in populated centers with air traffic, which means tourist facilities. In Tahiti, American Samoa, Suva, St. Thomas, Burmuda, Athens, Barbados, and many other places you can use credit facilities to buy stores and to obtain small sums of cash.

Mail is a problem that I have not solved. Our mail is sent to a friend who opens everything, throws out the junk mail, puts a collection of letters and magazines into a big envelope, and airmails it—a single parcel— to us after we have sent our latest address. If we are waiting for mail, we can leave as soon as the single parcel arrives, because we know there won't be a second unless we have asked for it.

We leave our friend a sum of cash for postage and for special purchases. He deposits any incoming checks at our bank. He does not forward mail unless he has definite instructions. This arrangement seems foolproof; in practice it is not.

The mail systems of the world seem to be more cluttered and dilatory than ever in spite of high postal rates. Delays can be tolerated but disappearances cannot. The present mail arrangements in the Galápagos Islands, for instance, are quite hopeless, and on a recent visit I elected to have no mail sent there at all. In Peru half the time the mail from New York or Europe comes in three or four days; the other half of the time it doesn't arrive at all. In Chile the clerk at one post office window charges rates that are different from the next window. In the heart of metropolitan Rio de Janeiro a mailbox may not be emptied for a week or longer.

Packages—all packages arouse suspicion—are another difficulty because they are promptly impounded by customs. The packages may contain urgent and important items, but the customs people of the world know no urgency. All you can do is to argue and hope. Once you have found out that the package has arrived and exists, at least you have a chance. Fifty percent of the time the package simply disappears. If it is really important, air freight, though costly, is safer. If you have the waybill number cabled to you in advance, at least you can meet the plane and, with luck, persuade the customs man to let you take the package on board as you sail away.

To succeed with money and mail in foreign lands, you need patience and an unflappable nature. I have neither.

Q. "*My wife and I are thinking of building a trimaran for ocean cruising. What is your advice?*"

A. This is a difficult question, because discussions of multihulls seem to be charged with strong personal feelings. Many catamaran and trimaran enthuiasts feel that any words said against multihulls are directed against the owners. This is not true. I have several good friends who own large trimarans. I like the owners a great deal; nevertheless I am not so keen on the vessels themselves for unlimited ocean sailing.

I am unimpressed with the accommodations in thirty- to forty-foot trimarans. The problems of securing the cross braces to the floats and hull have not been entirely solved, judging by the disparity of engineering approaches and the trouble that many owners continue to experience. The building efforts and costs of multihulls are about equivalent to those of a monohull of the same size. There are problems in marinas because of the extreme beam, and some marina managers try to charge berthing fees of two or three times that of a monohull, which is grossly unfair. Catamarans seem to have poor tacking ability, and I am unsure about the resale value of multihulls in general.

On the positive side, I think that flying in a big trimaran in smooth water is great fun. The acceleration and speed are superb. Easy beaching is a big advantage. It's a thrill to reach along at double the speed of an equivalent monohull.

In rough water the multihull is not as fast, and many ocean crossing times with average crews and small tris and cats are not much better than with monohulls. The giant trimaran *Pen Duick IV* of Alain Colas has made some remarkable passages, but after having climbed around his spidery aluminum colossus I would hardly consider it a comfortable vessel or practical for anything but flat-out racing (the accommodation reminded me of a wartime P-40 fighter aircraft). The problem of weight in a multihull is critical; you simply cannot pile on gear the same way you do in a monohull. The marvelous performance of large lightweight trimarans might be a good deal less if burdened with a few tons of cruising necessities.

If your sailing plans are for sheltered waters, shoal draft is a consideration, and if you like fast and exciting non-tippy sailing, then a multihull may be perfect. If you plan ocean passages with the trade winds in the proper seasons, a multihull may be excellent. For more rugged sailing in the higher latitudes I would choose a monohull.

In my judgment—all emotion aside—the key considerations for unlimited ocean cruising are ultimate stability and watertight integrity. All else is inconsequential, no matter how mellifluous are the arguments of multihull proponents. If a breaking wave flips a monohull over during a storm, its ballast keel will right the vessel. Plenty of monohulls have been rolled over and dismasted but have righted themselves and have been sailed to port with a jury rig. At the present design stage (with only one exception that I know of—see below) multihulls are not self-righting, and all arguments and specious words notwithstanding, they will not come back and most likely neither will their crews. The danger of capsize may be remote, but it exists. We know that the American Arthur Piver and the Australian Hedley Nichol—both well-known trimaran designers—were lost at sea in their vessels. In 1975, Dr. Roger Stewart, a prominent NASA scientist who was a diabetic, died from lack of insulin because his supply was lost when his trimaran *Meridian* overturned in hurricane Amy east of Cape Hatteras. The famous English sailor Brain Cooke disappeared from *Triple Arrow* near the Azores in early 1976. Without any great difficulty, this distressing list could be extended by a dozen more capsizes, including several grisly family disappearances in Australian waters.

Naval architect Dick Newick's sixty-foot, 13,460-pound trimaran *Gulf Streamer*, an outstanding performer if there ever was one, was flipped over by a rogue wave three hundred miles north of Bermuda on April 27, 1976. Owner Phil Weld suddenly found himself upside down standing on the ceiling in water rising rapidly to his hips. Weld and his crewman, Bill Stephens, were fortunately in warm water. They cut holes in the bottom of the hull (now the top) for access to the yacht's stores and rigged up an inside hammock for sleeping. After four and a half days of mole-like existence, the two sailors were rescued by the cargo ship *Federal Bermuda*. Weld thought the capsize was inconceivable; yet the accident occurred, and when it did the owner and his crew were quite helpless. They were fortunate to have been in warm water and in shipping lanes. If *Gulf Streamer* had capsized in a more remote and colder part of the ocean, the outcome might have been different.

Not only did Newick's *Gulf Streamer* capsize last year, but his trimaran *Three Cheers* disappeared with Mike McMullen aboard. If that wasn't enough, one of Newick's new *Val* trimarans sailed by Ham Ferris capsized four hundred miles southeast of New York while lying ahull in Force 8 winds. The evidence against ocean cruising in multihulls at the present stage of their development is overwhelming.

At the conclusion of the 1976 Observer Singlehanded Transatlantic Race I spoke with Nick Clifton, who made a good passage in *Azulao*, a trim thirty-one-foot trimaran designed and built by Dick Kelsall in England. Unlike *Gulf Streamer*, *Azulao* has built-in system of flooding and righting in the event of capsize. With the yacht in an inverted position, water is let into the bow section, which, becoming weighted with water, tips downward to bring the mast from an upside-down vertical position to a horizontal position on the surface of the water. Further water transfer presumably rights the vessel, after which she can be pumped out. A delicate and difficult business, no doubt, and a nightmare in bad weather, but at least there is a chance. This scheme is in a developmental stage but is a hopeful trend that we all should encourage and support.

But in the meantime, dear questioner, I suggest that for arduous ocean cruising you should stick to a monohull with its ballasted keel (lead mine, say the multihullers). In Chapter 1, I noted that a ballasted keel yacht can be made unsinkable with suitable flotation between an inner and outer skin.

If I were going to sail in San Francisco Bay or in Chesapeake Bay or in many sheltered places in the Caribbean or Mediterranean, however, I would certainly have a twenty-five- or thirty-foot, lightly loaded, speedy trimaran or catamaran. Zooming around, running up on beaches, ease of bottom painting, and a stable platform all add up to an exhilarating kind of practical fun. But keep the mainsheet free and ready to run, please!

Editor's Note: Azulao was later overturned (by a large wave breaking under a hull) off the Atlantic coast of the U.S.A. while lying a-hull in a Force 9 gale. The watertight cabin door broke open in the capsize, and once she was over the pressure of water surging inside the hull prevented the door from closing. The forehatch, never a very tight fit, was carried away, probably after the capsize. Had both remained closed, there would have been no water inside, rather than three feet of it. Clifton concludes that it is essential to think of force from inside the hull as well as outside when designing doors and hatches, and that these were not strong enough. Water surging in and out of a hull not only tends to suck out any loose gear, heavy or not, but also prevents effective flooding to alter the upside-down stability. There was no sail up, and the sealed mast stayed intact and watertight. Although *Azulao's* self-righting system had not been tried out, Clifton believes it would have been effective otherwise. Additional preparations for survival inside the boat worked well and Clifton stayed there for twelve hours. In order to keep a lookout, Clifton got into his liferaft, but its painter parted, and after two and a half days he was found by the U.S. Coast Guard. The foam-sandwich tri was eventually picked up by a container ship.

Running northward from Bermuda with 16 knots of wind, modest seas, and full sail. A preventer line going to the stemhead holds the boom forward while it is pulled down with a powerful vang tackle that leads to the genoa track. The headsail is held out with a spinnaker pole that is aligned parallel to the main boom. Two sails of roughly equal area, one on each side, are held before the wind and result in a balanced rig and easy steering.

17

Storm Management

Most blue-water sailors hope for trips with fair and steady winds. Lots of small vessels have voyaged thousands of miles and have never felt a gale or been tested by storm force winds. Sooner or later, however, a world-voyaging yacht is bound to encounter heavy weather, especially if she sails in latitudes higher than 30 degrees.

Personally, I think there is far too much talk and emphasis on gales and storms and tactics of desperation. If you leave port in the proper season, with settled weather, and shape a course to avoid bad weather systems, there is every likelihood that your weather will be reasonable. Not long ago Margaret and I completed a 4,000-mile passage from Brazil to Bermuda to Maine. Another long run was from California to Lima, some 5,500 miles. On both of these passages we had no winds over 26 knots. Twice in the past, however, we have been severely flattened in winter storms off the Oregon and northern California coasts of the United States—places we should never have been during the bad season.

Novice sailors are hopeless when it comes to judging wind strengths. During a strong wind the combination of unusual noises, violent motion of the yacht, spray coming aboard, and personal uncertainty generally combine to grossly exaggerate the wind velocity in the mind of an inexperienced sailor. A good sailing breeze when running becomes "a terrible wind" when close-hauled. A smaller yacht is influenced more by a strong wind than a larger vessel. A sailor in a twenty-five-foot yacht may speak of 40- or 50-knot winds ("It was really blowing"), while if he were in a vessel of twice the size, the wind might be judged to be appreciably less ("We had a good sailing breeze and were flying along").

There is a lot of difference between an occasional gust of 45 knots and a sustained 45-knot wind. The former is probably a momentary increase of a Force 7 gale (600 to 800 lbs. of wind pressure on a 100-sq. ft. sail), while the latter is Force 9 (1,100 to 1,400 lbs. of pressure on a 100-sq. ft. sail). When you hear someone say that it was blowing 60 or 70 knots, you can generally halve the numbers and be reasonably correct. I have read accounts in which sailors casually tossed off figures of 90 knots and talked of photographing the seas or drinking a bowl of soup in the cockpit. Believe me, in 90 knots no man can stand up to take a photograph. Indeed, his camera would be snatched away by the force of the wind and streaming spray; any soup would be long gone—including the bowl.

The only way to measure wind velocity is to use a calibrated mechanical or electrical instrument or for a man with considerable experience to judge the wind by the state of the sea. When you measure wind force during nasty weather, you are liable to be disappointed. I have found that it takes quite a strong wind to make my Swedish Ventimeter register 30 or 40 knots at deck level.

Wind pressure increases as the square of its velocity. The average wind, however, is not the whole story, because turbulence, especially around high land, can generate gusts some 40 percent higher.

When the wind increases, sail should be shortened promptly. The longer the delay, the harder the job. You should never go to sea without stout storm sails whose rigging details have been worked out in port. A gale at sea is no time to begin arranging headsail sheeting positions or to find that the tack pendant of the storm jib won't fit the deck hardware. Even worse is to discover that the trysail slides are too big for the mast track, that a wire halyard is too short, or that the roller reefing handle fouls the partially reefed mainsail.

Every seagoing yacht ought to have two hand-operated bilge pumps. One should be in the cockpit area and easily workable from the helmsman's position. The pump should be usable without opening any cockpit lockers. The second pump should be below, where it can be operated comfortably without going on deck. Each pump should be independent of the other and have as few right-angle bends as possible in its plumbing. Ideally, one piece of reinforced flexible hose should lead from the lowest point of the bilge to the pump. I recommend the Whale Gusher 25 (none smaller), which is a dependable, high-capacity device installed in thousands of yachts and fishing boats. My sailing friends assure me that the hand-operated Edson diaphragm pumps (one gallon a stroke) are superb. If possible, have both pumps of the same make so the parts are interchangeable. Electric and engine-driven pumps are nice if the engine is working or you have battery power. I want two hand-driven pumps in addition.

Sometime when you have your yacht alongside a dock, let water from a hose run into the bilge and try pumping for fifteen minutes (timed with a watch). You may get a few surprises.

The cockpit of a vessel that goes to sea should be small or nonexistent. Cockpit drains must be large and unobstructed. This point has been made for years, yet manufacturers continue to build yachts with 1- or 1¼-inch diameter pipes congested with bends and inferior valves and with the cockpit ends often capped with heavy wire mesh—ostensibly to keep foreign items out but quite successful in cutting down water flow too.

A high bridge deck, a stout hatch, and heavy washboards that fit together with overlapping joints should seal off the below-deck accommodation from the cockpit and outside. Portlights, skylights, and hatches should be small and well built. The cast aluminum skylight hatches of Goïot and Camper & Nicholson are superb. They are easy to open, don't leak, and let in plenty of light. Portlights ought to be through-bolted or constructed in such a way that they can't be pushed in by the force of water.

A flush-decked yacht is hardly practical under forty feet, but when you reach that length, it is certainly the best proposition for strength and watertight integrity. A coach roof and doghouse should be reinforced throughout. A fiberglass yacht should have plenty of layup to make strong sides. Perhaps a vertical centerline post should be erected inside the cabin to strengthen the coach roof. A wooden vessel should have metal tie rods placed vertically through the coach-roof coamings to strengthen them. Corresponding horizontal rods spaced every twelve inches or so between the carlines and shelves strengthen the deck structure a great deal and help to prevent leaks. I am surprised how many wooden yachts lack these tie rods, which are almost always specified by the best architects and then omitted by the builders.

A screw-in deck plate should be available for each ventilator in case it takes in water or is damaged. We have said earlier that the navel pipe that leads the chain below must have a foolproof arrangement to keep water out. It is incredible how much of the ocean can get through a small navel pipe closed with only a rag. Fuel-tank air vents must be

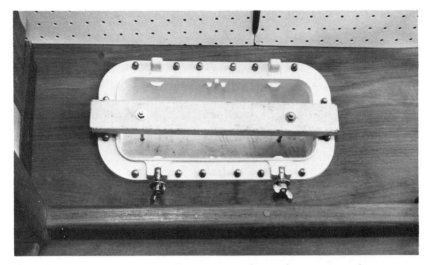

A yacht that goes to sea should carry some form of emergency closure for portlights in case of damage. We use a scrap of ⅜- or ½-inch plywood a little larger than the opening. The plywood is held in place with two bolts that run through a strongback made of 1- x 2-inch hardwood. I carry two such sets.

protected. Wooden skylights need close-fitting cloth covers. Masts require tight, well-painted mast boots. In short, you must be able to close off every leak, every source of flooding, and every access opening in a positive manner. The vessel should be as tight as possible.

Depending on her size and design, a yacht ought to be able to make progress on any point of sailing in Force 6 or perhaps Force 7 winds, making some allowance for sea conditions. Not many captains wish to hammer to windward in upper Force 7 or Force 8 winds (30 to 40 knots), because the distance made good is snail-like and the strain on the crew and the yacht is considerable.

Dutch sailor Dr. C. den Hartoog wrote about his thirty-five-foot Huismann-built aluminum sloop in the February 1976 issue of *Yachting World*: "*Senta* is very close-winded: even in Force 8 she still easily wins height, too easily sometimes, for under those circumstances the onrushing seas can deal such heavy blows that at some places the plating between the frames becomes dented, as I found out already during the voyage to Iceland last year."

With sufficient sea room it may be more sensible to heave to and wait for the wind to ease, or to change course a bit.

In *Whisper* we have found that we can make runs of 90 to 110 miles per day to windward in breezes of Force 5 and 6 (17 to 27 knots) in rough seas with a single- or double-reefed mainsail and one or two small headsails. With more wind the seas grow larger and increase the pounding and unpleasant noise. I ease the yacht by putting up the trysail in place of the double-reefed mainsail. It is important that the sails are not too small, for you need a certain amount of power and drive; otherwise the vessel sits and wallows. The ship must be sailed a little free to keep up speed in broken water. We find that about six points off the wind (67.5 degrees) or a little less is a realistic figure at sea.

There is much boasting about the close-windedness of modern yachts. I have read some remarkable claims, but these figures are presumably achieved in smooth water where head seas don't buffet the vessel and slow her headway. Severe pounding may not be popular with the crew or even tolerable for a long passage.

Running is another world. Out on the ocean we can go with Force 6 with ease and pleasure. When the wind gets over 30 knots (Force 7), we often furl the mainsail and run with a small headsail and perhaps the trysail. If we are far from land and the wind has been blowing from the same direction for perhaps half a day, the seas—though large—are often quite regular and we rush along splendidly hour after hour. Such sailing is exhilarating and you can make marvelous time toward the next port. The sails are full of wind and straining, the log line spins merrily, and the wind sings a tune in the rigging. Each sea picks up the yacht and pushes her forward a little with a whoosh of white as the seas overtake the vessel and hurry past. Wind-induced current adds to the mileage.

When we run in steady winds at Force 8—34 to 40 knots—the sailing is a bit more chancy, for a crest may rumble on board occasionally. We carry a second storm jib of 70 square feet for such winds and find that as soon as we hand the trysail and change to the smaller jib, the yacht slows down and we can go along tolerably well *depending on the sea conditions*. The danger in running with winds that are too strong is that the vessel may broach, that is, get sideways to the seas, with disastrous consequences. The headsail alone, however, is a pulling sail and helps to keep the ship tracking straight. Nevertheless, when heavy water commences to thump on board, you fill the cockpit a few times, and the course of the yacht becomes erratic, it is time to reduce sail further or to stop altogether.

If the wind is really strong, it will push you along without any canvas up at all. When Margaret and I sailed north through the Strait of Le

Maire between Tierra del Fuego and Isla de los Estados after rounding Cape Horn, a strong southwest gale blew up behind us. The wind increased rapidly. First I handed the main and then dropped the working jib. I began to hoist the small staysail, but the wind was about 40 knots and gusty; I was afraid the snapping halyard would tear the winch off the mast. I furled the sail and then realized that we were traveling at 4 knots or so under bare pole, that is, the windage of the yacht was sail enough. We continued under bare pole into the South Atlantic, where the wind was a little less so that we could hoist the small staysail.

Reaching in strong winds is halfway between windward work and running. The yacht goes faster and is sometimes difficult to manage. The behavior of various designs differs. Most yachts increase weather helm as they heel, which necessitates substantial reduction in mainsail area for a given headsail. With a yawl or ketch the mizzen can be dropped, or with stronger winds the mizzen can be left flying and the main handed directly. In reaching conditions it is harder to get the vessel to steer herself, because she tends to round up or fall off as individual seas push her one way or another. A lot of water thumps on the deck.

In bad weather the state of the sea is the critical thing. On smooth water in the lee of an island or in a protected strait or channel a sailing ship can make her way in almost any wind. But when the wind blows over the open ocean, it raises a swell whose size is proportional to the wind strength and the length of time the wind has been blowing. The seas tend to slow the ship if she is going to windward or reaching. If she is running, the yacht's speed may be boosted for a few moments when she surfs forward on a wave. There are simple mathematical formulas for wave periods, lengths, and velocities, but they are of little practical use to a sailor. Wave height is simply a matter of wind strength and the distance over open water—the fetch—that the wind blows.

If the wind came from one direction and stopped, the wave problem would be simple. But winds change and send out swells in advance of their arrival. Wave patterns from different directions interact and form complex and irrational wave trains—occasionally generating a sea of much greater than average height. The sea left on a windless ocean after a storm has passed can be gigantic, confused, and quite unpredictable, but fortunately soon dies down.

Another set of problems occurs when heavy ocean swells get into shoal water or meet an opposing current or tidal stream. Many vessels that have sailed with reasonable safety for hours in given sea and wind conditions have come to grief when they have entered shoal water or an opposing tidal stream. The problems of northerly gales in the Gulf Stream are well known. The waves become steeper, more crested, and heavy seas are likely to break on board. Wave height can easily be increased 50 to 100 percent in an opposing current as low as 2 or 3 knots.

"Then," as Maurice Griffiths has written, "the merry, sparkling sea—which tops the scales at 64 lb. for each cubic foot, or 35 cu. ft. to the ton —can be about as friendly as a ton of wet concrete when it chooses to break over a small vessel."[13]

Yachts seldom get in trouble at sea. It's the coastlines that are dangerous, doubly so when a strong wind opposes a tidal stream, or the ebb from a river sluices out to combat contrary seas. The prudent tactic is, of course, to stay well out to sea until conditions improve, or at least until the tidal stream or river ebb has turned.

The most violent scene I have witnessed in my life was at the mouth of Oregon's Columbia River when a spring ebb plus river flow from the east opposed a westerly storm force wind (Force 11) that spun the anemometer cups of the weather station at a steady 58 knots. The seas in the vicinity of the bar were utterly cataclysmic and powerful enough to fling channel buoys with 12-ton weights up on the beach. Margaret and I were on land at Cape Disappointment, where we watched from the Coast Guard observation station, whose massive concrete structure trembled and shook from the earthquake force of the water. No vessel on earth could have lived in that sea. Yet twenty miles to the west some small fishing vessels and several cargo ships were hove to waiting for the wind to veer to the northwest. Two days later—at high slack water—the ships crossed the bar and came in. The vessels were shaken and bruised but undamaged, demonstrating once again that one must keep to the sea in really bad weather.

I took this photograph while sailing between Punta del Este, Uruguay, and Ilha Santa Catarina, Brazil, while running northeast during a July storm from the west-southwest. Our mainsail is furled and we are logging about 5 knots under a staysail. The yacht is 55 miles offshore in a depth of 50 meters. Though the wind did not exceed 40 knots, the green-colored seas grew quite large and confused, perhaps because of the uneven sea floor on the shallow bank that extends offshore for 100 miles. Whisper was guided flawlessly by an Atoms pendulum-servo self-steering unit, a small but powerful gear made in Nice, France, and a favorite with long-distance sailors.

18

~~~~~~

Storm Tactics

The trouble with taking advice from sailing authors about storm maneuvers is that most small ship seamen have had experience in only one type of vessel. Each captain and each type of design react differently to bad weather. No single person has all the answers; indeed, he would be a very wise man who had *half* the wisdom to know what to do in truly severe weather at sea. Besides the human factor and the difference in ship behavior, there are a number of variables related to the sea and the storm itself. One's fortunes during a severe storm are a chancy business; yet a well-found small vessel properly handled is remarkably seaworthy.

The most authoritative book on storms vs. small ships is *Heavy Weather Sailing*, by Adlard Coles, a morose catalogue of chilling nautical disasters and near disasters. The book is gloomy but fascinating, and as you plow through one horror story after another, you can hardly put the book down. In fact, you can scarcely see the print through your tears. The best capsule summary of storm management that I know of is the appendix to Miles Smeeton's *Because the Horn Is There,* an excellent abstract by a great seaman. Another useful chapter is by Erroll Bruce in his book *Deep Sea Sailing.* Bernard Moitessier's *The Long Way* is perhaps my favorite, an absorbing study of long ocean passages, charmingly written, with a lucid discussion of swell and sea conditions and how they relate to passing weather depressions. Yet all these writers give advice with caution and readily admit to many unanswered questions.[14]

In the last twenty years there has been a great deal of ocean cruising and a good many accounts of different experiences and procedures. Let's see what a careful look can tell us.

The first rule of survival for a ship in a storm is to have adequate sea room. This is the fundamental rule of sailing. You must get far enough away from a lee shore so that adverse winds will not drive you ashore or put you into dangerous waters. If you are anchored near shore and no shelter is nearby, it is imperative to put up sail at once and to drive the vessel offshore as far as possible. Some storms are short-lived and twenty or twenty-five miles of sea room is enough—less if the wind is shifting so that it is not blowing directly onshore. But how are you going to know the duration of a storm? Eric Hiscock once got into a tempest near Tonga that lasted four days, during which he was blown to leeward 120 miles. Bad weather of this duration is unusual. Most storms move more rapidly—often performing to set, seasonal patterns. Usually there is a major wind shift in twelve or eighteen hours.

Only the foolish and inexperienced linger near shore when bad weather comes. The other captains have gone to sea. It is a good idea, incidentally, to routinely practice sailing an anchor out, a satisfying exercise that may save your life someday if an onshore wind blows up and you have to leave suddenly.

If you have sufficient sea room and there is so much wind that further sailing is undesirable, there are four possible tactics:

1. Heave to.
2. Lie ahull.
3. Run with the storm, perhaps streaming warps.
4. Lie to a sea anchor.

1. *Heave to.* This maneuver is simply to tack the ship without releasing the headsail sheet. As the yacht turns through the eye of the wind, the headsail is backwinded, which pushes the vessel's head to leeward. The tiller is then lashed to leeward. The backed headsail and opposite rudder tend to balance one another, and the forward drive of the ship is essentially stopped. You make a little headway and a lot of leeway. Suddenly the yacht floats quietly and easily even though the fury of the wind and seas continues. Generally, by the time you want to heave to, you have small sails up, so that there is no trouble with the clew of a backed genoa chafing itself to death on the weather shrouds. On *Whisper*

A permanent, sturdy boom gallows or crutch is important for a cruising yacht because it allows you to control the boom during heavy weather in case you drop the mainsail. A boom swinging from side to side can easily knock a sailor on the head or pitch him into the sea. In addition the gallows frame is a good handhold when going forward. This gallows is made of 1-inch and 1¼-inch stainless steel pipe and is quite strong in all directions.

we heave to quite well with a working jib (or smaller) and a reefed main (or trysail), either together or singly. The yacht heads up into the wind slightly, and the sails nicely stabilize the vessel.

We sometimes heave to for celestial sights or for a hot meal. When a sight is important, you often discover that the star or sun is to windward on a spray-lashed deck, or that a sail masks the moon or Polaris. It makes sense to stop. To heave to takes only a few moments, and you can then shoot the heavenly bodies from a relatively smooth platform in the direction you want without getting salt water all over you and the sextant. If you have been bashing to windward for days, it is nice to stop the vessel and let the cook operate in a galley that is not going wildly up and down. Sometimes you can make one stop for both a sight and a meal. (It's a useful idea to wear oilskins when cooking if the motion is severe. The oilskins are clumsy to work in, but they're a good way to prevent getting burned.) We have often hove to outside a strange port to wait for daylight.

The principal use of heaving to is to stop the vessel when the sea is too rough to continue. How far up into the wind a vessel will lie depends on the configuration of the keel, the windage aloft, and whether there is a mizzen. Generally, the longer the keel, the more a ship will put her shoulder into the wind. The ability of a long-keeled design like a Bristol Channel pilot cutter to head up when she is hove to is legendary. *Whisper*'s keel and attached rudder are about ten feet long; she lies about six points off the wind.

As the wind increases, the sail on the vessel pushes the ship more and more to leeward until she begins to labor like a half-tide rock. The balance between the rudder and the backed headsail may get upset by an irregular sea, which can shove the bow to windward, which means that the yacht will pay off and jibe and then head up again. Or the force of the wind on the backed headsail may be stronger than the opposing rudder, which will cause the bow to swing away from the wind. The bow will fall off to leeward and the ship will do a crab-like course downwind. All this will be accompanied by a great sail flapping and violent lurches as the yacht heels first to starboard and then to port.

With sufficient sea room most yachts can get through storms by simply heaving to. The sail(s) and rudder may have to be adjusted now and then, but heaving to is often quite enough. If, however, the storm increases and the yacht's motion and behavior are clearly unsafe, it is time for other action.

2. *Lie ahull.* This means letting the vessel skid slowly before the seas and wind without any sail up and the tiller lashed a little alee to keep the ship's head from falling off. Because of her keel, a ship will usually assume a position at right angles to the wind with the seas broad on the beam. This sounds dangerous, but if the wind has been blowing from one direction for a number of hours and there is plenty of water depth, the seas are often quite regular and the yacht will ride reasonably well before the storm. If you're near a weather shore, the seas will have had no time to build up.

When lying ahull, the ship appears to make a slick to windward and the seas slide past. At first the noise and motion are alarming, but as long as there are no breaking or irregular seas, you can get along tolerably well. One problem is that when you lie broadside to the sea without any sail up, the rolling is terrible (some say ghastly). Under these circumstances, a schooner may have some advantages because the considerable windage of her mainmast and main boom may keep her partially headed up into the storm.

The great danger in lying ahull with the seas broad on is that if the swells are confused, there is a wind shift, or the tempest becomes truly colossal, the seas may get out of phase with one another and a whopper may break near or on top of the vessel and overwhelm her with tons of water. Even a small breaking sea is extremely dangerous. Think of a waterfall suddenly landing top of the ship and shoving her bodily to leeward. The impact from being pushed into the sea is the same as being dropped on concrete. Damage almost always ocurs on the leeward side of the vessel and can mean a stove-in coach roof or collapsed portlights. The force of the water can easily carry away pulpits as well as furled sails, dinghies, and deck gear.

"Every cubic meter of sea water contains slightly more than one ton of mass," writes Captain William Kielhorn. "A breaking sea wave may easily contain 500 tons or more, curling and racing downslope at speeds up to 20 or 30 knots."[15]

It has been amply documented that a breaking sea can flip a ballasted monohull right over. The yacht will right herself, but the damage may be considerable. I have always marveled at the account of Joe Byars' thirty-nine-foot yawl *Doubloon* when she was rolled over twice in aggravated seas churned up by a tropical cyclone blowing in the opposite direction to the Gulf Stream. *Doubloon* not only lost her entire rig and almost everything on deck, but the force of the water even bent her ¾-inch bronze centerboard and partially tore off a sheet winch. Think of the power to do that!

In *Whisper* we have lain ahull perhaps a half dozen times, certainly under easier conditions than *Doubloon* faced. Twice *Whisper* was in upset water, which shoved us to leeward hard enough to put the spreaders in the water. During one storm the force of the sea destroyed both the bow and stern pulpits, the rudder shaft head fitting was shattered, and we lost a storm jib.

The direct lessons we learned were never to lash the tiller with heavy line, but to use a bit of marline or thin manila or shock cord that will break or stretch. I have also learned never to furl sails along the lifelines but to bag the sails and carry them below or put them in a locker. Large canvas bunk cloths or automotive-type seat belts will keep you safely in your berth. Lockers with heavy items should be stoutly hinged along one side and have positive, strong, bolt-type closures so that you will not be attacked by flying tools, avalanches of canned goods, or showers of glass fragments from broken bottles. When singlehander Eric Hall was rolled over in the roaring forties west of Chile three days before

Christmas in 1971, he was almost killed by an anchor and chain that he had stowed in *Manuma*'s bilges.

The unnerving part of lying ahull is to be in your bunk listening to the seas hissing past outside hour after hour and wondering whether the next one will break on top of you. The seas slide up and then race away with great bubbling sounds; in the distance you hear a crash as a monster topples into a mass of white foam. When this begins to happen frequently, it is time to change your tactics before solid water lands on board. These are the hours you will need to bestir yourself, to summon your reserves of energy, to think clearly, and to wear your safety harness.

If you continue to lie ahull in big seas that have begun to break, you are going to get into real trouble. This has been documented in all oceans again and again. To take just one example from among a dozen I could quote, the June 1976 issue of *The Telltale Compass* recited the doleful account of the Contest 31 sloop *Banjo* on passage from Bermuda to Long Island. On July 26, 1975, the crew went through the usual sail reductions as the giant winds of hurricane Blanche began to swirl around the Dutch-built vessel. Crewman Alfred Boylen reported that in a few hours the seas had built to "fifty feet or more with big surfs." The captain and the two crewmen were in their bunks while the vessel lay ahull.

"About 2000 we felt a big lift, an almost weightless drop and a sudden stop with a crash that reverberated as though we were inside a kettle drum," wrote Boylen. "A second later another shudder ran through the ship along with a slashing roar as the crest of the wave from which we had dropped fell on top of us while we lay in the trough. We estimated that we had dropped fifty feet on our side from a crest into a trough."

Poor *Banjo* was severely damaged. Her rudder was jammed and water poured in along a six-foot split in the fiberglass hull. In spite of five pumps, the crew's damage control efforts failed. Sixteen hours later, with the storm over and a big ship standing by, the three men abandoned the yacht.

In a postmortem discussion the crew blamed faulty yacht construction. My feeling is that no vessel—large or small—can be expected to survive fifty-foot drops and avalanches of tons of water without serious damage, no matter what the hull material. In my judgment the crew should have run *Banjo* off before the storm.

3. *Run with the storm, perhaps streaming warps.* When sea conditions become chaotic and it is no longer safe to take a chance with a breaking sea, the next step is to turn tail and flee before the storm, having, one

hopes, plenty of sea room. Of course, if you are traveling away from your destination, you will want to sail as slowly as possible. You can run under bare poles, or perhaps hoist a small storm jib to make steering easier. Some sailors stream warps to slow and steady their ships, as Joshua Slocum did in *Spray* during a frightful gale near the western shore of Tierra del Fuego. Other men speak out strongly for keeping the yacht moving at 4 or 5 knots without warps and bearing off a little at the approach of a big sea. Certainly the ship's way through the water should not get close to hull speed, because the greater the disturbance made by the hull, the more likely it is that a following sea will break. Often a slight easing of speed immediately reduces the evil-looking crests sliding up astern. Sometimes a steering vane will work perfectly in these conditions. Note, however, that no steering vane "will bear off at the approach of a big sea."

Tom Steele, who circumnavigated twice in *Adios*, wrote in *Yachting* (January 1965) about his adventures with two hurricanes off the coast of Baja California:

Our procedure in a tempest, where there is sea room, is to run before the wind and sea under bare poles and drag 300 feet of one-inch nylon line* with an anchor on the end. This has proved very effective in keeping an even, powerful strain at all times so that she lies stern-to. The one-and-one-half to two-knot headway gives steerage way so as to take the oncoming sea properly. I find this method far superior to using a warp, which usually skips when the boat surges ahead and the total strain is needed most. Full advantage of the line's length and resistance is gained by the single weighted length, yet the strain is never excessive as is the case with a sea anchor. I am totally afraid to lie a-hull in a great sea. A small craft lying a-hull or hove-to in such conditions, even though well ballasted, presents a greater area to the sea with danger of being stove in, or capsizing due to beam-on conditions minus a stabilizing drag.

Robin Knox-Johnston, an extraordinary seaman who sailed the structurally marginal thirty-two-foot *Suhaili* to win the solo round-the-world race in 1968–69, wrote about his experiences in *A World of My Own*. Knox-Johnston, like Tom Steele, used an extremely long warp but preferred a U-shaped bight of floating line with some stretch. He used no weight. Knox-Johnston had plenty of opportunities to perfect his scheme during ten and a half months of non-stop sailing.

* Recent studies of nylon suggest that 5/8-inch diameter line will be adequately strong and allow more stretch.

WIND FORCE TABLE

| Beau-fort number | Wind speed | | | | Seaman's term |
	knots	mph	meters per second	km per hour	
0	under 1	under 1	0.0–0.2	under 1	Calm
1	1–3	1–3	0.3–1.5	1–5	Light air
2	4–6	4–7	1.6–3.3	6–11	Light breeze
3	7–10	8–12	3.4–5.4	12–19	Gentle breeze
4	11–16	13–18	5.5–7.9	20–28	Moderate breeze
5	17–21	19–24	8.0–10.7	29–38	Fresh breeze
6	22–27	25–31	10.8–13.8	39–49	Strong breeze
7	28–33	32–38	13.9–17.1	50–61	Moderate gale
8	34–40	39–46	17.2–20.7	62–74	Fresh gale
9	41–47	47–54	20.8–24.4	75–88	Strong gale
10	48–55	55–63	24.5–28.4	89–102	Whole gale
11	56–63	64–72	28.5–32.6	103–117	Storm
12	64–71	73–82	32.7–36.9	118–133	
13	72–80	83–92	37.0–41.4	134–149	
14	81–89	93–103	41.5–46.1	150–166	
15	90–99	104–114	46.2–50.9	167–183	Hurricane
16	100–108	115–125	51.0–56.0	184–201	
17	109–118	126–136	56.1–61.2	202–220	

I nearly lost *Suhaili* in the Southern Ocean because I was handling her badly. I had always left her beam-on to the seas before, in gales, but the size of the seas in the Southern Ocean were such that *Suhaili* was being battered to breaking-up point. I found that by streaming a warp as a bight, with both ends made fast to the kingpost forward and leading down on either side of the boat and out astern, and then setting the 40 sq. ft. storm jib with both sheets tight so that it was held hard amidships, *Suhaili* would lie very comfortably stern to wind. To start with I streamed a full 100 fathom coil of 2-inch [circumference] polypropylene rope, but later I used to reduce this slightly, depending on the state of the sea, when I wanted to move the boat to

U. S. Weather Bureau term	Estimating wind speed	
	Effects observed at sea	Effects observed on land
	Sea like mirror.	Calm; smoke rises vertically.
Light	Ripples with appearance of scales; no foam crests.	Smoke drift indicates wind direction; vanes do not move.
	Small wavelets; crests of glassy appearance, not breaking.	Wind felt on face; leaves rustle; vanes begin to move.
Gentle	Large wavelets; crests begin to break; scattered whitecaps.	Leaves, small twigs in constant motion; light flags extended.
Moderate	Small waves, becoming longer; numerous whitecaps.	Dust, leaves, and loose paper raised up; small branches move.
Fresh	Moderate waves, taking longer form; many whitecaps; some spray.	Small trees in leaf begin to sway.
Strong	Larger waves forming; whitecaps everywhere; more spray.	Larger branches of trees in motion; whistling heard in wires.
	Sea heaps up; white foam from breaking waves begins to be blown in streaks.	Whole trees in motion; resistance felt in walking against wind.
Gale	Moderately high waves of greater length; edges of crests begin to break into spindrift; foam is blown in well-marked streaks.	Twigs and small branches broken off trees; progress generally impeded.
	High waves; sea begins to roll; dense streaks of foam; spray may reduce visibility.	Slight structural damage occurs; slate blown from roofs.
Whole gale	Very high waves with overhanging crests; sea takes white appearance as foam is blown in very dense streaks; rolling is heavy and visibility reduced.	Seldom experienced on land; trees broken or uprooted; considerable structural damage occurs.
	Exceptionally high waves; sea covered with white foam patches; visibility still more reduced.	Very rarely experienced on land; usually accompanied by widespread damage.
Hurricane	Air filled with foam; sea completely white with driving spray; visibility greatly reduced.	

leeward. She drifted to leeward slowly with this system but was never subjected to jerking even when riding over the steepest waves. The stretch in the rope provided sufficient give to prevent the waves smashing into the boat. I found the foredeck dry in a Force 10 on one occasion when hove-to like this, and the waves never pooped her.[16]

In the June 1973 issue of *Yachting Monthly*, Knox-Johnston underlined the long length, 100 to 120 *fathoms*, and the importance of the floating elastic polypropylene line, which allows "a smoother running passage, shocks being absorbed instead of increased as might be the case with a short but heavily weighted bight which would skip and drag by turns."

In *Whisper* we have run before a Force 10 storm dragging warps on the ends of which I chained several tires. But from time to time big seas would carry the tires up alongside the yacht. My failure was in having out only 150 feet or so of line. I think I needed twice as much. Fortunately, about this time the winds began to ease and the following seas stopped filling the cockpit.

I must mention the considerable physical effort required to stream a warp, to deal with storm sails, or other special problems. All warps, sails, and heavy-weather gear should be accessible and as ready to use as possible. For example, if you decide to stream a warp with a couple of tires, it may easily take an hour to get the warp out, secure one end to a mooring cleat, wrap some chain around the tires, and shackle the chain to the warp. You use up half your energy merely hanging on. You may be encumbered with oilskins, it may be night, and you may be steering as well. This sort of work coupled with lack of food and sleep, the noise of the storm, and water all over the place can easily lead to nervous and physical exhaustion.

To illustrate the degree of lethargy and weakness that a severe storm induces, let me mention the following incident to demonstrate what one is up against.

I have worked as a professional editorial photographer for many years and am well used to taking photographs under trying conditions. Fortunately, I do not suffer from motion sickness and I am generally able to deal with the ship and her management.

In a Force 10 storm off the Oregon coast I was aware that the sea conditions were truly spectacular and that I should take some photographs. At the time the motion of the yacht was appalling, because we had the sails down and were lying ahull. I distinctly remember thinking that I might never again be out in such seas and that I should take a few photographs to record the conditions. My camera, however, had no film in it. I recall trying to decide whether to load the camera with black and white or color film. I was quite unable to choose. My mind refused to function properly. In the end I took no pictures at all because the camera had no film. I was unable to make a simple decision. . . .

During a severe storm the roar of the wind and water, the rolling and pitching of the ship, the problems of navigation and sailing all combine to make one's reactions slow and puppet-like.

4. *Lie to a sea anchor.* The theory of a yachtman's sea anchor is a drogue or drag of some kind put into the sea to hold the ship's head to the wind to expose the strongest and most streamlined part of the vessel

to the storm. The crew is then supposed to set a small riding sail on the mizzenmast or to hoist a storm jib on the mainmast backstay to keep the ship's head into the wind. According to marine artists of the nineteenth century and the writings of Captain Voss, the ship will then easily ride out the storm while the crewmen retire below to smoke their pipes.

This is a nice fairy tale, which unfortunately is nonsense. In the first place, a small sailing ship will lie at roughly right angles to a 30-inch drogue because of the ship's keel and windage aloft. An aft riding sail will head the vessel up a little, but in a storm of any consequence an ordinary sail will flog itself to death as the ship's heading changes with passing seas. It's hard to think of a more appalling strain on the rudder and its fastenings than when the ship makes sternway in a rough sea and the full weight of a yawing and bucking vessel slams against the rudder. Erroll Bruce recalls that when he was in a storm in the South China Sea in a naval whaler, the rudder broke clean off while lying to a sea anchor. The small yacht *Nova Espero* had the same trouble during an eastward crossing of the Atlantic in 1951.

The chafe problems with a sea anchor are severe, and time after time sailors have hauled in the warp to find that the drogue has either disintegrated or the warp has chafed through and the yacht has actually been lying ahull. A stout, funnel-shaped sea anchor of heavy Dacron seems possible only for sailing vessels under thirty feet at best. The sea anchors sold by chandlers are utter rubbish. It's incredible how such trash continues to be sold as storm equipment for yachts. For rowboats in an estuary, yes; for yachts at sea, no. A New Zealand model of plywood and angle iron is certainly more realistic.

Rather than to stream a sea anchor from the bow, a better scheme may be to let go a sea anchor or weighted warp—the terminology is imprecise—from the stern, which takes advantage of the mast windage and keel shape. "Like that she will lie with her stern or quarter to the sea and present a smaller target," writes Eric Hiscock. "As she is moving ahead there will be no abnormal strain on tne rudder, and within limits she should answer the helm, which may be of great importance if there is some danger to leeward."[17]

During the 1970–71 Antarctic circumnavigation of the fifty-three-foot cutter *Awahnee*, Bob Griffith and his crew lay to a sea anchor or stern drogue time after time. *Awahnee*, however, had a strong crew and used a sea anchor that not many yachts would be able to produce or manage. "We hove to with the stern into the wind and swell held by a sea anchor consisting of about 100 yds. of line with half a dozen car tires and a small anchor on the end," wrote crewman Pat Treston in the New Zealand magazine *Sea Spray*.[18] During several giant Antarctic storms the crew of *Awahnee* set as many as three drogues—one of 80 feet of $\frac{7}{16}$-inch chain, a second of two or three car tires on 200 feet of line, and a third of 600 feet of line with an anchor and a tire on the end. "However we had to steer all the time to try to keep the quarter to the wind and waves," wrote Treston. Broken water flew everywhere. There was some damage, but the yacht and crew came through unharmed.

When I read the *Awahnee* account, I wondered how a nylon aerial parachute would have worked as a drogue, either from the bow or from the stern. Certainly there must be an easier drogue scheme than the *Awahnee* crew used.

In the May and September 1975 issues of *Sail* magazine Captain William Kielhorn wrote of an extended study he made for the U.S. Coast Guard. Kielhorn also used parachute drogues to hold oceanographic vessels steady while instruments were lowered to the ocean floor. On one occasion he employed a 24-foot surplus nylon aerial parachute on a 40-ton motor vessel in winds of 30 knots and seas with a significant height of 18 feet. The parachute drogue was streamed from the bow on a $\frac{5}{8}$-inch diameter nylon warp 600 feet long, the average wave length at the time.

"Earlier her high bulwarks had been crested port and starboard and the oversized freeing ports had been unable to handle the sweeping seas," wrote Kielhorn. "But from that moment on, the cook didn't even have to mount the storm racks on the mess table."

Kielhorn suggests freeing a nylon aerial parachute of all unnecessary fittings to make the water drogue as light and simple as possible. He says that it is of utmost importance to support the entire sea anchor and line with a small float attached to the top, or apex, of the parachute. The apex-to-float line should be a floating lanyard equal in length to the diameter of the parachute. No trip line is necessary. Kielhorn advises three-strand nylon with a swivel where it is attached to the parachute's shrouds. The nylon needs protection from chafe where it leads from the vessel. The ship's rudder should be firmly lashed amidships.

Kielhorn's remarks make sense for motor vessels, but whether his technique will work with a sailing yacht in a storm at sea is unproven and at present must remain an experimental procedure (I have bought a nylon parachute to try in the next storm). Unlike a fishing boat or motor vessel, a yacht has more windage forward because of her mast and rig; the lateral area of her hull is aft of center. As the yacht drifts astern, she pivots on her keel and takes up a position broadside to the storm. The New Zealand seaman Ross Norgrove told me that this was his exact experience with a small sea anchor in his eleven-ton *White Squall* during a violent Pacific storm. "As soon as we streamed the sea anchor at the bow, the yawl turned sideways on and I knew it was a disaster," he said.

But hopefully a 20- or 24-foot nylon parachute will slow the rearward drift and keep a yacht headed up.

All these problems are reversed when the sea anchor is put over the stern. This position, however, offers the transom, cockpit, and coach-roof openings to the seas, better than broadside-on lying ahull, but a poorer second choice than the bow-on position, which may be impossible for a sailing yacht to achieve in a storm in the ocean.

Awahnee's adventures and the experiences of others strongly favor stern drags, yet when towing a mélange of warps, weights, and nets from the transom of his forty-foot steel ketch *Joshua*, Bernard Moitessier got into a great storm in the high latitudes of the Southern Ocean in which colossal breaking seas from different directions threatened to overwhelm his vessel. Moitessier was almost pitchpoled. He cut loose all the drags, and at 5 knots under bare poles he was able to bear off 15 or 20 degrees as the giant seas passed, and to skid away from "the acres of boiling water."[19]

The storm tactics of Bob Griffith's *Awahnee* and Bernard Moitessier's *Joshua* were quite different. It's obvious that the storms were different too. It may have been that Moitessier was dragging too many warps, which made his vessel sluggish, but in any case the differing experiences show the problems of trying to suggest optimum bad-weather management. Nevertheless, one truth pennant seems to wave in the wind: lying ahull, beam on, in confused seas is asking for trouble. All the authorities agree, and anyone who studies heavy-weather accidents must concur. "Once the breaking tops of the waves are higher than a yacht's freeboard, it would be folly to offer the whole length of the ship to them," writes Erroll Bruce.[20] The veteran sailor W. A. Robinson says that the yacht must be allowed to take her natural position with her stern before the storm. She should be run just fast enough so the helmsman can retain good steering control, using drags as a brake to prevent her going too fast.[21]

The Polish engineer, C. A. Marchaj, has recently published a paper which—in theory at least—seems to reconcile the differing types of storm management when running before a severe tempest as a survival tactic. As I have mentioned, one scheme favors towing warps to reduce speed and to increase control. The other suggests no warps at all, to run at speed, and to bear off slightly to take large waves on the quarter. As we have seen, each procedure has very experienced adherents.

Professor Marchaj suggests that both may be correct. In the early stages of a severe storm the waves may be very steep and may well cause broaching. However, after a high wind—say 50 knots or more—has been blowing for a number of hours, the waves become longer and not so steep as their velocity increases. Marchaj postulates that early in the storm the best tactic is to stream warps to stabilize the vessel directionally and to prevent broaching and dangerous surfing. Later in the storm, however, when the velocity of the waves is greater, the use of warps should be discontinued. The yacht should be speeded up to minimize the difference in velocity between the vessel and the overtaking seas. In other words, warps early in the storm to control broaching; running at near hull speed later on to lessen the chance of getting overwhelmed by a huge wave.[22]

There is one additional weapon that can materially aid these techniques, and that is to use oil, which is a remarkable tranquilizer for nasty seas. The oil can be dripped into the sea from an oil bag or from a can that has been pricked with an ice pick, or pumped slowly from a marine head. Not one cruising yacht in a hundred has cans of fish oil aboard, but you may have diesel oil, lubricating oil, cooking oil, or kerosene. Even if it works only partially, it may be just enough to help you win the battle.

Somewhere I have read an account of an Englishman who crewed aboard a large fishing boat when he was a lad. During one trip the vessel got into a terrible North Atlantic storm and was soon running before big seas. The lad was sent to the afterdeck to pump a little oil through the head every few minutes. The oil immediately eased the overtaking seas. The young man was there for many hours and finally dozed off, but whenever he forgot to pump a little oil, the waves knew the difference at once. Their cold spray woke him up and alerted him to pump more oil quickly.

Two other heavy-weather weapons are a storm trysail and an extra-small storm jib. In my experience, the average storm jib is necessary but needs to be supplemented by a second storm jib with 30 or 40 percent less area. On *Whisper* we have run for days with a 70-square-foot storm jib. Heavy-weather sails—reinforced with multiple tapes along the edges— can be very sturdy and still be light and easy to stow and handle, because Dacron of seven or eight ounces is quite strong in the small areas we are discussing. I have mentioned earlier that a trysail ought to have a row of worked grommets along the luff so the sail can be laced to the mast if there is any difficulty with the track. With a cutter or double headsail rig both running backstays can be set up when the trysail and/or storm jib are hoisted to make a very secure rig.

To summarize the complex subject of storm tactics, I suggest the following action when a yacht gets into winds and seas of increasing force:

1. *Heave to.* If you are unsure of your position and the sky is clear, take sights if possible. At the earliest stage do your best to cook a simple, hot, nourishing meal. Drink no alcohol. If you are wet, change to dry clothes and put on oilskins followed by a safety harness. Lash down any loose gear. Put unused sails in bags out of the way. Reassure the crew.

2. When the yacht becomes too hard pressed, *lie ahull* until big seas begin to break near the yacht.

3. *Run with the storm,* trailing a 300-foot warp with a small anchor or an 80- to 120-fathom floating line streamed in a U-shaped bight from the quarters. If there are dangers to leeward, you may wish to increase the drags or to use a sea anchor from the stern. If necessary, you can steer a little to get away from dangers to leeward. If you have unlimited sea room and the wind is blowing in the direction of your journey, you can perhaps use a very small storm jib, depending on conditions, which will make the motion and steering easier.

4. If truly enormous seas threaten to engulf the vessel, you can try oil, perhaps pumped slowly from a head or allowed to drip from a can that has been pricked with an ice pick. You can cut away some or all of the warps and begin to steer by hand, bearing off a little when the yacht rises on a big sea. This will require careful steering, and crew exhaustion will become a factor. Let us hope you will never get to this point.

A final cheering thought is that most tempests are fairly fast moving in relation to the slow speed of a yacht. You need only play for time while the weather depression moves off. With luck it will be gone in twenty-four or forty-eight hours, and you will be sailing again in normal conditions and wondering what all the fuss was about.

19

~~~~~~

Schooling at Sea

One of the queries we've heard most in our travels concerns children on board. What about their schooling and safety? Are there any special problems? How old should they be?

Whisper's great friend is Mary Adams, who is eleven years old. She has been living on the forty-foot Canadian ketch *Eileen* for almost two years. Her father—Doug Adams—is a doctor and her mother—June— is an attractive shipboard wife who keeps *Eileen*'s brass lamps polished brighter than any others that we have ever seen. We met the Adams family in Canada several years ago when they were moving aboard and getting ready for a long cruise. At that time Mary—aged nine—was a bit shy and introverted. We used to see her coming down the dock at Van Isle Marina on Vancouver Island, but she seldom had much to say. Some eighteen months later when we met *Eileen* near the United States– Mexican border, the change in young Mary was surprising. No longer was she the bashful and diffident girl we had known in Canada. The Mary we now met was friendly and outgoing. Of course, the change in her behavior and attitude may have been simply one of growing up a little, but I like to think that living on board, traveling to new places, sharing a little of the responsibilities and work on *Eileen*, and meeting

Mary Adams busy with a history lesson aboard Eileen.

a variety of children in similar circumstances had something to do with it.

Mary spends each morning from 0900 to 1100 or 1130 studying her elementary correspondence school lessons from the Department of Education in Victoria, British Columbia. The cost is $76 a year, which includes all books, lessons, examinations, teaching instructions, and even specimens for science (a preserved shrimp, for example). In short, everything except a patient parent to keep an alert eye on the whole business. Included among the books are many paperbacks—easier to stow—but Mary also received a hefty atlas, a big dictionary, a book of poetry, and various hardbound textbooks. Supplementary books can sometimes be borrowed from a local library—if there is one.

"When we first left Canada, Mary missed her friends at school," said Mrs. Adams. "She was unhappy for a few days but soon got over it. We discovered that children waste an inordinate amount of time at school. The lesson plans of the correspondence courses are excellent; Mary can accomplish more in two hours in the quiet saloon of *Eileen* than she did in five hours at school. To make up for the lack of social life, we find that she soon makes friends in each port that we visit.

"Make no mistake about the parents' role," continued Mrs. Adams. "Even with the teaching instructions written out by experts, there is quite a bit of reading to do. It's amazing how much I've learned! We find that a child should have reasonable reading skills, because most of the instructions are detailed and need to be followed closely. There are many composition-type exercises which cover topics of different choices, including stories of the trip, new friends, and personal experiences. Laboratory science situations are sometimes difficult, but there are various alternative lessons. We were told that correspondence lessons don't work for some children, so we tried the system out a little before we left.

"Both the parents and the child need a bit of organizing," said Mrs. Adams. "It is surprising how many things must be completed before a set of lessons is ready to be mailed. Mary always breathes a big sigh of joy when she finally puts a lesson envelope in the mail."

Some of the Canadian pupils are in the Arctic, some live in Africa, while other children travel with parents who are engineers, diplomats, military people, or consultants for various United Nations or other foreign programs in remote areas. According to Mrs. Adams, there were seventeen children living on ships who were taking British Columbia schooling courses in 1972. The Canadian program has a number of full-time teachers, who like to meet the children if possible or at least to exchange a snapshort or two. A pupil has the same instructors all year, and little notes are sent back and forth. In other words, the school staff tries hard to make the student and teacher—who may be separated by thousands of miles—a little closer in spirit. A brown envelope can be pretty impersonal.

"Sometimes it's hard to keep to a regular schedule," said Mary's father, Dr. Adams. "Things are a little more hectic and irregular on a boat. Guests and workmen and officials arrive without notice, or we may have the yacht hauled out of the water while we paint her bottom. But by and large Mary puts in the required hours. I see to that."

The school prefers to have tests administered by a responsible disinterested person (lawyer, local school official, port captain, etc.). The arrangement, however, is flexible as required.

The Canadian school is only one of many correspondence programs that are used by children and adults of every age. Practically all countries have correspondence schools of some kind—programs for elementary, junior high, high school, and beyond. State universities often have extensive programs and will send you a thick catalogue in exchange for a postcard. Witness the success of navigation schools that are run entirely by mailed-in lessons.

Many American and foreign children on world cruising yachts have been educated by the Calvert School (Tuscany Road, Baltimore, Md. 21210), founded in 1897, which offers instruction from kindergarten through eighth grade by a teaching staff of fifty-four professionals. The courses are constantly being updated and evaluated by educational experts and offer the latest in new mathematics and science. The Calvert School deals with basic reading instruction in addition to scores of other subjects, and furnishes detailed daily lesson plans plus general instructions.

For example, the third-grade course has reading, composition, spelling and phonics, arithmetic, history and mythology, geography, science, picture study, poetry, and drawing. The school recommends its advisory teaching service, which provides special guidance for the parent and child, information on the grading of papers, suggestions for improvement, and advice to the home teacher (who often has no experience) on how to encourage and teach the pupil.

The Calvert School is a non-profit organization approved by the State of Maryland; the school's certificates of completion are readily accepted by most authorities. The tuition charge is $150 for each school year, which includes all lesson materials, books, and the teacher advisory service. The shipping weight of a typical Calvert course is twenty-two pounds.

"The Calvert people are not kidding when they claim to furnish everything," said Al Kohlwes, the owner of *Proesa*, a handsome forty-six-foot steel yawl built in Germany and based in San Francisco. "When we enrolled our boys Jeff and Chris in the fifth and seventh grades, we were flabbergasted at the mountain of things that arrived. The boys got both hard- and soft-cover books, paper, pencils, crayons, rulers, drawing paper, compasses—everything except thinking caps.

"We soon found out that the supervision aspect requires considerable adult time," said Kohlwes. "The instructions are planned for a nine-month school year with each of our two boys working five days a week for two to five hours a day. A typical instruction plan starts out with the phrase 'Today your student will study . . .' We think the boys are getting excellent schooling in both hard-core and cultural subjects, although we realize that correspondence work doesn't replace a normal school.

"Preparatory to enrolling at the Calvert School, a student takes a test to evaluate his knowledge," said Kohlwes. "Jeff was OK for arithmetic but a poor speller like his father. Chris needed help with composition and handwriting."

The schooling can go leisurely or be more rushed, depending on the student. Mrs. Liev Kennedy, recalling her son's schooling in Australia aboard *Kelea*, wrote the following: "One morning, less than a week after our arrival in Gladstone, a shout sounded from the after cabin. 'Hooray! I've finished grade five.' We all cheered. Curtis had done well. Working only while in port, he had waded through thirty-six lessons of arithmetic, English, social studies, science, and spelling. His working day would generally start around seven and continue late into the afternoon. He would always join us, however, on any excursion we might take to a new area. He was his own boss and set up his own work schedule; it was up to him how much he got done."

When I began to collect material for this chapter, I had no idea there were so many children on yachts and elsewhere being educated by correspondence. I found out that there are dozens of schools (for more names and addresses, check your local library). The two I've detailed are typical, however, and have been well tried by the children of the sailors to whom I've talked at length. Many of the home-study schools are concerned with completing high school.

Where regular correspondence and the mailing of lessons is troublesome, the Parents' National Education Union (PNEU), based in England, may be a good choice. The non-profit PNEU scheme gives the parents a complete term's work at one time together with answers.

Address: PNEU, Murray House, Vandon Street, London SW1H OAJ.

Mrs. Carol Hogan wrote a wonderful article, "The Kids Made the Cruise," in the April 1975 issue of *Sail* magazine. The Hogan family had a nine-year-old girl and an eleven-year-old boy to educate but no funds for formal correspondence courses. Mrs. Hogan asked for help from the principal of the school that her children were attending. The principal thought that the proposed cruise was the best education possible. She helped Mrs. Hogan prepare an extensive study outline and supplied seventy-five books, including some teacher's editions.

For the first six months the Hogans tried to maintain regular study periods ("OK, everybody down below for some arithmetic"). In Panama, however, after the children had passed achievement tests with ease, the approach was changed to put more emphasis on current experiences and less on schoolbooks. Instead of writing on abstract topics, the children were encouraged to prepare compositions about their trip and the things they were experiencing. The Hogan youngsters did a great deal of reading from children's literature, which included fiction and the classics (available in paperback). Geography and language books helped develop other skills, while foreign-language practice itself was easy with local children when the yacht was in distant ports. The ship's library was supplemented by additional books and pamphlets from the U.S. Government Printing Office and the Pan American Union in Washington, D.C.

After the first few months of cruising, the year ended and we didn't have a calendar so we improvised with home made [wrote Mrs. Hogan]. These were always colorful and had pictures and notations added by the whole crew. We kept careful track of days spent at sea and noted special events that took place. A special event could be anything. Our daughter became publisher/editor/reporter, and typed a weekly newspaper entitled *Discovery Press*. It contained poems, straight news, special events, and lottery results. Small prizes were awarded for accurately guessing ETAs, and winners were announced in the paper. Other diversions at sea included cards, puzzles, and games. Scrabble was an educational and stimulating favorite.

Birthdays and holidays were exciting events. We always managed to bake and we had a supply of candles and cake decorations. Boat-baked cakes became works of art. To accompany the cakes, the children filled many hours designing and creating holiday decorations and cards from our supply of crayons, colored pencils, glue, and glitter. Additional craft items aboard included a watercolor set, construction paper, wrapping paper and ribbon, writing paper, masking tape, Scotch tape, oil paints, small canvases, and even a supply of mosaic tile and cutters. We kept a list of birthdays for family and friends and all cards and gifts made at sea were mailed to them from the next port.

Even on the high seas we celebrated Christmas with a small, stowable, artificial tree hung with brightly-colored, home-made decorations. The cabin lamp was usually hung with paper trees and bells too.

We had a small portable sewing machine on board, and using a gasoline generator on deck for power, we could sew on calm days at sea. The sewing kit included embroidery hoops, thread, every kind of miscellaneous sewing notion, and extra blue, green, and red yardage. This we used to make our own courtesy flags before entering ports. For reference we used a United Nations flag chart.

Once in port the local stores supplied small playthings that would be of interest to kids. Almost every town had souvenir items that made good toys. For example, in Mexico Sharri found a large variety of small pottery dishes and was able to purchase them for a few pesos. On board Sharri played with her small dolls and pots for hours, and every item imaginable went into making doll clothes and doll houses.

The children had a few small pets on board, and in foreign ports the youngsters became fishermen and local explorers in the sailing dinghy. There was hiking, surfing, and swimming with fins and masks. The children also collected shells, which they cleaned, categorized, labeled with correct Latin names, and stored. At sea the youngsters towed a plankton net and inspected their daily harvest with a simple microscope. As the yacht's latitude changed, there were new constellations of stars to identify. When the Hogan family crossed the equator, a fatherly King Neptune made his appearance—bearded, crowned, wearing a white sheet, carrying a trident—and solemnly presented hand-lettered shellback certificates. Obviously, the conscientious parents had as much fun as the children.

The major teaching problem turned out to be the everyday distractions involved with cruising, e.g., a reading lesson interrupted by my husband catching a fish, with the result that reading turned into biology [wrote Mrs. Hogan]. Because of this we realized the need to be flexible, and whenever possible we made everything into a learning situation, not getting frustrated by interruptions. We found we needed books to cover every topic from astronomy to zoology. I recommend a fairly new encyclopedia set published by the World Publishing Company called *The Ocean World of Jacques Cousteau*.[23]

Mrs. Hogan learned that, with the whole world as a classroom, you don't need formal teaching credentials to wind up with some fairly well-educated children at the end of the voyage. It's not necessary to be a nuclear physicist to teach a nine-year-old some arithmetic.

Margaret and I have seen young people of all ages on yachts. Three times we have got acquainted with children who were *born* afloat. Unless you are a real diehard and enthusiast, however, I think that very young children have no place on board the restricted quarters of a small yacht (maybe my age is showing). When infants are in a crib, the diaper difficulty is an appalling problem. At walking age the children are liable to crawl up the companionway steps and toddle right over the side unless an adult keeps an eye on them. Certainly youngsters should be obliged to wear life jackets whenever they go on deck.

From four or five years of age and onward, however, I think a child can fit in with life afloat. He can learn simple jobs at first and gradually master more complex procedures with age and experience. He or she can soon learn to steer and to take daylight watches. In fact, to keep up crew morale and interest, it's good for *everyone*—wives, children, friends, mothers-in-law—to participate in some phase of running the ship. Certainly all hands should have safety harnesses and should practice man-overboard drills and recovery.

If young people are given their head, it's surprising how much they can learn about navigation and pilotage and sail handling. I immediately think of Curtis Kennedy, Reid Griffith, and Ronald Mitchell, respectively a Canadian, an American, and an Australian, who started sailing with their world cruising parents when they were small boys. Now, after periods of five to ten years and with thousands and thousands of sailing miles behind them, these youths are no longer boys but experienced and resourceful young men. Each has a well-developed sense of judgment and achievement and an enviable background of visits to the far corners of the world—the unique reward of life under sail.

I think also of the daughter of a friend who has taken his family on one colossal sailing passage after another. The daughter was seventeen and her beauty and figure were breathtaking. Her smile would have opened the door to Heaven itself. At each island where the yacht stopped, a swarm of suitors soon collected. The daughter fell madly in love with one young man and announced that she was staying. Her father counterannounced that the yacht was leaving on Tuesday and that she had better be ready to leave with it.

"But, father," she wailed. "You can't. I'm in love!"

"It's Tuesday, child, and that's final," said her father in a stern voice.

On Tuesday the yacht left with a weeping and miserable daughter who was prostrate with grief. ("Oh, daddy, what'll I do?") On Wednesday she was standing watches as usual. On Thursday she had forgotten her suitor's name. On Friday she was anxiously scanning the horizon for a new landfall.

CAPITAN DEL PUERTO

DANILO EGRED HEREDIA
ALFEREZ DE NAVIO- UN.

ARMADA DEL ECUADOR

SANTA - CRUZ

RTO - AYORA

POR LA PRESENTE SE CERTIFICA PARA LOS FINES NECESA

" WHISPER " DE BANDERA NORTEAMERICANA, DE 8.99 T
OR CAPITAN HAL ROTH; CON DOS TRIPULANTES Y SIN
A RRECORRIDO DE ISLAS.

CAPITAN DEL PU

DANILO EGRED HE
ALFEREZ DE NAVIO.

REPUBLICA DEL ECUADOR

CAPITANIA DEL PUERTO

GUAYAQUIL

CERTIFICADO DE ZARPE

nte se certifica, para los fines necesarios

ue el buque yate turismo "WHISPER"

Bandera _norteamericana_ 8.99 toneladas netas, al

_____ toneladas brutas _____

ndo del señor Capitán: Hal Roth _____ sin _____ pasajeros

_____ dos _____ tripulantes y

sido despachado previo el cumplimiento de los requisitos deter-

nados en el **Código de Policía Marítima**, con destino al

erto de _____ Recorrido por el Archipiélago _____ y escalas en

San Cristóbal, Guayaquil, a 29 de _____ Enero _____ de 1973

ZARPE

EL CAPITAN DEL PUERTO

Offset Imp. Yzquieta-86

es Ochoa-Aguirra 118

20

~~~~~~

Foreign Paperwork

One of the mysteries of modern travel is that you can fly all over the world and whiz in and out of country after country and hardly ever spend more than a few minutes dealing with entrance and exit formalities. Yet when you switch from the air to a small ship, the same country-to-country border formalities often become tedious and complex. Certainly many of the procedures are archaic. In an age of computerized tourism and vast international commerce, can you imagine hoisting a signal flag to ask for permission to enter a country? It wasn't long ago that suspect ships were fumigated with pots of burning sulphur.

A ship must satisfy four classes of regulations: customs, immigration, health, and agriculture. *Customs*, of course, deals with restrictions on the transit of many items—machinery, whisky, foodstuffs, tobacco, clocks —a million things. The gear, fittings, and spares of a transient vessel are exempt, but you must be scrupulous in not selling things from the ship to locals without telling the customs people. You can get into terrible trouble trying to make a few dollars on the sly. If you want to help someone, you are much better off to *give* the item away, but even then you should inform the officials. Not only are there possible penalties against you, but you ought to think of the yachtsmen and travelers who come after you. It can be very nasty to follow a ship whose crew has misbehaved. The thing to aim for when you leave a country is to have people on the dock waving and smiling, not throwing rocks and shaking their fists.

Some countries do not allow private ownership of firearms. The customs agents in Papeete and Kobe and Bermuda, for instance, will ask for all guns and take them from you in exchange for a receipt which will be honored for the weapons when you get your final clearance. Canada allows rifles but no handguns. Other countries have varying restrictions.

Parts, stores, and equipment for a vessel and personal items for the crew can usually be shipped in free of duty. Such packages are addressed: "USA Yacht *Smile* in transit" and theoretically pay no customs charges. Each country has different procedures, however, best looked into when you are there. Sometimes a customs agent may be necessary; perhaps a friend in the country can help. By the time such shipments actually arrive on board, the costs are high and are usually only worthwhile for high-priority items.

Immigration is concerned with your physical presence within a country and what you will be doing while there. Generally, yachtsmen are classed as tourists or merchant seamen and you are not allowed to compete with local citizens for employment. Sometimes you are asked to secure permission to visit a country in advance—a visa—and in a few places you must post a bond to guarantee your exit transportation by commercial means. To visit French Polynesia, for example, every non–Common Market citizen must put up a bond equivalent to the cost of air travel out of the territory. This anti-beachcomber guarantee is $280 and must be posted by the owner, passengers, and each member of a yacht's crew, notwithstanding the fact that their vessel is their transport to and from the area. Incidentally, it's a good idea to get visas in advance when you visit French Polynesia; otherwise the officials in the outer islands tend to hurry you along to Tahiti, when you might wish to spend time in the outlying islands beforehand.

The various customs and immigration regulations apply to each member of a ship's crew, for whose presence and behavior and bills the captain is entirely responsible. Sometimes it is very tedious to make crew changes. If a new crew member is flying to meet the vessel at point X, it may be prudent to see a consul of the country in question *beforehand* and get an official letter from him detailing any special procedures.

Each consul is a special problem, and his demands for fees must be judged according to how important his special permissions are to you. Some consuls are paid very little and must eke out their salaries with fees. A few try to take advantage of yachtsmen. If you feel you are being victimized, you can complain to the ambassador or to the head of the department of tourism of the country in question, sometimes with startling and immediate results. Don't be too quick to complain, however. Even if you feel there has been some injustice, it may be simpler in the long run to pay a small fee and to forget it.

The sums for visas and port charges for many countries are trifling. In 1967 we stayed in the Gilbert Islands for five weeks and paid only about $5, which included harbor dues, buoyage charges, fresh-water fees, and all else. But port regulations are ever changing and are generally out of date before they are written down. I think the best scheme is to make inquiries among yachtsmen who have been to the country you are planning to visit (sailors in their home country seldom realize the requirements for foreign yachts; taxation, registration, residence, sale, chartering are by no means simple and may be unacceptably expensive).

If I am unable to find out anything about a country that I want to visit, I simply go. If the information is conflicting, seems unreasonable, or comes from a doubtful source, I ignore it.

If you have no knowledge of a confused foreign situation and want to ask for authority or permission, a good way is to pay a personal call on the naval attaché at the country's embassy. Sometimes a naval attaché will take an interest in your voyage and secure special seasonal weather reports or port information for you. For example, when we were in Japan and ready to leave for the Aleutians, Margaret called on the naval attaché at the U.S. Embassy in Tokyo. (We had heard that the Griffiths on *Awahnee* had stopped at the U.S. Navy base at Adak the year before and had almost been arrested because they arrived unannounced during war games.) Margaret asked the attaché to send a message informing the commander that we were coming and requesting permission to use the harbor at Adak for a few days. By originating the request with an official, we had the system with us and a sort of quasi-authority to visit a place that we had heard was tough on transient vessels.

When we sailed south from Lima, we had no knowledge of southern Peru. The air attaché at the U.S. Embassy introduced me to an aide of a principal Peruvian admiral who was both a keen small boat sailor and a native of the area. He made valuable suggestions.

I don't want to overemphasize this and suggest a run on attachés or people in high positions, but I think one can ask for a little assistance occasionally. Sometimes a few bits of information can lead to a slight change in plans and turn a routine passage into an exciting experience. We met a man in Ponape in the eastern Caroline Islands who told us about the bay on southern Guam that Magellan had entered in 1521. We sailed to that little bay and our visit was memorable.

I often think of the wise words of Miles Smeeton regarding official clearances. "Never ask too many questions," Miles told me once. "Somebody might say no! Then what would you do? Just go and the officials will have to deal with you."

Besides customs and immigration, a vessel must satisfy *health* regulations. When you enter a country the first time and hoist the yellow Q flag (beneath the courtesy ensign of the country) up to the outer part of the starboard spreader of the mainmast, the flag is signaling: "My vessel is healthy and I request free pratique." The port captain's office or the health department will send out a doctor to decide whether the people on the incoming ship are healthy and "free of plague." If your inoculations for smallpox or tetanus or whatever have expired, you will sometimes be injected on the spot or be sent to a local hospital. Supposedly, if one had the mumps or whooping cough, the vessel would be obliged to remain in a quarantine anchorage until the danger passed (yet you can travel by bus or plane or automobile and never be questioned). Animal quarantine (for rabies, generally) comes under health. Most countries pay no attention to dogs and cats and parrots, but Hawaii and England, for example, have extremely strict rules for pets.

Spain is a special case regarding the Q flag, which, when seen, appears to terrify the local officials and makes them believe that you have grave infectious illnesses on board. On the basis of the experience of many yachtsmen, I would not use the Q flag in Spain.

The inspector for *agriculture* is concerned with stopping harmful insects and plant diseases from entering his country. In Rarotonga in the Cook Islands, where the orange crop is of great importance, all incoming citrus fruits and their containers are routinely destroyed to prevent introduction of pests. In islands that raise coconuts there may be special inspections for the rhinoceros beetle. The United States prohibits any fresh meat from abroad except under closely controlled conditions, because of the chance of foot-and-mouth disease in foreign cattle. And so on.

The four inspections are sometimes handled by four men, or one man may come on board and deal with several or even all of the inspections, depending on local arrangements. A yacht and her people are often an amusement for the officials, who like to come on board, look around a bit, and have a cup of coffee or the traditional brandy. Since the men live in the area, they will be knowledgeable about the port and can generally answer any pressing questions.

The inspections are usually handled through a port captain's office, which may also be charged with controlling your anchorage or docking, dealing with pilotage and watchmen, collecting small sums for harbor dues, fresh-water services, and navigation light maintenance. The various charges are often computed on ship tonnage.

Foreign officials expect you to have the flag of their country prominently displayed on your vessel. Some port captains are insulted if they do not see their flag and can levy substantial fines. The countries of South America are particularly touchy on this point, especially Chile, Peru, and Uruguay. In general, be sure to have 20 x 30-inch or larger courtesy flags for all countries on your itinerary. Most flags are easy to make, and since they are viewed at a distance, the fine points of sewing aren't too important. The main things are the colors and general form. Brazil, Canada, Antigua, and Barbados, for example, have complicated colors or patterns and you may have to buy these flags. A foreign yachtsman with a ketch who visits Uruguay and is used to flying his national flag at his mizzen top (higher than the mainmast spreaders with the courtesy flag of Uruguay) will soon learn that the Uruguayans want their flag higher and will stand for nothing else. No matter how illogical these demands may seem, the best thing is to agree at once and to change the flag flying to the local custom.

It's best to enter a port during regular working hours; overtime charges for night and Sunday officialdom are high. Generally, you must enter a country at a large port or a major harbor, where officials are present. It is customary for you not to conduct any business or for anyone to go ashore until the ship has been cleared. If no one comes in response to the yellow flag after a period of hours, I row ashore and either telephone or walk to the port captain's office. I take a crew list, the registration paper for the ship, passports, vaccination certificates, and any special clearance papers. If there is a language problem, you will have to find an interpreter or else fight it out with a dictionary. No matter what happens, I try to keep calm and remember that I am a guest of the country. Keep smiling no matter what happens.

I never pay any charges at this time, because (1) I don't know the local rules, (2) the "charges" may be dropped, and (3) you generally have no local funds anyway. I try to stall off compliance with anything that seems ridiculous until I can inquire at a yacht club or talk with the captain of a merchant ship. Sometimes the ship's papers and passports are taken from you and a receipt is given, but you should try hard to keep these documents after showing them. You can argue that if a wind comes up in the night and you have to clear out you must have your papers.

If all else fails, you may have to engage an agent. If this is the only way, I shop around and try to find an agent or shipping company that deals with vessels from my country. Most agents are reputable, but a few are crooks and will try to charge you the moon. In Peru I had the experience of being told that an agent was obligatory ("There is no other way, señor. I can suggest a reliable man."). I went to see the agent and was told that the initial fee would be $100. A second agent told me that the first agent was the brother of the man I first spoke to and who got a percentage of all business he originated. The second agent—with whom I became great friends—dealt with my problems and charged me nothing at all!

When you leave a country, you should have an outgoing clearance of some kind. Anything will do just as long as it looks vaguely official with a few stamps and signatures on it. Authorities prefer big sheets of paper with a lot of words and a counter-signature or two if possible. The last three times I have left the U.S. mainland, however, the customs people have declined to give me papers of any kind. Yet on leaving Guam, Western Samoa, Bermuda, and Japan, for instance, I was given an outbound clearance, which is the first thing the next country's officials asked for. An Ecuadorian official told me that his country didn't issue outbound clearances; the next country, of course, demanded an outbound clearance from my last stop and threatened me with a big fine. On one trip I got a formal health certificate, which stated that I had no infected rats on board. But no one was interested in this intriguing document, and after carrying the paper around for years, I finally threw it away.

If the preceding pages seem vague and conflicting, it is because ship's paperwork is one of hazy cross-purposes. The only thing certain is that there are no rules. Confusion is normal. No matter what paper you have, you need something else. In blue, green, and red. And six copies of each. Perhaps one should carry a printing press, red ribbons, a notary stamp, wax, and signet rings. Certainly a bottle of brandy. For the captain.

A startling example of poor construction and the force of breaking water. This 37-foot Chris-Craft Apache sloop was damaged severely (and lucky not to have been sunk) by a wave that broke on board a little southwest of San Francisco's Golden Gate. The force of the water found weaknesses in the coach roof, which in this case was a kind of foam sandwich construction without proper fiberglass layup above and below the foam. Notice the long cracks in the brittle filler (unstrengthened by fiberglass), the missing portlights, and the crushed companionway. A vertical post inside the cabin near the hatch might have helped support the coach roof. One liter of water weighs one kilo, which seems little enough. But the weight of water increases enormously with larger volumes. One cubic meter of water weighs about 1,000 kilos. A wall of water only two meters high, three meters long, and two meters from front to back weighs almost 12,000 kilos or 12 metric tons. No wonder yachts that sail on the ocean need to be strong.

The Chris-Craft company quickly had this yacht withdrawn from sight. The camera's eye is often damning, however, and this visual evidence is hard to explain away or to laugh off.

21

~~~~~~

Which Yacht for Me?

The very first, the basic question to ask yourself when choosing a yacht is: "What am I going to do with her?"

If you want to win big-league ocean races, by all means go to a specialized naval architect like Dick Carter or Sparkman & Stephens and sign up for a sleek, high-ballasted aluminum beauty that will fly to windward quicker than a sea gull sniffing sardines. The yacht will cost the earth—$100,000 hardly opens the action—and she will require a crew of expensive and temperamental experts to sail her. You will need truckloads of nautical jewelry—ant hills, cross-connected three-speeds, hydraulic vangs and babystays, electronic consoles, disappearing spinnaker poles—and such exotic sails as tallboys, flankers, runners, and big boys.

Ocean racing is a high-pressure league of nautical lawyers and mathematical wizards who study each rule change more closely than Hebraic scholars working on the Dead Sea Scrolls. You will have to learn a new language so you can casually throw around such terms as "tight leeching," "rudder ventilation," "Barber hauling," "negative RSAT," and "slot control." Though your nifty yacht will initially get acclaim in all the sailing magazines, in two or three years she will be obsolete. The yacht brokers will have a hard time selling her even at a big loss, because if she has a winning pedigree, "she may be strained and worn out." If she hasn't won, "she's no good anyway."

Yet if ocean racing is your life, you'll sell your soul to have her.

If you want a motor sailer because of demanding time schedules or for use in poor sailing areas, then hire Phillip Rhodes or Eldredge-McInnis and outline your requirements. If you like to sail but hate wind and spray, or your wife has reservations about the whole thing, the shelter of an enclosed deckhouse and steering position may be ideal. A six-cylinder Caterpillar engine gives marvelous performance. I know one couple whose whole life exists around afternoon bridge games in their deckhouse, from which they can see their friends and other boat life in the harbor. Sometimes motor sailer owners who keep track of engine and sailing hours find that they sail only 10 percent of the time and that they would be better off with a powerboat or a bus-type mobile home. Yet the prestige of a large and well-kept motor sailer is rewarding; lovely varnished wood and immaculate teak decks give a feeling of pride and perfection.

If you are a Sunday-afternoon enthusiast who likes to sail a Folkboat or a Cal 20 in a windy area and not use an outboard, then by all means have the best Folkboat or Cal 20 on the bay and learn to be an authority in intricate maneuvering under sail. My friend John O'Brien races his Cal 20 keenly and hard and realizes that his little fiberglass sloop is an interesting hobby and nothing more. "She's perfect for me," says O'Brien. "She's a pleasant diversion from the pressures of being an architect and designing houses and apartments and commercial buildings from Monday to Friday."

If the yachtsman's concern is with long-distance coastal cruising—perhaps the west coast of Mexico or the islands of Yugoslavia northwest of Dubrovnik—he travels in a different sort of vessel. This man goes from bay to harbor to island and prefers a familiar mountain to be within handy binocular distance; he anchors or ties up each night and may travel in company with a second yacht. If a storm comes up, shelter is nearby. Some might say that such a captain is timid, but maybe he is more sensible than one who crosses oceans and gets flattened in storms. It is wonderful to enjoy a quiet anchorage, to see a new town from your own vessel, and to have a brisk sail on the smooth water of a cloud-dappled fiord.

A four- or five-foot draft and masts in tabernacles are an advantage with this class of cruising vessel, especially if the captain elects to use canals on his travels. The deep-sea aspects of this yacht are not so critical, and the crew need not be so strong. A big cockpit with a good-sized awning for the sun, perhaps building to less rigorous standards (see the discussion of Lloyd's below), and more emphasis on the engine, electrics, and deluxe accommodation are the hallmarks of the larger coastal cruiser.

Jack Jensen, who founded Jensen Marine, the manufacturer of Cal yachts, is quite aware that his Cal Cruising 46 is not an ocean crossing powerhouse. "She wasn't designed to be," said Jack when we discussed this point. "She was made for easy coastal cruising, which is exactly what Hale Field and I, who have the prototypes, use them for. We have traveled from California to Alaska, but we do the trips from point to point when the weather is good and the sailing or motoring is pleasurable."

There is a smaller class of coastal cruising vessel best exemplified by the pocket cruiser designed by Maurice Griffiths for the southeast coast of England, a world of tidal estuaries, shimmering sands, inquisitive shorebirds, strong winds or no winds, and muddy anchorages. In my home state of California I think of sailing in sheltered Tomales Bay in a lightly built, inexpensive twenty-five-foot daysailer with a retractable keel and the fun of running this small cruiser up on an isolated beach, camping overnight, catching a salmon, and building a big fire to cook Sunday dinner. In a thousand places in the world, weekend enthusiasts sail to nearby sheltered islands, anchor for a day or two, and have an informal meal or a scratch race with similar small coastal cruising vessels.

Quite another sort of yacht is required for unlimited ocean cruising. If this is your game, you need a robust and seaworthy vessel built to specifications that have been worked out and refined by generations of patient and hardworking naval architects. A few years ago in Tahiti, I interviewed the owners of sixteen round-the-world yachts, and I can tell you something about the typical small vessel that is crossing the oceans of today.

She is a monohull between thirty and forty feet in length with a beam of ten or eleven feet and a draft of six feet. She is of medium displacement, has outside ballast of perhaps 30 or 35 percent of her tonnage, and is about ten years old. Her hull is made of steel, fiberglass, or wood and has short or moderate overhangs. The hull may have wineglass sections, although a surprising number of these vessels have hard chine construction and are built from steel or plywood. Or she may have a roundish bottom with a fin keel and a rudder attached to a hefty skeg.

She might be rigged as a ketch, but this sail plan—while offering more sail combinations—is losing favor becouse of the added expense and complication of a mizzenmast, a bowsprit, and sometimes a bumpkin. The mizzen sail is often useless while on the wind or running.

Our typical Tahiti cruiser will be rigged as a Bermudian cutter or sloop with a variety of headsails. Her mast will be tall so she can set plenty of canvas for light airs, but she also carries storm sails. There will be a long pole or two hanging from the mast to wing out headsails for running. Her cockpit will be of modest size and she will have small portlights. On board you will see a sailing dinghy, a bicycle, and a couple of tires for use as drogues or fenders. On the afterdeck an odd-looking steering vane turns nervously as each gust of wind passes.

The little ship will have a small diesel engine, three or four slightly rusty anchors spaced around the deck, and she will be four or five inches down on her designed waterline because of all her gear and stores. The paint on the topsides may have a few scratches, and the boot topping line may be a bit wavy—reminders that haulout facilities in many places are primitive and expensive and that the captain and his crew were hurried when painting (also it rained).

There will be a radio transmitter which is likely to be out of order because it hasn't been used for a year or more, since there is no communications network and no one to talk to. You will see two (or one or three) people on board with maybe a child or two scampering along the side decks. The captain will have ten years of sailing experience, having started with dinghies and worked up. He is confident, resourceful, clever with his hands, and has a big smile, for though he is sometimes harried, he is a happy man. The captain and crew will be typically short of money but will be having the time of their lives. In short, our ocean crosser is an ideal mini-ship for blue-water sailing, a little small perhaps and sometimes with an unpleasant motion, but a satisfactory compromise.

I believe a prospective yacht owner should think hard about what he wants to do with his vessel before he buys it or has it built. If this sentence reads like a kindergarten instruction, it is only because I have seen dozens and dozens of people in yachts quite unsuitable for them. A prospect would be well served if he wiped the glitter from his eyes and the sweet words of the salesmen from his ears; instead he should sit down for an hour in a quiet place with those who will be with him and write out on a single sheet of paper exactly what he intends to do with his small craft. He might be wise to seek out owners of his intended design and talk with them; he might even build a scale model of her to familiarize himself with every detail.

The prospective yacht owner should realize that ocean racing is a great deal different from ocean cruising. Racing gets a lot of attention and many owners do lip service to competition, but it is clear that most yachts are bought for pleasure sailing, not racing (of course, some men consider that racing is pleasure). Similarly, local overnight cruising is one thing; long-distance coastal cruising can be quite another. For many kinds of harbor and local area enjoyment the choice of a power yacht may be quite sensible. A motor sailer can be a marina show-off piece or a unique way to enjoy both power and sail, but its design requirements are particularly severe if it is to enjoy the best of both worlds.

Boating advertisements often seem designed to confuse the poor prospect. We see a full-page color photograph for a forty-foot sloop with an enormous headsail and accompanying advertising copy that implies that a man and his wife "in their retirement years" can easily handle a 150 percent genoa in a rising wind. Yet if we look closer at the beautiful color photograph, we see two or three muscular men crouched along the weather rail. The photograph is always taken in sheltered water, although the copy suggests a go-anywhere approach.

I think there should be a rating system of all yachts so that each buyer knows in unmistakable terms exactly what he is getting. With the proliferation of coastal and world cruising, some kind of offshore and onshore classification is necessary and would clearly help everyone, particularly the commercial yacht builders, for a satisfied customer is the best of all possible advertisements.

Professional naval architects are accountable for their work, and the men I know are quite willing to suggest specific designs for certain trips. Respectable building yards clearly guard their reputations. Amateur designers and slipshod builders have no place in our world, because a sometimes cruel sea makes no distinction. Twice I have met yacht plan sellers who promise a would-be adventurer that he can build a yacht from scratch for a few thousand dollars and sail around the world. Such claims are ridiculous and not only hurt the poor plan buyers—who are often incredulous when they find out what they have got into—but give a bad name to the whole world of small ship sailing. If I had a dollar for every ferro-cement and trimaran building disaster I have seen, I would have a suitcase full of money. Ferro-cement is a useful hull-building material and trimarans certainly have their place in the sailing world; however, plan sellers who exploit these mediums and grossly overpromote their wares and try to minimize costs and building times make me ashamed that such people are in my sport.

To upgrade the general standards of yachts, I am in favor of building to

A broken spade rudder on an Islander 37. The rudder came with a new yacht made by a supposedly reputable company. In spite of naval architect Bill Tripp's careful drawings that showed a full-length heavy-walled stainless steel pipe the entire length of the rudder, an appalling iron weldment was substituted by the builder. Externally the rudder looked perfect, with the required rudder stock disappearing into a carefully streamlined fiberglass foam section. But just below the surface there was no strength at all; the first time owner John Warren took his new yacht Beyond out into the ocean, the rudder folded like a piece of paper. Mr. Warren hired an attorney to file a damage suit, but was mollified by the company, which supplied a new rudder and an excuse that a subcontractor was responsible.

the Lloyd's Register of Shipping classification scheme. Lloyd's is an international organization, is well set up for small vessels, and is active and respected. The procedure means having the naval architect's plans

A close-up of the broken Islander 37 rudder shows no rudder stock at all. Instead, there is a piece of flat iron totally lacking in athwartship strength. The man who ignored the naval architect's plans and built this rudder certainly never went to sea.

approved by Lloyd's engineers, having the construction inspected by Lloyd's surveyors, and having periodic checks to establish the current condition. A vessel so classed is listed in the latest *Register of Yachts*.

The advantage to the buyer is that an independent authority is on his side. The advantage to the reputable builder is that an independent authority certifies his product. The advantage to everyone is that slipshod building and designing are eliminated and we get better vessels. On an expensive yacht (all yachts are expensive) Lloyd's fee is perhaps 2 percent of the total cost, which is more than offset by the buyer's peace of mind and the ease of resale.

It is a well-established custom to have surveyors inspect and certify the condition of used yachts when they change hands. I think it is equally important to have a tough surveyor—hired by the buyer— *look over a new vessel as well*. In fact, the logical plan is to have the surveyor inspect the yacht when it is under construction and to check each system at different stages of building.

A most important aspect, of course, will deal with the fiberglass hull— the verification of the resin type and age, the requisite number of various glass materials, good layup techniques, the checking of ballast weight, supervision of bulkhead installation, and so on, right up through the engine, the plumbing, and the stepping of the mast.

The time for inspections is when a bulkhead is being put in, not after joinery work has hidden part of the framework. If an independent surveyor with reasonable authority is on hand and sees a problem, he should be able to say, "Hey, wait a minute, fellows. Before you cover over that bulkhead area with those nifty teak panels, I want to see the proper amount of fiberglass on those hull-to-bulkhead joints." A few hundred dollars' worth of time and glass at an early stage can prevent thousands of dollars' worth of agony and trouble at a later time. *For both the buyer and the builder.*

Another function of an independent endorsing authority is to make sure that the plans of the architect are being followed *and continue to be followed.* What a naval architect draws and what is actually built are often quite different. Among electronic equipment installers, who cut holes in hulls for speed indicators and depth sounders, it is an old story that each year the hull plugs cut from the same models get thinner and thinner.

New yachts always have growing pains. Good builders use feedback from buyers to improve the vessels. No. 25 of a series should be a much better yacht than No. 2. These changes and improvements should be discussed and planned with the buyer's representative—the independent surveyor.

A further advantage of inspections is that rumors and whispering campaigns can be stopped. Perhaps advertising should be more truthful. Yachtsmen are gossipy types by nature, and no news travels faster than fanciful stories and half-truths about some yacht or other. ("Have you heard about the Snowflake 41?" "Yep, the steering vane supports caved in the whole transom. Weak as a piece of cardboard.")

I know that if an independent engineering authority routinely inspects plans for any complex product, you always get better final results. I have looked at drawings for hull-deck joints on glass boats that are simply impossible to build. I have seen deck structures that are grossly overbuilt and not only affect stability but waste a lot of money. Some of our best yacht designers are more artists than hard-boiled engineers. The gimlet eyes of a structural engineer can be a welcome and leavening influence. In addition, the surveying agency should be intimately concerned with materials. Aluminum pop rivets, inferior wiring, badly seasoned wood, cheap plywood, chopper gun layups, self-tapping screws, shoddy rigging hardware, and so on, have no place in our world.

Large sums of money are involved in boatbuilding. Generally one-quarter of the delivery price is paid when the keel is laid, another quarter when the hull is completed, and so forth. My friend, Don Street, has suggested that the money might be put into an escrow account with the release conditional on the signature of the surveyor. The builder would get his money as soon as he satisfied the surveyor at each step.

To my knowledge, not one yacht builder in the United States or Canada offers work to *Lloyd's Register of Shipping* classification, even though I believe the plans and construction of many contemporary yachts would meet the strict standards. It seems to me that it is only a question of time until a discerning builder offers the added assurance of Lloyd's inspections and gets a lot of orders as a result. Then, of course, all the major builders will follow.

Some builders will scream that such inspections will cost too much. I counter that an independent engineer or firm with wide experience may be able to recommend procedures that are not only more satisfactory but less expensive as well. In the long run, expert advice is always cheap. I don't mean to wave a flag for *Lloyd's Register of Shipping*, but for some reputable independent expert(s) to certify yacht construction and equipment.

A yacht used for less rigorous sailing possibly could qualify for Lloyd's classification with certain exceptions—perhaps lighter scantlings and ground tackle, which would make the vessel weigh less and not be so expensive. Of course, this vessel would be clearly identified. Even a certificate with exceptions (or however the classification might be handled) would be valuable.

It's not a question of one yacht being better than another; it's simply that different vessels are built for different purposes. There is little need for a coastal cruising yacht to be built like an Alaskan trawler. It is a waste of money and effort to use a powerful, deep draft ocean racer with cramped accommodation for a live-aboard home in a marina when a light and airy power yacht with lots of big windows and a large outdoor afterdeck is much more sensible.

My hope is that all yachts can be made safer and more pleasurable to sail. Whether you elect an ocean greyhound to go slashing to windward toward a distant horizon or meet after church for a Sunday sail, the yacht must fit your needs and be proper for the job. Getting the right vessel is the responsibility of the designer, the builder, and the buyer, all working together.

*Here is a wide-angle photograph of Whisper's interior. We look forward
with the chart table in the port foreground and the galley to starboard. The
saloon arrangement has a dinette to starboard and a settee to port and allows
unimpeded passage to the head area and forepeak beyond. An athwartship
bookshelf for large volumes is on the main bulkhead above the table. A
six-foot bookshelf runs along the port settee, and two additional six-foot
bookshelves are on the outboard sides of the forepeak berths. Ten drawers are
in the saloon, three are in the head, two are under the chart table, and four
are in the galley plus several dozen bins and lockers. Ten-foot grab rails run
along each side of the cabin at a convenient height. A vertical metal post in
the center of the cabin both strengthens the coach roof and is a convenient
handhold. The galley work area is of stainless steel with a high lip around
the edges. There are both fresh and salt water hand pumps (we have
one sink, but two would be better). A CO_2 fire extinguisher is on the inboard
side of the galley. Three brass kerosene wick lanterns plus a few electric
lamps spotted around at strategic reading spots provide light. The cabin
has eight 5 x 12-inch Fuller opening portlights (they do not leak and the
design is superb). The interior woodwork is teak, all solid except for teak
veneer over the bulkheads. The teak cabin sole is easy to scrub and keep clean.*

22

~~~~~~

The Accommodation Puzzle

The living and stowage arrangements in a small yacht are a miracle of ingenuity. Or they should be. Settees turn into comfortable bunks. An engine box doubles as a chart table. You open a galley drawer and find both a cup holder and a knife rack. A seat back pulls forward to reveal a clever tool locker. A folded storm sail slips neatly into the back of the oilskin locker. A hundred nautical charts disappear into a flat box slung beneath the deckhead in the forepeak. You have long-term stowage (paint, galley pumps, engine spares) in difficult-to-reach lockers, while items you need daily (flashlight, binoculars, navigation books, a hand-bearing compass) are at your fingertips in handy racks and shelves.

In a length of thirty-five feet or so, designers often show two quarter berths, two settee berths, and two forepeak berths. Sometimes one settee berth pulls out to form a double, making seven berths in all. I would certainly hate to be aboard a thirty-five-foot yacht with seven people sleeping or trying to sleep, however, not to speak of the eating, toilet, and washing problems. In my opinion, jamming six or seven berths into a yacht of this size is idiocy. I suppose it's done in the name of sales competition, but who is kidding whom? Why must the first question of newcomers be: "How many does she sleep?" A sailing yacht is not a sleeping dormintory. If it is, a yacht is certainly an expensive way to bed down for the night.

Four people are plenty; two or three are even better if you are going to sail together for several months. A long cruise means a lot of gear, food, clothes, and personal things. Suppose that bulky cold-weather sailing clothes for one person occupy space x. $2x$ is one thing; $4x$ is another; $7x$ means that one or more berths are going to get piled high with woolens, oilskins, and boots. And don't forget food stores, extra sail bags, bedding, spare warps, hats, ordinary clothes, laundry bags—a hundred things—plus any special equipment of the crew (an accordian, hiking boots, cameras, etc.). The designer who makes most of the interior space into berths is not being realistic. You need a few berths, of course, but you must allocate a reasonable amount of space for personal necessities and the specialized requirements of long-distance sailing. Life at sea can't be all work. You want a few things for outright pleasure, perhaps a chess set for the captain or a dozen jigsaw puzzles for a youngster.

A yacht broker in Sausalito named Dick Miller once showed me a thirty-six-foot wooden ketch named *Voyageur*. She had five berths. I noticed she had no sails bent on.

"Where are the sails?" I asked.

"Oh, she's got two complete sets," said Miller. "They're stored in the owner's garage."

"Where do you put the second set when cruising with the five people?" I asked.

"If you take the sails, you lose your crew," said Miller.

A vital point in the accommodation plan is the suitability of berths *for use at sea*. Forepeak V berths are quite impractical except during settled weather because the motion of the boat is too severe. What long-distance sailing vessels require are *sea berths*, places to sleep amidships or a little aft with narrow (not over 24 inches), deep, well-cushioned berths provided with strongly secured lee cloths of stout material 15 inches or higher. A lee cloth (a board is too hard and is usually too low) has one function: to keep you firmly in your berth no matter what the ship does. Within the last few years two of my sailing friends, Jerry Cartwright and Marge Petersen, were seriously injured in separate accidents by being flung across a saloon during violent weather.

Ideally, each person on board a yacht should have his own pilot berth with curtains (for privacy and daytime sleeping), a reading light, and a small drawer for personal items. He can make up his berth to suit himself. Quarter berths half under the cockpit (the French call them "coffin berths") are sometimes wet from flying spray and noisy from the engine and people climbing in and out of the cabin. A quarter berth is hard to make up if it is part way under the cockpit area. Like the pilot berths, the quarter berths should not be over 24 inches wide at the shoulders, a dimension that designers are particularly prone to overlook because the head of the quarter berth is in a wide part of the vessel.

As Arthur Beiser has pointed out, naval architects have been designing vessels for two thousand years or more, an interval during which the dimensions of the human body have changed very little. One would assume that a berth would be fitted perfectly to the human body, much as an automobile seat fits the driver. Unfortunately for sailors, the design of sleeping arrangements is far from ideal, and we are obliged to put up with berths that are too short, too hard, too wide, too shallow, or too wet. Structural details such as chainplates, winch bases, locker doors, or bundles of wiring project lethally into the berths, which are frequently ill-ventilated and appallingly uncomfortable—even by submarine standards. Sometimes a potential sleeper must be an acrobat to enter or leave his bunk. Handholds or strategic foot guides might well be provided. Once I spent a horrible night in a fold-up berth that was so close to the overhead that when I wriggled into the bunk I felt like bread going into a toaster. My nose was only a few inches from the ceiling and turning over was impossible. On another trip I recall sleeping in the forepeak of a Hand-designed ketch. Again there was scarcely any room to get into the berth. In the middle of the night there was a crisis and all hands were called. I sat up suddenly from a deep sleep and automatically cracked my head on a big oak beam.

Permanent bunks ready for use are much to be preferred over berths that have to be made up before you can turn in. If a berth is readily available, it is easy for a person to take a nap or to slip into it at his pleasure. Sometimes he may wish to get away by himself for a few hours. His berth can be his own private little world. Some sailors like sleeping bags. Margaret and I prefer smooth sheets and blankets together with soft pillows and fresh pillowcases.

On *Whisper* our present layout (Fig. 1) shows two forepeak berths, two settee berths, and one quarter berth. In port we often sleep in the forepeak berths, which can be left made up. The quarter berth then becomes a general catchall. At sea we use the quarter berth (with a snap-in curtain to keep out spray) and one or the other of the settee berths, depending on the tack on which the yacht is sailing. It is more comfortable to sleep with your back to leeward and to have your back firmly pressed into soft and resilient cushions. At sea we use the forepeak for general stowage.

I consider an athwartship chart table (with seat) an absolute necessity.

You have all the navigational equipment and current charts in a place that is comfortable to use. In port the chart table makes a useful desk. The top of the table can be hinged at its forward end and a chart stowage box built underneath. The dimensions of the chart table should be as large as possible so that the chart stowage box underneath can take most nautical charts folded in half. Attention to this point is worthwhile because an increase of an inch or two can mean that the chart capacity can be doubled if the charts don't have to be folded twice.

In *Whisper's* galley the stoves are outboard while the sink and work areas are athwartships. The engine box is both a seat for the cook and a handy worktable. Aft of the galley to starboard is an oilskin locker.

Margaret and I are completely sold on the dinette arrangement, which has proven perfect over many years. The design of the saloon gives an unhindered passage fore and aft (no dodging around a finger-crunching table leaf), and the table is an excellent place to write or eat. Often we have one or two couples for dinner; five or six people can sit around the table, and it makes a pleasant social center. Note that our dinette arrangement is U-shaped so that people can sit around the table on four sides. The dinette table will descend to form a double berth.

Structurally, the table can be made very strong by using a pedestal base with wide supporting flanges at the top and bottom. The flanges can be through-bolted to the cabin sole and the table to make a firm, non-moving piece of furniture. How often I have seen flimsy folding tables that tend to collapse at the touch of a finger or knee.

Again referring to Fig. 1, we see that the head area has doors both forward and aft so the compartment can be closed off. Opposite the toilet is a washbowl and tap. A hanging locker is outboard of the toilet.

Throughout the interior, fiddles or fiddle rails keep dishes or charts or tools or sextants or cooking pots in place. The saloon table should have fiddles of ¾ inch, because you tend to drape your arms and elbows on them while eating or working. Other fiddles should be higher, particularly in the galley and on bookshelves, where 1½ or 2 inches is a good height. Ship carpenters and builders who never go to sea invariably make tiny ornamental fiddles that are much too fancy and much too low and weak.

If we were to make any improvements in *Whisper's* accommodation, it would be in the sleeping arrangements, especially for sea berths. In Fig. 2 you will see that we have got rid of the forepeak berths entirely and have put the toilet amidships and forward. The area at the bow is for general stowage. The saloon comes next, aft of which we show a sleeping cabin with made-up berths on either side. This is followed by the chart table–

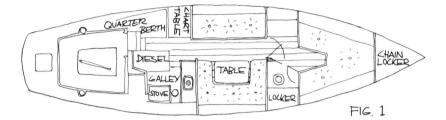

FIG. 1

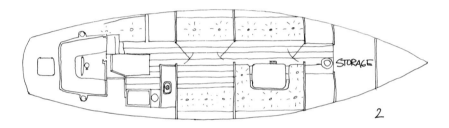

2

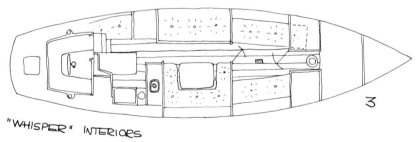

3

"WHISPER" INTERIORS

quarter berth–galley area. Note that leg space for the sleeping cabin extends beneath the chart table and galley worktable.

To get room for all this, I have cut down on the cockpit size and show a wheel instead of a tiller. The cockpit is quite large enough for a cruising vessel, and four people can easily sit around it. (In port, if you have a group of guests on deck, half of them tend to sit on the coach roof anyway.) The profile of the yacht is low, so the long coach roof doesn't visually overpower the hull. A disadvantage of arrangement 2 is that the cook is removed from any social group in the saloon and that food has to be passed a long distance. Also, the yacht is less open and is somewhat chopped up into compartments.

In Fig. 3 we have switched the saloon and sleeping cabins. This puts the cook closer to the people in the saloon and makes the food handling simpler. The forward sleeping cabin is quite private, and a person can be asleep and apart from activity in the saloon. (Note that leg room for the sleeping cabin extends into the head area.) The dividers at the forward end of the galley and chart table are partial bulkheads, which means an open accommodation from the main hatch all the way forward to the sleeping cabin after bulkhead. A possible disadvantage of arrangement 3 is that you have to pass through the sleeping cabin to reach the head from the after part of the vessel. Everything considered, however, we think this plan is quite good for a thirty-five-foot cruising vessel. At least for us.

On *Whisper* we carry about 240 books, both large and small volumes. Some are sailing books, some for navigation, and others for leisure and special-interest reading. We have a six-foot fore-and-aft shelf above the settee on the port side, a dozen navigation books on a shelf above the quarter berth, and an athwartship shelf for large books above the forward seat of the cabin table. In addition, we have a six-foot bookshelf above and along each side of the forepeak berths. The bookshelves should have 1¾-inch fiddles at the bottom to keep the books in place. To help the permanent wooden fiddles (the books are heavy), we tie strong string (stretched between small brass screw eyes) along the front of each bookshelf at the top to keep the books in place at sea. The motion is most violent in the forepeak, and these books need to be tied in securely. We have learned to put the string ties in place *before we go to sea*, not after the storm is over and the books are spread around like confetti.

The biggest problem with book stowage is large volumes. H.O. 249* and

* I prefer the British edition (A.P. 3270), which has permanent, well-made hard bindings for the three volumes.

Ocean Passages for the World, for instance, are big books and should be at hand *when the bookshelves are constructed*. Otherwise the shelves will certainly be made too small in all dimensions. Big books without a permanent niche get moved from place to place, and not only can you never find such a volume when you want it, but the books get dog-eared, wet, and ruined.

For ventilation we have eight opening portlights (5 x 12 inches) made of ABS plastic by the Fuller Brush Company. The design is excellent, with the spigot angled downward at 15 degrees so the portlight will drain outboard and can be left open in light rain. I fastened each of the portlights to the coach-roof sides with sixteen stainless steel bolts. A ¼-inch plastic finish ring went over the countersunk bolt heads on the outside to make a second barrier to water. The opening window is made of ⅝-inch Plexiglas sealed with a neoprene O ring and is secured at four points. There is a snap-in screen for insects. During the five years we have had these portlights installed on *Whisper* we have had no leaks. Whether the ABS plastic—the same material from which telephones are molded, I am told—will hold up is a question. Being a super-conservative, I would prefer metal. With the exception of the very expensive Goïot and Palmer-Johnson aluminum portlights, however, all the bronze and aluminum designs I have seen are incredibly poor and leaky, and are miles behind the Fuller portlights.

In addition to the ventilation from the portlights, we have two dorade vents in the saloon, two mushroom vents outboard of the cockpit coamings, and a 4-inch cowl vent at the stem (which we replace with a bronze screw-in plate when going to windward). Our transparent front hatch is made of ⅜-inch acrylic mounted in an aluminum molding. The hatch is manufactured by Camper & Nicholson and has a clear opening of 19½ x 19½ inches for access, light, and air. The C & N product (similar to the excellent French Goïot hatches) is low in profile, weighs 23 pounds, requires no maintenance, and the design is simple and functional. Also, the hatch doesn't leak a single drop—unless you forget to close it!

For light at night we have three polished brass kerosene wick lamps spaced around the saloon. These lamps give a pleasant glow and furnish a little heat. Sometimes at sea at night we keep one lamp turned very low. For reading we have small 12-volt electric lamps at the head of each berth, one above the chart table, two in the galley, one in the head, and a few in key storage areas (why grovel around in the dark with a flashlight?). We are set up to get along without any electricity (and have), but if a little power is available, why not use it for a few handy lights?

In Chapter 8 we mentioned that the hull and some of the coach roof of *Whisper* are well insulated against condensation with two layers of ¼-inch indoor-outdoor carpet (Ozite) tacked on with contact cement (the rest of the coach roof is of foam sandwich construction with built-in insulation). We have also discussed in detail our diesel heating stove. Both insulation and heat are necessary as well as plenty of ventilation and fresh air.

Comfort and pleasure on a vessel are related to an accommodation keyed to your activities. If you're an artist, you want space for an easel. If you're an underwater biologist, you may need a place for scuba tanks, a compressor, a wet suit, and a small marine laboratory. If you're a photographer, a small darkroom is the thing. Or if you just plan to sail and sleep and eat, your vessel can be simpler still. Whatever you want from your home afloat, it must be warm and dry in bad weather and open and airy on summery days. The layout and detailing of the little ship on which a man lives and travels ought to be as personal as his fingerprints.

23

The Dream and the Reality

The role of fantasy in men's dreams is too strong to be ignored. The answer for me is to accept the dream but to control the fantasy with a big dose of realism. We all have our dreams, which are important to us because they represent hope, anticipation, and a world beyond the present. Within the circle of small ships and ocean cruising, however, there is more hot air and phony scheming—call it fantasy and make-believe—than perhaps in any other activity, simply because a trip around the world or a sail to island X represents the ultimate adventure.

Only a few men can be astronauts. Mountaineering has strict age and physical requirements. Free balloons and soaring in a glider are too transient an escape. But who hasn't become Walter Mitty and decided to captain his own ship through true peril, fierce storms, and adverse shores to reach the ultimate palm-studded paradise?

I remember so well having *Whisper* tied up in a fisherman's berth at

The famous yacht Jester *with Blondie Hasler aboard at the start of the 1964* Observer Singlehanded Transatlantic Race *in Plymouth, England. Although* Jester *is only 25.9 feet in length, she made double Atlantic crossings in 1960, 1964, 1968, and 1972, plus many shorter trips. Engineless, and built around a wooden Folkboat hull, she is propelled by a single 237 square foot fully battened Chinese lugsail set on a stout unstayed mast. (Photo by Eileen Ramsay)*

False Creek in the city of Vancouver a few years ago. I had shown a film and given a lecture about a sailing trip at a nearby prominent theater. During subsequent weeks a number of people came to see the yacht and to talk with Margaret and me. To be quite honest, *Whisper* looked like all the other yachts. Her mast and gear might have been a little heavier, but she seemed much the same. But to visitors who had seen the film, *Whisper* was entirely different, *for she had been there.*

Among the people who came to see us was a pleasant couple whom we will call Will and Maxine Ariel. Will was in his early fifties and a successful stockbroker. "I'm tired of the rat race," he said. "I want to buy a yacht and get away to sea. I've always loved sailing, and I've saved enough for a forty-five-foot vessel, which should be ample for Maxine and me to live on comfortably now that we have married off our last daughter. If we get short of funds, we can do some chartering in the West Indies."

Will and Maxine asked a hundred questions. What kind of yacht should they get? Did we like a ketch? Was there plenty of room in the marinas? Did we think wood was better than fiberglass? How did you cook when the vessel rolled? And so on. In fact, Will and Maxine had so many questions they came back to see us a second night.

Then I asked a few questions: How much sailing had Will and Maxine done? "We had a daysailer many years ago when the children were young. We used to go out on weekends in the summer." Have you ever crewed on a thirty- or forty-foot yacht or made an ocean passage? "No, but we're anxious to." Have you ever slept aboard a yacht? "No, but it sounds exciting." Do you know anything about coastal or celestial navigation? "I've ordered the book by Dutton that is said to be very good." What do you know about the charter business? "Not much, really. I guess I've never thought about it. We would have a sort of neat little floating hotel in the tropics."

"Excuse me for speaking up," I said, "but you have a bad case of romantic nonsense about yachts and world cruising. Ocean sailing in small vessels is a complex business and requires a captain who is a mechanic, rigger, carpenter, painter, navigator, and diplomat plus assorted other skills. People speak of the glory of sailing, but let me tell you that it can be damned hard work. You've got to get some experience before you go off on these long trips under sail.

"If I went to your office with $50,000 to invest, I am sure you wouldn't let me put one cent into stocks and bonds until you satisfied yourself as a professional stockbroker that a company's growth record was good, its product had a future, its management was capable, and its price-to-earnings ratio and other figures were favorable," I said. "You would be a hard-

*What fun to see this delightful carving going to sea! Some anonymous
carpenter with the soul of an artist has turned the forward end of this
taffrail into a thing of pleasure and beauty. Any clod could have screwed
a piece of wood between the upper and lower rails, but only an inspired man
could have fashioned this frolicking fish for all the world to see and admire.*

boiled, prudent businessman. Yet you tell me that you want to invest a
similar sum, and you have no idea of what you're getting into.

"You must get some experience. Sign up for sailing lessons. Sail with
other people on local trips. Try to crew on longer cruises. Advertise in
the newspapers and magazines for berths. Inquire around and pin up
notices that you are available on yacht club bulletin boards. Write to
cruising associations. Make some sailing friends. Take classes in navigation. Study the books of famous cruises. Subscribe to a couple of magazines that specialize in cruising. In short, apply a yardstick to your
capabilities and limitations. If you find yourself short of knowledge in an
area, undertake some special study.

"You talk blithely of chartering in the West Indies," I continued. "Yet you know nothing about it. Chartering is particularly demanding work. Not only do you have to be a master at handling your ship, keeping the yacht in good order, shopping for difficult-to-buy foodstuffs in remote islands, and clever at overcoming a dozen small and large problems every day, but you must be an entertainer and know how to amuse people. The preparation of deluxe meals in a tiny galley is a major part of the game, because your customers expect to be fed well and fancily because they are paying first-class hotel rates.

"You can make money if you're good, but it can break your heart if you're not a gregarious, convivial, party-every-night type," I said to Will and Maxine. "The most successful charter captains run large, superbly equipped vessels that take four or six charterers in two or three separate cabins, which suggests a sixty-five-foot vessel or larger. To take just one point, I can tell you that dealing with laundry for six or eight people in an out-of-the-way place can be a real hassle. And you won't be the only one in the game. There is competition, plenty of it. You have to advertise or sign up with an agency. If there is an economic squeeze or an airplane strike, your customers will vanish faster than ice cubes in the sun.

"What I suggest you do is to hire a yacht run by a successful charter couple for two weeks. Then you can see how the cruising and sailing life works. You can ask questions all day long."

"What will it cost?" asked Will.

"I think Michael and Jane DeRidder charge $900 a week, which includes everything. I know the DeRidders well. Marvelous people. They have a perfect setup on *Magic Dragon*, a modern deluxe sloop. You will have a wonderful time. You can consider it both a vacation and a business learning experience."

"Nine hundred dollars!" said Will. "I haven't got that kind of money."

"Yet you just told me you were going to spend $50,000 or more for a yacht and try to get into a way of life and a business you know nothing about," I replied. "You are successful in a demanding line of work, yet when you speak of the sea and ships, your business disciplines are clouded by romantic fantasy.

"It's folly to get involved with a large and expensive yacht until you try the life a little," I continued. "I can't tell you how many people Margaret and I have met who decided that world cruising was not for them and sold their dream yachts at substantial losses.

"Let me tell you a story about a chap in San Francisco who built a Garden-designed Porpoise cruising ketch, a splendid yacht of its type but difficult and complicated to construct. The building went on in the man's back yard for six years. He used the finest of everything—Everdur fastenings, selected mahogany, and the whitest of oak. The hull was first-class, and the saloon had some of the best joinery work that I've ever seen. Finally the great day came and the yacht was launched with flags and fanfare. The owner and his wife moved aboard and began buying charts and ordering stores. A few weeks later the masts were stepped, the sails bent on, and the proud owners went out for their first sail.

"When the yacht heeled to the wind, the owner's wife was terrified. 'It's tippy,' she said. 'I can't stand this. It feels to me as if the yacht is going to turn upside down.' The upshot was that the vessel was sold. Six years of sacrifice and hardship and planning and dreaming went up in smoke. How much better it would have been to have chartered or to have crewed on other yachts!

"I'm sure you know that ocean cruising is not all glorious landfalls and quaint natives lorded over by tall colonials in pith helmets and Palm Beach suits," I continued. "There may be some of this, but there are times when you're covered with oil from a recalcitrant engine. You may be very tired and long for a port and a night of untroubled sleep. You may be doubled up in a bunk with a foreign bug in your guts. You may be sick to death of upside-down meals and rolling madly in an anchorage somewhere. You may be plagued by local officials who subject you to petty regulations. You may have trouble with thieves, or unpleasant experiences with crewmen. You may be overcharged by shopkeepers. You may be at sea with a cloudy sky and be desperate for a sextant sight. There may not be a stitch of dry clothing on board.

"You may experience all of these things or none of them," I said, "but you should be aware of them."

Later I worried a lot that I had been too negative, too discouraging, and too pontifical when I spoke with Will and Maxine. I have often thought of this pleasant couple and have wondered whether they sold their comfortable home and took to the sea for their world trip. Margaret and I have met Wills and Maxines in many places, and such experiences always make me think about my reasons for sailing.

To me, cruising is the excitement of traveling to new places in a small sailing ship of your own in a leisurely and unhurried manner, taking into account the awkward and poky nature of sailing. When you travel this way, you have your home with you—everything you need to exist pleasantly and comfortably. You can sail to the ends of the earth or to a river five miles away and you still have your bed, favorite books, a writing table, and a few possessions with you. A ship of your own is a total convenience and is the only way to visit many distant islands and remote coastlines. You alone decide the pace at which you go—whether it be to a bay around the corner or to an estuary a continent away. Your vessel is a tiny, self-contained city with suitable supplies and equipment so that you can be quite independent for a time and look after yourself no matter what happens.

I like the quietness, the closeness to nature, and the small feelings of achievement when you successfully complete a passage or a simple maneuver. There are negative aspects, of course, but I try hard to minimize the bad experiences and to work around them.

Yacht cruising is, I suppose, the ultimate way to get back to first principles, independence, and self-determination. This must explain the wide appeal of this life style to men of all countries. In the years that I have been sailing and entering strange ports in faraway places, I can tell you that no matter where you go someone *always* appears and tells you that he is planning to do the same thing.

My grandest memories of sailing are of the wonderful people I've met. Wherever Margaret and I have gone, local residents have come down to the yacht to see us.

"Where have you been? Where are you going?" they have typically asked us. "What have you seen? What have you felt? Are the islands of the South Seas as lovely as we've heard? Are the Cape Horn seas as big as the stories? Do you ever get scared out there? Which place is your favorite?"

We have listened to these questions hundreds of times. The visitors have come aboard for a look around, a little talk, and to sign our guest register. Our new friends have often assisted us and have freely given us help and hospitality of many kinds. Though we are ordinary people, we have been on great adventures, the kind that many men and women dream of, and with which they can identify. Perhaps by helping us they have participated a little in our journey.

In the cruising world there are many types of vessels because there are many kinds of owners, each with different goals and ideas. An astonishing number of yachts never leave the dockside, although their owners talk a good game. They live for new varnish, the mythical gale, and the new bit of gadgetry carried lovingly from their homes. They work to perfect the dream of distant shores they will never see under sail. Every year they buy a new Nautical Almanac and throw away the unused one from the

The choice of a yacht is difficult and fascinating, and can be the work of a lifetime or an instant. Here in the Lesser Antilles in the West Indies we see glimpses of three types of cruising vessels—a schooner, a cutter, and a ketch— each as different as the personality of her owner.

year before. The owners spin endless, repetitious, pathetic yarns with one another. I met a fellow once who bought each new cruising book as it came out and then sat in his harbor-bound yacht reading and storing away volume after volume.

"Much easier this way, and I don't get wet and nasty," he said.

All the harbors of the world have these dreamers. Certainly nothing is wrong with owning a stationary yacht and dreaming if it gives the owner a bit of pleasure. It seems to me, however, that it cheats the enthusiast of a good deal of self-satisfaction if he doesn't at least try to put his dream into practice.

Whether a yacht owner elects the coast or the ocean or some combination is up to him. In the ports of the world you meet every sort of person —from a millionaire with a large luxury yacht and an expert crew (and chef!) to a singlehander with a little vessel and not much money. Each finds a measure of pleasure and delight and contentment in his own manner if he brings an untroubled nature with him (you can't run away from yourself; sailing may ease personal problems but it can't solve them).

What are the qualifications? Some money. A stout, small vessel well fitted out. A trial cruise or two. An adaptable captain and, one hopes, an enthusiastic wife or daughter or friend. As much experience as possible.

One makes his preparations quietly and privately. Under no circumstances does an outward-bound captain give his friends a departure date, for he will not be ready. Delayed sailing dates are embarrassing to everyone. Little by little our captain collects his gear and stores and crew and completes his sea trials. One day he is ready and slips away.

Our captain is honest with himself. If the cruising life is not for him and he finds himself delaying and endlessly putting off his trip, maybe he should forget it. If he is genuinely afraid of the deep sea (many are; it's no sin to admit fear), he doesn't taunt himself with recriminations. The hell with it. He sells out and takes up something else.

But if you want to try a sailing venture, by all means go ahead. Sometime in your life (before big jobs, between big jobs, or after big jobs) you can certainly snatch away a year or two. The experience will change your life. But don't wait too long or the game may be up. The frail flesh lasts only so long. Throw up the job and get under way. You only live once.

Notes

1. Guy Cole, *Ocean Cruising* (London: Adlard Coles, Ltd., 1959), pp. 5–6.

2. For a look at how a clever designer can lower a racing yacht's rating, see "Inside the IOR," by Daniel Charles, in *Yachting World*, October 1976.

3. John Teale, *Designing Small Craft* (New York: David McKay Company, Inc., 1977), p. 81.

4. Quoted from a letter from Captain Johnson to William Stelling, dated August 27, 1973, in possession of the author.

5. See "Anchors and Anchoring," in *Yachting Monthly*, January 1969; "Ground Tackle and Anchoring Techniques," by Jack West, in *Yachting*, November and December 1975; "Anchors and Anchoring," by R. D. Ogg, a booklet published by Danforth, Portland, Maine.

6. For an excellent discussion of boating fuels, see "A Landlocked Fuel Goes to Sea," by Robert W. Magnusen, in *Sail* magazine, October 1976.

7. "Searchlight on a Silent Service," by John Brown, in *Yachting Monthly*, September 1975.

8. *Yachting World*, January 1971 and other issues, is the source for these figures.

9. *Sail*, November 1973.

10. E. G. Martin, *Deepwater Cruising* (New York: Yachting, Inc., 1928), p. 72.

11. University of California (Berkeley) weekly press clip sheet for June 21, 1966.

12. *Yachting Monthly*, March and April 1966.

13. *Yachting Monthly*, May 1967, p. 233.

14. Adlard Coles, *Heavy Weather Sailing* (New York: De Graff, 1975); Miles Smeeton, *Because the Horn Is There* (Sidney, B.C., Canada: Gray's Publishing Co., 1971); Erroll Bruce, *Deep Sea Sailing* (New York: Van Nostrand, 1953), a modern book but curiously dated because of the style and layout; Bernard Moitessier, *The Long Way* (New York: Doubleday, 1975).

15. "Sea Anchors," an article by William V. Kielhorn, in *Sail*, May 1976. Also see Letters to the Editor in the September 1975 issue.

16. Robin Knox-Johnston, *A World of My Own* (London: Corgi, 1971), pp. 234–35.

17. Eric Hiscock, *Voyaging Under Sail* (London: Oxford University Press, 1970), p. 178.

18. Pat Treston in *Sea Spray*, a New Zealand yachting magazine. The account of the epic Griffith trip ran in the 1972–73 issues.

19. Bernard Moitessier, *Cape Horn: The Logical Route* (London: Adlard Coles, 1969).

20. Bruce, *Deep Sea Sailing*, p. 186.

21. William Albert Robinson, *To the Great Southern Sea* (London: Peter Davies, 1967), p. 221.

22. "Heavy Weather," *Sail*, March 1973.

23. Letters to the Editor, *Sail*, August 1975, p. 9.

Appendix 1

Ahlemann & Schlatter, Postfach (P.O. Box) 448540, 2800 Bremen 44, West Germany. Navigation lights.

John Atkin, Noroton, Connecticut 06820. Naval architect.

Atoms, Boîte Postale 171, 06 Nice, France. Wind vane steering devices.

Barient Company, 936 Bransten Road, San Carlos, California 94070. Winches.

Barlow Winches, 52 Wentworth Street, Granville, New South Wales, Australia. Winches.

James Bliss & Co., Inc., 100 Route 128, Dedham, Massachusetts 02026. Marine chandlery.

Buck-Algonquin, Second Street and Columbia Avenue, Philadelphia, Pennsylvania 19122. Marine chandlery.

Calvert School, Tuscany Road, Baltimore, Maryland 21210. Correspondence school for children.

Camper & Nicholsons Marine Equipment, Ltd., 55–61 Northam Road, Southampton SO9 1WB, England. Skylight hatches.

J. B. Cartwright, 226 Bellevue Avenue, Newport, Rhode Island 02840. Naval architect.

Robert Clark, 55a Welbeck Street, London, W.1., England. Naval architect.

Tom Colvin, Fiddlers Green, Miles, Virginia 23114. Naval architect.

Defender Industries, Inc., 255 Main Street, New Rochelle, New York 10801. Marine chandlery.

Dickinson's Marine Products, Ltd., 3737 Napier Street, Burnaby 2, B.C., Canada. Marine cooking and heating stoves.

Edson Corp., 460 Industrial Park Road, New Bedford, Massachusetts 02745. Hand-operated diaphragm bilge pumps.

Farymann Diesel, 684 Lampertheim bei Mannheim, Postfach 100, West Germany. Marine diesel engines.

Thomas Foulkes, Lansdowne Road, Leytonstone, London E11 3HB, England. Marine chandlery.

Fuller Brush Company, Box 729, Great Bend, Kansas 67530. Portlights.

M. S. Gibb, Ltd., Warsash, Southampton SO3 6ZG, England. U.S. agent: Gibb-Henderson, Inc., 82 Border Street, Cohasset, Massachusetts 02025. Hasler steering vanes; yacht rigging hardware.

Laurent Giles & Partners, Ltd., 4 Quay Hill, Lymington, Hampshire SO4 9AR, England. Naval architects.

Goïot, 26 rue du Frère-Louis, 44200 Nantes, France. U.S. agent: Goïot US, Inc. 809 Aquidneck Avenue, Middletown, Rhode Island 02840. Skylight hatches, winches, and rigging equipment.

Gougeon Brothers, Inc., 706 Martin Street, Bay City, Michigan 48706. Cold-molded hull construction using the wood epoxy saturation technique (WEST).

The Guest Corporation, 107 Vanderbilt Avenue, West Hartford, Connecticut 06110. Anchor and overboard lights.

Mrs. John Hanna, 636 Wilkie Street, Dunedin, Florida 33515 (widow of the deceased naval architect).

Peter Haward, 1 Blenheim Gardens, Warblington, Havant, Hants, England. Safety harnesses.

Järnföradling, S-640 30 Halleforsnas, Sweden. Self-feathering propellers, anchors, marine chandlery.

Michel Joubert, rue Jeanne d'Albret, La Rochelle, France. Naval architect.

Lands' End Yacht Stores, Inc., 2317 N. Elston Avenue, Chicago, Illinois 60614. Marine chandlery.

Lister Marine, Dursley, Gloucestershire GL11 4HS, England. Marine diesel engines.

Paul Luke, Inc., East Boothbay, Maine 04544. Fisherman anchors, marine stoves, feathering propellers.

Manhattan Marine, 116 Chambers Street, New York, N.Y. 10007. Marine chandlery.

Marine Vane Gears. Northwood, Cowes, Isle of Wight, England. Aries wind vane steering devices.

Merriman Holbrook, Inc., 301 River Street, Grand River, Ohio 44045. Marine chandlery.

Moonlite Marine Corporation, 776 W. 17th Street, Costa Mesa, California 92627. Mast steps, and running backstay levers and sheaves.

Morriss Marine, Saltmarsh Lane, Hayling Island, Hants, England. Gunning wind vane steering devices.

Munster Simms Engineering, Ltd., Old Belfast Road, Bangor, County Down, Northern Ireland. Whale bilge pumps.

Navik, Plastimo, Boîte Postale 162, 56104 Lorient, France. Wind vane steering devices.

The Nicro Corporation, 206t West Avenue 140th, San Leandro, California 94577. Blocks and rigging fittings.

Petters Limited, Staines, Middlesex TW18 3AR, England. Marine diesel engines.

Dominique Presles, Le Parc du Belloy, Mesnil le Roy, Par Maison Lafitte, France. Naval architect.

J. Read, Ltd., 327 Shirley Street, Southampton, England. Sewing machines.

E. S. Ritchie & Sons, Inc., Pembroke, Massachusetts 02359. Compasses.

RVG, Madeira Marine and Manufacturing, Inc., P.O. Box 1218, Pinellas Park, Florida 33565. Riebandt wind vane steering devices.

Sabb Motor A.S., P.O. Box 2626, 5010 Bergen, Norway. Marine diesel engines.

Schaefer Marine, Industrial Park, New Bedford, Massachusetts 02745. Rigging hardware.

Sea Spray, magazine, P.O. Box 793, Auckland 1, New Zealand.

Sharp and Company, Ltd., Richborough Hall, Ramsgate Road, Sandwich, Kent, England. Autopilots and wind vane steering devices.

Simpson-Lawrence Ltd., 218/228 Edmiston Drive, Glasbow G51 2YT, Scotland. Marine chandlery, anchors, and anchor windlasses.

Spar Craft, 770 West 17th Street, Costa Mesa, California 92627. Masts, booms, spinnaker poles, and hardware.

Spencer Boats, Ltd., 1240 Twigg Road, Richmond, B.C., Canada. Yacht builders.

Tamaya & Company, Ltd., 5–8, 3-chome, Ginza, Chuo-ku, Tokyo 104, Japan. Sextants.

Taylor's Para-Fin Oil & Gas Appliances, Ltd., Downs Road, Maldon, Essex STD 0621, England. Marine cooking and heating stoves.

The Telltale Compass, The Yachtsman's Newsletter, 18418 South Old River Drive, Lake Oswego, Oregon 97034. A handy and useful newsletter of opinion and information. No advertising.

Tillermaster, Box 1901, Newport Beach, California 92663. Autopilots.

The Tilley Lamp Co., Ltd., Dunmurry, Belfast, Northern Ireland. Cooking stoves and storm lanterns.

AB Volvo Penta, Box 392, Göteborg 1, Sweden. Marine engines.

Thomas Walker & Son, Ltd., 58 Oxford Street, Birmingham B5 5NX, England. Ship's logs.

Captain O. M. Watts, Ltd., 48 Albemarle Street, Piccadilly, London W1X 4BJ, England. Marine chandlery.

Westerly Chandlers & Service, Aysgarth Road, Waterlooville, Portsmouth PO7 7UF, England. Safety harnesses.

West Products, 161 Prescott Street, East Boston, Massachusetts 02127. Marine chandlery.

Wilcox-Crittenden, 699 Middle Street, Middletown, Connecticut 06457. Marine chandlery.

Wishbone Marine Products Inc., 780 S.W. 9th Terrace, Pompano Beach, Florida 33060. Anchors.

Yachting Monthly, Kings Reach Tower, Stamford Street, London SE1 9LS, England.

Yachting World, Dorset House, Stamford Street, London SE1 9LU, England.

CONVERSION TABLE FOR METERS, FEET, AND FATHOMS

Meters	Feet	Fathoms	Meters	Feet	Fathoms	Feet	Meters	Feet	Meters	Fathoms	Meters	Fathoms	Meters
1	3.28	0.55	61	200.13	33.36	1	0.30	61	18.59	1	1.83	61	111.56
2	6.56	1.09	62	203.41	33.90	2	0.61	62	18.90	2	3.66	62	113.39
3	9.84	1.64	63	206.69	34.45	3	0.91	63	19.20	3	5.49	63	115.21
4	13.12	2.19	64	209.97	35.00	4	1.22	64	19.51	4	7.32	64	117.04
5	16.40	2.73	65	213.25	35.54	5	1.52	65	19.81	5	9.14	65	118.87
6	19.68	3.28	66	216.54	36.09	6	1.83	66	20.12	6	10.97	66	120.70
7	22.97	3.83	67	219.82	36.64	7	2.13	67	20.42	7	12.80	67	122.53
8	26.25	4.37	68	223.10	37.18	8	2.44	68	20.73	8	14.63	68	124.36
9	29.53	4.92	69	226.38	37.73	9	2.74	69	21.03	9	16.46	69	126.19
10	32.81	5.47	70	229.66	38.28	10	3.05	70	21.34	10	18.29	70	128.02
11	36.09	6.01	71	232.94	38.82	11	3.35	71	21.64	11	20.12	71	129.85
12	39.37	6.56	72	236.22	39.37	12	3.66	72	21.95	12	21.95	72	131.67
13	42.65	7.11	73	239.50	39.92	13	3.96	73	22.25	13	23.77	73	133.50
14	45.93	7.66	74	242.78	40.46	14	4.27	74	22.56	14	25.60	74	135.33
15	49.21	8.20	75	246.06	41.01	15	4.57	75	22.86	15	27.43	75	137.16
16	52.49	8.75	76	249.34	41.56	16	4.88	76	23.16	16	29.26	76	138.99
17	55.77	9.30	77	252.62	42.10	17	5.18	77	23.47	17	31.09	77	140.82
18	59.06	9.84	78	255.90	42.65	18	5.49	78	23.77	18	32.92	78	142.65
19	62.34	10.39	79	259.19	43.20	19	5.79	79	24.08	19	34.75	79	144.48
20	65.62	10.94	80	262.47	43.74	20	6.10	80	24.38	20	36.58	80	146.30
21	68.90	11.48	81	265.75	44.29	21	6.40	81	24.69	21	38.40	81	148.13
22	72.18	12.03	82	269.03	44.84	22	6.71	82	24.99	22	40.23	82	149.96
23	75.46	12.58	83	272.31	45.38	23	7.01	83	25.30	23	42.06	83	151.79
24	78.74	13.12	84	275.59	45.93	24	7.32	84	25.60	24	43.89	84	153.62
25	82.02	13.67	85	278.87	46.48	25	7.62	85	25.91	25	45.72	85	155.45
26	85.30	14.22	86	282.15	47.03	26	7.92	86	26.21	26	47.55	86	157.28
27	88.58	14.76	87	285.43	47.57	27	8.23	87	26.52	27	49.38	87	159.11
28	91.86	15.31	88	288.71	48.12	28	8.53	88	26.82	28	51.21	88	160.93
29	95.14	15.86	89	291.99	48.67	29	8.84	89	27.13	29	53.04	89	162.76

30	98.42	16.40	9.14	54.86
31	101.71	16.95	9.45	56.69
32	104.99	17.50	9.75	58.52
33	108.27	18.04	10.06	60.35
34	111.55	18.59	10.36	62.18
35	114.83	19.14	10.67	64.01
36	118.11	19.68	10.97	65.84
37	121.39	20.23	11.28	67.67
38	124.67	20.78	11.58	69.49
39	127.95	21.33	11.89	71.32
40	131.23	21.87	12.19	73.15
41	134.51	22.42	12.50	74.98
42	137.80	22.97	12.80	76.81
43	141.08	23.51	13.11	78.64
44	144.36	24.06	13.41	80.47
45	147.64	24.61	13.72	82.30
46	150.92	25.15	14.02	84.12
47	154.20	25.70	14.33	85.95
48	157.48	26.25	14.63	87.78
49	160.76	26.79	14.94	89.61
50	164.04	27.34	15.24	91.44
51	167.32	27.89	15.54	93.27
52	170.60	28.43	15.85	95.10
53	173.88	28.98	16.15	96.93
54	177.16	29.53	16.46	98.76
55	180.45	30.07	16.76	100.58
56	183.73	30.62	17.07	102.41
57	187.01	31.17	17.37	104.24
58	190.29	31.71	17.68	106.07
59	193.57	32.26	17.98	107.90
60	196.85	32.81	18.29	109.73

90	295.28	49.21	27.43	164.59
91	298.56	49.76	27.74	166.42
92	301.84	50.31	28.04	168.25
93	305.12	50.85	28.35	170.08
94	308.40	51.40	28.65	171.91
95	311.68	51.95	28.96	173.74
96	314.96	52.49	29.26	175.57
97	318.24	53.04	29.57	177.39
98	321.52	53.59	29.87	179.22
99	324.80	54.13	30.18	181.05
100	328.08	54.68	30.48	182.88
101	331.36	55.23	30.78	184.71
102	334.64	55.77	31.09	186.54
103	337.93	56.32	31.39	188.37
104	341.21	56.87	31.70	190.20
105	344.49	57.41	32.00	192.02
106	347.77	57.96	32.31	193.85
107	351.05	58.51	32.61	195.68
108	354.33	59.06	32.92	197.51
109	357.61	59.60	33.22	199.34
110	360.89	60.15	33.53	201.17
111	364.17	60.70	33.83	203.00
112	367.45	61.24	34.14	204.83
113	370.73	61.79	34.44	206.65
114	374.02	62.34	34.75	208.48
115	377.30	62.88	35.05	210.31
116	380.58	63.43	35.36	212.14
117	383.86	63.98	35.66	213.97
118	387.14	64.52	35.97	215.80
119	390.42	65.07	36.27	217.63
120	393.70	65.62	36.58	219.46

Appendix 3

Exact relationships shown by asterisk (*)

Area

1 square inch	=6.45162581 square centimeters
1 square foot	=144 square inches*
	=0.09290341 square meter
	=0.00002296 acre
1 square yard	=9 square feet*
	=0.83613070 square meter
1 square (statute) mile	=27,878,400 square feet*
	=640 acres*
	=2.58999847 square kilometers
1 square centimeter	=0.15499969 square inch*
	=0.00107639 square foot
1 square meter	=10.76386736 square feet
	=1.19598526 square yards
1 square kilometer	=247.1043930 acres
	=0.38610061 square statute mile
	=0.29155335 square nautical mile

Length

1 inch	=25.4000508 millimeters
	=2.54000508 centimeters
1 foot (U.S.)	=12 inches*
	=1.00000373 British feet
	=⅓ yard*
	=0.30480061 meter
	=⅙ fathom*
1 yard	=36 inches*
	= 3 feet*
	=0.91440183 meter

Length

1 fathom	=6 feet*
	=2 yards*
	=1.82880366 meters
1 cable	=720 feet*
	=240 yards*
	=219.45643891 meters
1 statute mile	=5,280 feet*
	=1,760 yards*
	=1,609.34721869 meters
	=1.60934722 kilometers
	=0.86897798 nautical mile
1 nautical mile	=6,076.10333333 feet
	=2,025.36777777 yards
	=1,852 meters*
	=1.852 kilometers*
	=1.15077715 statute miles
1 meter	=100 centimeters*
	=39.37 inches*
	=3.28083333 feet
	=1.09361111 yards
	=0.54680556 fathom
	=0.00062137 statute mile
	=0.00053996 nautical mile
1 kilometer	=3,280.83333333 feet
	=1,093.61111111 yards
	=1,000 meters*
	=0.62136995 statute mile
	=0.53995680 nautical mile

Volume

1 cubic inch	=16.38716233 cubic centimeters
	=0.01638670 liter
	=0.00432900 gallon
1 cubic foot	=1,728 cubic inches*
	=28.31622363 liters
	=7.48051948 U. S. gallons
	=6.22882272 imperial (British) gallons
	=0.02831702 cubic meter
1 cubic yard	=46,656 cubic inches*
	=764.53803813 liters
	=201.97402597 U. S. gallons

Volume

	=168.17821354 imperial (British) gallons
	=27 cubic feet*
	=0.76455945 cubic meter
1 cubic centimeter	=0.06102338 cubic inch
	=0.00026417 U. S. gallon
	=0.00021997 imperial (British) gallon
1 cubic meter	=264.17046733 U. S. gallons
	=219.96747874 imperial (British) gallons
	=35.31445483 cubic feet
	=1.30794276 cubic yards
1 quart (U.S.)	=57.75 cubic inches*
	=32 fluid ounces*
	=2 pints*
	=0.94633213 liter
	=0.25 gallon*
1 gallon (U.S.)	=3,785.43449592 cubic centimeters
	=231 cubic inches*
	=0.13368056 cubic foot
	= 4 quarts*
	=3.78532851 liters
	=0.83267248 imperial (British) gallon
1 liter	=1,000.028 cubic centimeters
	=61.02508662 cubic inches
	=1.05671146 quarts
	=0.26417786 gallon
1 register ton	=100 cubic feet*
	=2.83170166 cubic meters
1 measurement ton	=40 cubic feet*
	=1 freight ton*
1 freight ton	=40 cubic feet*
	=1 measurement ton*

Volume-mass

1 cubic foot of sea water	=64 pounds
1 cubic foot of fresh water	=62.428 pounds at temperature of maximum density (4° C=39°.2 F)
1 cubic foot of ice	=56 pounds
1 displacement ton	=35 cubic feet of sea water*
	=1 long ton

Mass

1 ounce	=437.5 grains*
	=28.34952673 grams
	=0.0625 pound*
	=0.02834953 kilogram
1 pound	=7,000 grains*
	=16 ounces*
	=0.45359243 kilogram
1 short ton	=2,000 pounds*
	=907.1848554 kilograms
	=0.90718486 metric ton
	=0.89285714 long ton
1 long ton	=2,240 pounds*
	=1,016.047038 kilograms
	=1.12 short tons*
	=1.01604704 metric tons
1 kilogram	=2.20462234 pounds
	=0.00110231 short ton
	=0.00098421 long ton
1 metric ton	=2,204.622341 pounds
	=1,000 kilograms*
	=1.10231117 short tons
	=0.98420640 long ton

Index

Accommodations, 289–296
  aboard *Whisper*, 291–296
  berths, 289–291
  for books, 294–295
  for comfort and pleasure, 296
  dinette, 292
  navigation equipment, 291–292
  permanent bunks, 291
  ventilation, 295
  See also Stowage
Adams, Doug, June, and Mary, 263–265
Adios, 64, 253
Admiralty Chart 5308, 142
Admiralty charts, 142, 147
Admiralty Pilots, 142, 143
Aeromarine Plastics Company, 30
Agriculture inspectors, 274–275
Ahlemann & Schlatter, 153–154, 157, 158
Alcard, Edward, 44
Alcohol, flash point of, 133
Alden, John, 18, 38
Aldis signaling lamp, 158–159, 228
Aleutka, 230
Allied yachts, 40
Aluminum dinghy, 217
Aluminum foil, 162
Aluminum hulls, 27–28

Aluminum portlights, 295
Amazing Grace, 102
America Jane III, 7
American Plywood Association, 25
Anchors and anchoring, 85–124
  aboard *Whisper*, 86–90, 93–94
  in broken rock, 102–103
  buoying, 114–116
  in coral, 101–102
  CQR anchor, 85, 88, 94, 97, 98
  Danforth anchor, 86, 94–95, 97, 98, 99
  fisherman anchor, 96–99
  freeing fouled anchors, 116–117
  holding ground, 102–103
  in kelp, 103
  logbook bearings, 112
  mooring, 114
  nylon line, 90–94
    advantages, 92
    disadvantages, 90–92
    warp stowage, 92–94
  in ooze and clay, 103
  in pebbles and shingle, 103
  ratio of cable to depth, 101–102, 112
  and sailing out, 117–118
  in sand, hard mud, shells, broken shells, 103

Anchors and anchoring (*continued*)
second anchor, 107–109
in smooth rock, 102
storm conditions and, 118–121
around the clock watch, 121
gale force, 119–120
on a lee shore, 121
lines ashore, 120–121
shock loading factor, 118–119
windage problem, 118
summary of, 121–124
technique, 109–112
tidal considerations, 112–114
types of anchors, 96–99
uniform strength, 103–104
bow roller, 103–104
nylon and chain, 103
in weed and grass, 103
weight factor, 99–101
Animal quarantine, 274
Archer, Colin, 53
Aries vane gear, 74, 80
Athwartship chart table, 291
Athwartship floors, 21–22
Atoms vane gear, 74, 81
Autopilot, 78–79
Avon inflatable dinghy, 220
Awahnee, 29, 257–258, 259, 273
Awning, for water-catching, 171–172, 173, 214
Azulao, 236–237

Bacchus, 76
Ballast arrangement, fiberglass hulls, 33–34
Ballast keel, 22
Banjo, 252
Bankia (shipworm), 25
Baquerizas, Julio, 69
Barient winches, 232–233
Barlow winches, 232–233
Battens and batten pockets, 225–227
Baugh, Ian, 30
Because the Horn Is There (Smeeton), 247
Beiser, Arthur, 291
Bermudian rig, 53, 62
types of sails for, 223
Berths, 289–291
Beyond, 27

Bilge pumps, hand-operated, 240–241
Bingham, Bruce, 29
Birmabright (aluminum alloy), 27
Bluejacket, 120
Boden, Ed, 219
Books, accommodations for, 294–295
Bosun's chair, 174
Boyce, David, 102
Boylen, Alfred, 252
Brandlmayr, John, 39, 40
Bread, 163–164
Brewer, Edward, 7
Broken rock, anchoring in, 102–103
Broken shells, anchoring in, 103
Bruce, Erroll, 247, 257, 259
Bumboats, 230–232
Buoyancy, dinghy, 218
Buoying the anchor, 114–116
safest arrangement for, 115
Butane stoves, heating and cooking with, 133–135
Byars, Joe, 251

Cable, length, in anchoring, 101–102, 112
Cal yachts, 40, 280, 281
Caledonien, 230
Callegari inflatable dinghy, 220
Calvert School, 265–266
Camper & Nicholson Company, 158, 241
Canned foods, 162, 165, 166
Cappeliez, Guy, 193
Carpenter, Ed, 85–86
Cartwright, Jerry, 33, 290
Carvel planking, 23
Caterpillar engine, 280
Chapelle, Howard, 13
Charts, 190, 193–194. *See also* types of charts
Cheeses, 162, 169
Chichester, Sir Francis, 74, 77
Children, schooling at sea, 263–269
Calvert School, 265–266
Canadian program, 264–265
correspondence programs, 265
PNEU program, 266–267
Chinese lugsail rigs, 62
Clamp (or sheer clamp), 22
Clark, Robert, 38
Clay, anchoring in, 103

Clifton, Nick, 236–237
Clinker planking, 24
Clyde Cruising Club, 143
Coastline storm management, 245
Cockroaches, 181
Colas, Alain, 235
Cold-molded hulls, 24
Cole, Guy, 3
Coleman, William, 30
Coles, Adlard, 247
Columbia yachts, 40
Colvin, Tom, 62, 204–205
Conversion tables:
    area, 314
    length, 314–316
    mass, 318
    for meters, feet, and fathoms, 312–313
    volume, 316–317
    volume-mass, 317
Cooke, Brian, 236
Cooking. *See* Heat and Cooking
Cooper, William, 67
Coral, anchoring in, 101–102
Courtesy flags, 275
CQR anchor, 85, 88, 94, 97, 98
    buoying, 114
    design, 94
    freeing fouled, 116, 117
    handling, 88–90
Credit cards, 234
Cruising Club of America, 5
Cruising Guide to the New England Coast, A (Duncan and Ware), 143
Cruising under sail:
    dream and reality, 299–306
    pleasure and freedom of, 1–19
    popularity of, 2–4
    racing yachts and, 5–17, 282–283
    types of yachts, 12–13
    See also Long-distance sailing costs; Yacht, choice of
Curved construction, dinghy, 218–219
Cutter mast, 53–54

Dacron line, 227
Dacron sailcloth, 62, 71
Danforth anchor, 86, 94–95, 97, 98, 99
    buoying, 114–115

    cost of, 96
    design, 94–95
    flukes and shank foulup, 95–96
    freeing fouled, 116, 117
    Hi-tensile, 96
Darroch, Colin, 5, 80
Davey oil lamps, 154
Davidson, Hamish, 218–219
Deck plate, screw-in, 241
Decks:
    plywood, 25
    secure footing on, 178–179
Deep Sea Sailing (Bruce), 247
Deepwater Cruising (Martin), 164–165
DeRidder, Jane, 197, 302
DeRidder, Michael, 76, 137, 197, 302
DeRidder auxiliary trim tab gear, 76–77
Design and construction, 37–48
    naval architects and, 37–38
    problems of, 38
    Whisper's, 39–48
        bilge drainage and ventilation, 46–47
        bow, 39
        bulwarks, 43
        coach roof, 44–45
        cockpits, 44, 45–46
        decks, 43–44
        drainage and damp problem, 48
        galley, 45
        hull and deck moldings, 42–43
        keel, 40–41
        rudder, 40
        stern and midship sections, 39–40
        storm shutters, 44
        toilet facilities, 46
        water and fuel tanks, 47–49
        waterline and beam, 39
Devogué, Jean, 5
Dickinson diesel stove, 135–138, 194
Diesel engines, 201–205
    filters, 203–204
    fuel blockage, 203–204
    fuel consumption, 201
    horsepower, 204–205
    propeller, 203
    reduction gears, 203
    weight of, 203

Diesel stove, heating and cooking with, 135–138
  during cold weather, 137–138
  fuel, 136–137
  lighting, 137
  models for, 136
  soot and, 127–128
Dijkstra, Gerard, 79
Dinghy, 213–221
  bumper strip, 218
  buoyancy, 218
  construction materials, 217
  curved construction, 218–219
  flat-bottomed, 219
  functions of, 213
  inflatable, 219–221
  keel rubbing strip, 218
  pram boats, 219
  rowing, 213–214
  rowlocks (or oarlocks), 215–217
  scull technique, 217
  stowage, 215
  types of, 218–221
Dolphin Book Club, 14
Double headsail rig, 55
Doubloon, 251
Duffin, Bill, 192
Duncan, Roger, 143

Ebeling, Walter, 181
Eggs, 162
Eileen, 263–265
Electrolux Company, 161
Engines, 199–210
  accessibility of, 209
  arguments for and against, 199
  availability of parts, 205–208
  competent sailing maneuvering and, 199–200
  diesel, 201–205
    filters, 203–204
    fuel blockage, 203–204
    fuel consumption, 201
    horsepower, 204–205
    propeller, 203
    reduction gears, 203
    weight of, 203
  with hand-cranking capability, 205
  special tools for, 208–209
  water-cooled models, 209
English gaff cutters, 55

Farymann engine, 205, 209
Fast Lady, 167–168
Federal Bermuda, 236
Ferris, Ham, 236
Ferro-cement hulls, 28–30
  cost of, 30
  insulation, 29
Fiberglass dinghy, 217
Fiberglass hulls, 30–35
  ballast arrangement, 33–34
  bulkheads and framing, 33
  construction of, 31–32
  drawbacks of, 31
  gel coat, 31
  glass filaments, 30–31
  keel area, 32–35
Field, Hale, 281
Finisterre, 5
Finn dinghy, 68
Fishing, 167–169
Fisherman anchors, 96–99
  drawback to, 97
  Herreshoff pattern, 97, 99
Flare gun, 228
Flat-bottomed dinghies, 219
Floors, 21–22
Food, 162–169
Food-stowage areas, 178
Foreign ports, entrance and exit, 271–276
  agriculture inspections, 274–275
  courtesy flag, 275
  customs and immigration, 272–274
  health regulations, 274
  outgoing clearance, 276
  Q flag, 274
  visas, 272, 273
Forepeak berths, 290
Fouled anchors, freeing, 116–117
Foulkes, Thomas, 186
Frames, hull, 21–22
Franklin, Nick, 80
Frers, Germán, Sr., 24, 38
Frers & Cibels Company, 32
Fresh winds, estimating, 255
Fruit and vegetables, 161, 162
Fuller Brush Company, 295

Gaff rig, 53
Garden, Bill, 38
Gau, Keane, 120

Gazelle, 204–205
Gel-coated fiberglass hulls, 31
Genoa sail, 223
German Hydrographic Office, 154
Giles, Laurent, 12–13, 38
Goïot Company, 241
Goïot portlights, 295
Gougeon Brothers, 25
Graham, Robin Lee, 5
Grass, or gravel, anchoring in, 103
Gribble (shipworm), 25
Griffith, Bob, 3, 29, 257–258, 259
Griffith, Nancy, 29
Griffith, Reid, 269
Griffiths, Maurice, 245, 281
Gulfstreamer, 18, 236, 237
Gunning vane gear, 74
Gypsy Moth IV, 24
Gypsy Moth V, 24

Halibut anchor, 97–98
Hall, Eric, 78, 251–252
Halyards, 68–69
Hanna, John, 53
Hantke, Phil, 39
Harbor dues, 194
Hard mud, anchoring in, 103
Hartoog, Dr. C. den, 242
Hasler, Blondie, 62, 73, 173–174
Hasler pendulum servo gear, 73–74, 80
Hayman, Bernard, 156
Headsails:
  with deep reefs in the foot, 68
  removing and bagging, 55
  tacks, 225
Heat and cooking, 127–138
  butane or propane stoves, 133–135
  diesel stove, 135–138
    during cold weather, 137–138
    fuel, 136–137
    lighting, 137
    models, 136
    soot and, 127–128
  difficulties with charcoal, 128–129
  kerosene stove, 129–133
    alcohol for, 132–133
    burners, understanding, 131–132
    disadvantage of, 133
    successful operation of, 132
    warmth and comfort, 130–131

Heave to (storm maneuver), 248–250, 261
Heavy gear, handling, 232–233
Heavy Weather Sailing (Coles), 247
Helmsmanship, 73
Herreshoff, Francis, 13, 37
Herreshoff (fisherman) anchor, 97, 99
Hinkley Company, 158
Hiscock, Eric, 186, 248, 257
Hogan, Carol, 267–268
Hulls, 21–35
  aluminum, 27–28
  ballast arrangement, 33–34
  cost of, 21
  ferro-cement, 28–30
    cost of, 30
    insulation, 29
  fiberglass, 30–35
    ballast arrangement, 33–34
    bulkheads and framing, 33
    construction of, 31–32
    drawbacks of, 31
    gel coat, 31
    glass filaments, 30–31
    keel area, 32–35
  planked or plated, 22
  steel, 25–27
    maintenance, 27
    rust, 26–27
    zinc-spraying, 26
  stem, keel, sternpost, and frames, 21–22
  wood construction, 22–25
    carvel planking, 23
    clinker planking, 24
    cold-molded, 24
    frames, 25
    plywood, 24
    strength of, 25
    strip planking, 24
    WEST system, 25

Ice, 162
Icebox, 161, 162
Illingworth, Capt. John, 55
Inflatable dinghies, 219–221
  cost of, 221
Insecticides, 181
Insurance, 194
International Offshore Rule (IOR), 5–7, 12

International Regulations for Preventing Collisions at Sea, 151–152
Iota, 230
Islander, 16
Island to Myself, An (Neale), 102

Jachtwerf Zuiderzee B.V. Company, 219–220
Jacubenko, Alex, 26
James Bliss Company, 99
Jennings, Tee, 164
Jensen, Jack, 281
Jensen Marine Company, 281
Jester, 174
Jib and staysail, 54–55
Jiffy reefing, 65–67
Johnson, Capt. Irving, 92
Jolie Brise, 164
Joshua, 259
Joubert, Michel, 56
Journal of Ferro-Cement, 30
Jumpers, 55

Keel, 21–22, 40–41
  dinghy rubbing strip, 218
  shapes, 40
Kelea, 266
Kelp, anchoring in, 103
Kelsall, Derek, 236–237
Kelvin engine, 205
Kemp, Dixon, 67
Kennedy, Curtis, 266, 269
Kennedy, Mrs. Liev, 266
Kerosene appliances, priming device for, 182–186
Kerosene iron, 229
Kerosene lantern, 154
Kerosene refrigerators, 161
Kerosene stove, heating and cooking with, 129–133, 135, 138
  alcohol for, 132–133
  burners, understanding, 131–132
  disadvantage of, 133
  successful operation of, 132
  warmth and comfort, 130–131
Ketch rig, 55–56
  mainmast of, 56
Kielhorn, Capt. William, 251, 258
Kittiwake, 219

Knox-Johnston, Robin, 253, 255–256
Kohlwes, Al, Jeff, and Chris, 266
K'ung Fu-ste, 27

Laser dinghy, 68
Laundry, 228–229
Lecky, S. T. S., 171
Lecky's Wrinkles to Practical Navigation, 171
Letcher, John, 82, 230
Letcher, Pati, 230
Lewman winches, 232–233
Lie ahull (storm maneuver), 250–252
Lie to a sea anchor (storm maneuver), 256–260
Liggett, Al and Beth, 76
Lighting. *See* Night lighting
Limnoria (shipworm), 25
Lister engine, 205, 209
Lloyd's Register of Shipping, 284–285, 287
Long-distance sailing costs, 189–198
  aboard *Whisper* (1976), 196–197
  in big ports, 192–193
  charts, 190, 193–194
  fuel, 194
  getting vessel ready, 190–192
  harbor dues, 193, 194
  individual demands and, 189–190
  insurance, 194
  maintenance, 196, 197
  per person per year, 194–196
Long-distance shipping, 229–230
Long-keel design, propeller of, 41
Long Way, The (Moitessier), 247
Lou, 81
Luke (fisherman) anchors, 99

McInnis, Eldridge, 280
MacLear, Frank, 56
McLeod, Jock, 62
McMullen, Mike, 236
Magic Dragon, 76, 197, 302
Mainsail, 223
  without battens, 225–226
Malabar, 18
Manual of Yacht and Boat Sailing, A (Kemp), 67
Manuma, 252
Marchaj, C. A., 259–260

Martin, Cdr. E. C., 164–165
Martinson, Lennart, 210
Massachusetts Institute of Technology, 7
Mast boots, 242
Masthead lights, 153–154, 156–159
Masthead strobe light, 159
Mast steps, 174–176
Matangi, 85
Mercedes-Benz engine, 205
Meridian, 236
Merriman-Holbrook Company, 99
Milk and cream, 166–167
Miller, Dick, 290
Miranda wind-vane steering gear, 77–78
Mischief, 174
Mitchell, Ronald, 269
Mizzen sail, 55–56
Moitessier, Bernard, 247, 259
Money and mail, 233–234
Moonlite Marine Corporation, 55
Mooring, 114
Mud, anchoring in, 103
Muraccioli, Antoine, 56
Myth of Malham, 55

National Oceanic and Atmospheric Administration, 190
Nautor Company, 31, 158
Naval architects, 37–38
Navik trim tab pendulum servo unit, 74
Neale, Tom, 102
Newick, Dick, 18, 236
Nichol, Hedley, 236
Nicro Corporation, 104, 158
Night lighting, 151–159
    Aldis lamp, 158–159, 228
    battery power, 158
    Davey oil lamps, 154
    importance of, 152–155
    masthead, 153–154, 156–159
        strobe light, 159
        xenon flashers, 159
    problem areas, 151–152
    sidelights, 152, 158
    starboard lantern, 152
    white stern lights, 155–156
    worthless schemes, 154
Night work, 227–228
Noot, Tim, 102

Nosgrove, Ross, 259
Nova Espero, 257
Nylon line for anchor cables, 90–94
    advantages, 92
    disadvantages, 90–92
    warp stowage, 92–94

Oarlocks, 215–217
Oars, 200
O'Brien, Conor, 66
O'Brien, John, 280
Observer Singlehanded Transatlantic Race (1976), 153–154, 236–237
Ocean Passages for the World, 142, 144, 146, 147
Om, 56
Outgoing clearance, foreign ports, 276
Outlaw, 5

Paille-en-Queue, 15
Palmer-Johnson portlights, 295
Pan American Union, 267
Parents' National Education Union (PNEU), 266–267
Paul Luke Company, 99
Pebbles, anchoring in, 103
Pen Duick IV, 235
Pen Duick VI, 24
Perkins engine, 205
Petersen, Marge, 290
Pidgeon, Harry, 16
Pilot charts, 142–144, 190
    cost of, 147
    studying, 146
    up-to-date, 146–147
Pirelli inflatable dinghy, 220
Piver, Arthur, 236
Planning the trip, 141–150
    basic guides, 142–148
    care in, 141–142
    commercial shipping lanes and, 149
    schedule, 149
    tidal current and height tables, 148
Plow anchor. *See* CQR anchor
Plywood decks, 25
Plywood hulls, 24
Portlights, 44, 295

Pram boats, 219
Preciosa, 147
Primus burners, 128, 129, 131, 132, 138
  priming of, 132
Procax, 193
Proesa, 266
Propane stoves, 133–135
Propeller, fin-keel design, 40
Prout Marine Company, 219

Q flag, 274
Quarter berths, 290–291

Racing sails, 227
Refrigeration, managing without, 161–169
  fishing, 167–169
  foods that keep, 162–167
  shopping in port, 161–162
Rhodes, Phillip, 30, 280
Riebandt auxiliary rudder device, 80–81
Rig, 51–69
  Bermudian, 53, 62
  chafe problem, 53, 66
  Chinese lugsail, 62
  cutter, 53–55
  double headsail, 55
  English gaff cutters, 55
  gaff, 53
  jib and staysail, 54–55
  to jibe, 63
  jiffy reefing, 65–67
  ketch, 55–56
  roller furling headsails, 67–68
  sails, hoisting, 68–69
  sloop, 53
  staysail schooner, 56–58
  twin headsails, 63–64
  trysails, 58–61
  unstayed mast, 62
  wind conditions and, 53, 62, 68
    downwind work, 64–65
  yawl, 56
Roberts-Goodson, Bruce, 14
Robinson, W. A., 259
Roller furling headsails, 67–68
Roller reefing, 65
Rope ladder, 174
Rowlocks, 215–217

Royal Cruising Club, 5
Royal Ocean Racing Club, 5, 154
Rubbing strip, dinghy, 218
Running backstays, 55
Run with the storm (maneuver), 252–256, 261

Sabb engine, 203, 204–205
Sail (publication), 7, 29, 258, 267
Sailcloth, 62, 71
Sailmakers, 224–225
Sails:
  hoisting, 68–69
  what kind to buy, 223–227
  See also types of sails
Sand, anchoring in, 103
Scull technique, 217
Search for Speed Under Sail, The (Chapelle), 13
Sea Spray, 258
Second Life, 79
Self-steering equipment, 71–82
  learning about, 72
  power from wind on sails, 81–82
  See also Wind vane gear
Self-Steering for Sailing Craft (Letcher), 81–82
Senta, 242
Service Hydrographique et Oceanographique de la Marine, 148
Seven Seas Cruising Association, 14
Sheer clamp, 22
Shells, anchoring in, 103
Shilshole Bay Marina, 39
Shingle, anchoring in, 103
Shipworms, 25
Sidelights, 152
Simpson, S. A., 230
Simpson-Lawrence Company, 94
Slab or tied reefs, 65
Slocum, Joshua, 16, 253
Slocum Society, 224
Sloop rig, 53
Small Ocean-going Yacht, The (O'Brien), 66
Smeeton, Miles, 247, 273–274
Smooth rock, anchoring in, 102
Spar Craft Company, 181
Sparkman & Stephens, 7
Spencer Boats, Ltd., 39, 45
Spinnaker poles, 179–181
Spinnaker sail, 223–224

Spray (Slocum), 16, 253
Spray (publication), 224
Staysail schooner rig, 56–58
Steaming lights. *See* Masthead lights
Steele, Tom, 64–65, 253
Steel hulls, 25–27
    maintenance, 27
    rust, 26–27
    zinc-spraying, 26
Stem, 21–22
Stephens, Bill, 236
Stern lights, 155–156
Sternpost, 21–22
Stewart, Dr. Roger, 236
Storm conditions:
    anchoring and, 118–121
        around the clock watch, 121
        gale force, 119–120
        on a lee shore, 121
        lines ashore, 120–121
        shock loading factor, 118–119
        windage problem, 118
    setting trysail in, 58–61
Storm jib, 58, 223, 260
Storm management, 239–246
    bilge pumps, 240–241
    coastline, 245
    cockpit drains, 241
    difference between gust and force
        gale, 240
    fuel-tank air vents, 241–242
    mast boots, 242
    portlights, skylights, and hatches,
        241
    progress under sail, 242–243
    reaching and, 244
    running, 243–244
    screw-in deck plate, 241
    watertight integrity, 241
    wave patterns and, 244–245
    wind velocity and, 239–240, 244
        measurement of, 240
Storm shutters, 44
Storm tactics, 247–261
    books on, 247–248
    first rule of survival, 248
    summary of, 260–261
    techniques, 248–260
        heave to, 248–250, 261
        lie ahull, 250–252
        lie to a sea anchor, 256–260
        run with the storm, 252–256,
          261

wind force table, 254–255
Storm trysail, 58, 223, 260
Stormvogel, 24
Stoves, priming device for, 182–186
    See also types of stoves
Stowage:
    compartment, 176–178
    dinghy, 215
    for food, 178
    See also Accommodations
Street, Don, 287
Stringers, 22
Strip planking, 24
Suhaili, 253
Sykes, Raith, 217

Taberly, Eric, 24
Tahiti ketches, 53
Taylor, Geoffrey, 94
Taylors kerosene stove, 129–130, 135,
    138
Taylors Para-Fin cooker, 128
Teale, John, 7–12
Telltale Compass, The (publication),
    252
Teredo (shipworm), 25
Thomson, Andy, 121
Three Cheers, 18, 236
Tiburon, 102
Ticonderoga, 13
Tidal conditions in anchoring, 112–
    114
Tilley burners, 131, 132
Tilley wick clip-on device, 131, 182–
    186
Tilman, Bill, 174
Topping lift, adjusting, 186
Trade-wind rigs, disadvantages of,
    63–64
Transverse floors, 22
Treston, Pat, 258
Trimarans, building, 235–237
Trim tab vane gear, 74–77
Triple Arrow, 236
Trysails, 58–61
Twin headsails, disadvantages of, 63–
    64
Tyler of England (builders), 31

Uniform strength, anchoring and,
    103–104

Uniform strength, anchoring and (*continued*)
bow roller, 103–104
nylon and chain, 103
U.S. Government Printing Office, 267
U.S. Pilots, 142–143

Vagabond, 210
Vang tackle, 63
Ventimeter, 240
Vessey, Ed, 102
Visas, 272, 273
Volvo-Penta engine, 203, 205, 208–209
Voss, Capt., 257
Voyageur, 290

Ware, John, 143
Washington Stove Works, 128
Water, fresh, 167
Water collection, 171–174
awning, 171–172, 173, 214
coach roof, 173
using deck with low battens, 173–174
Waterwitch ketch, 230
Watts, Capt. O. M., 186
Weeds, anchoring in, 103
Weld, Phil, 236
WEST system, 25
Westerbeke engine, 205
Whale Gusher 25 bilge pump, 240–241
Whisper:
accommodations, 291–296
anchors and anchoring, 86–90, 93–94
cruising costs (1976), 196–197
design and construction, 39–48
bilge drainage and ventilation, 46–47
bow, 39
bulwarks, 43
coach roof, 44–45
cockpit, 44, 45–46
decks, 43–44
drainage, 48
galley, 45
hull and deck moldings, 42–43
keel, 40–41
rudder, 40
stern and midship sections, 39–40
storm shutters, 44
toilet facilities, 46
water and fuel tanks, 47–49
waterline and beam, 39
ground tackle, 86–87
Hasler unit, 71, 80
launched, 127
running rig on, 63
sails, hoisting, 68–69
twin forestays, 56–58
White rocket flares, 158, 228
White Squall, 259
Wilcox-Crittenden Company, 99
Wilcox-Crittenden rowlock sockets, 217
Wind blades, 71–72
Wind velocity, 239–240, 244
measurement of, 240
Wind Force Table, 254–255
Wind vane gear, 72–81
Aries, 74, 80
Atoms, 74, 81
Gunning, 74
Hasler, 73–74, 80
mechanical schemes, 78–80
Miranda, 77–78
trim tab, 74–77
Windward Passage, 24
Wire halyards, 69
Wood dinghy, 217
Wooden hulls, 22–25
carvel planking, 23
clinker planking, 24
cold-molded, 24
frames, 25
plywood, 24
strength of, 25
strip planking, 24
WEST system, 25
Working jib sails, 223
World of My Own, A (Knox-Johnston), 253
World War II, 17, 96
Worth, Tom and Ann, 27

Xenon flashers, 159

Yacht, choice of, 279–287
for long distance coastal cruising, 280–281

Yacht, choice of (*continued*)
    ocean racing and, 282–283
    time schedule factor, 280
    for unlimited cruising, 281–282
    upgrading standards, 283–287
    See also Cruising under sail
Yacht Club Argentino, 157
Yachting (publication), 64–65, 253
Yachting Monthly (publication),
    143, 255–256

Yachting World (publication), 156,
    242
Yachts and Yachting (Cooper), 67
Yankee, 92
Yanmar engine, 205
Yawl, 56

Zinc-spraying, steel hulls, 26
Zodiac inflatable dinghy, 220

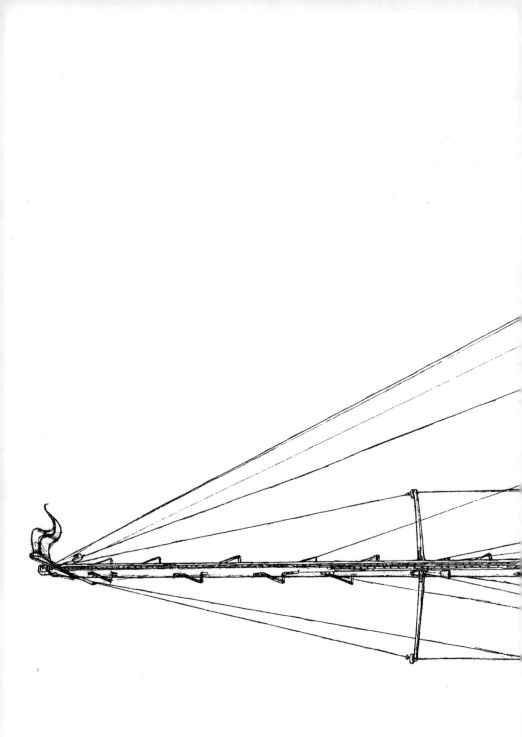